State Enterprise Zone Programs

Have They Worked?

State Enterprise Zone Programs

Have They Worked?

Alan H. Peters
and
Peter S. Fisher

2002

W.E. Upjohn Institute for Employment Research
Kalamazoo, Michigan

Library of Congress Cataloging-in-Publication Data

Peters, Alan H.
    State enterprise zone programs : have they worked? / Alan H. Peters
and Peter S. Fisher.
        p. cm.
    Includes bibliographical references and index.
    ISBN 0-88099-249-2 (pbk. : alk. paper) — ISBN 0-88099-250-6
(hardcover : alk. paper)
        1. Enterprise zones. I. Fisher, Peter S. II. Title.
    HD1393.5 .P484 2002
    307.3'42—dc21

                                                            2002013032

© 2002
W.E. Upjohn Institute for Employment Research
300 S. Westnedge Avenue
Kalamazoo, Michigan 49007-4686

Cover design by J.R. Underhill.
Index prepared by Nancy Humphreys.
Printed in the United States of America.

Contents

List of Figures

List of Tables

x   Contents

Preface

We started this project in September 1997, soon after finishing our previous book for the W.E. Upjohn Institute for Employment Research. At that time we were fairly confident that enterprise zones were one of those good ideas that could actually work in practice. Our reasons for this confidence were both theoretical and empirical. Enterprise zone programs seemed to target those in most need of employment and thus were likely to raise fewer economic red flags than other place-based economic-development strategies. Moreover, there was reason to believe that the major incentive instrument used in enterprise zones, tax breaks, could be effective. Indeed, the evidence seemed to support the idea that taxes (and thus tax incentives) could materially alter the geography of business investment. And some of the earlier work that looked directly at enterprise zones indicated that they could be effective in creating local growth.

As will become clearer later, our empirical results have made us much more skeptical of the usefulness of enterprise zones, at least to the extent that zones are primarily a tax incentive program. We find that their effect on growth is close to minimal, they often encourage the use of capital rather than labor, their power to influence business decisions has been diminished by the growth in non-targeted incentives, and they do not alter the wider spatial functioning of urban labor markets. Of course, all of this does not prove that state and local enterprise zones cannot work or even that they do not currently work effectively in a few states. But it certainly does suggest that their implementation at the state and local level in the United States has not been a success.

More so than any other research we have done, the work on this book has been information technology intensive. Not only have we been able to use a wide variety of data sets that are huge but nevertheless accessible (compared to the past), but by the end of the project we were astounded at the amount of software we had found it necessary to buy, license or, in quite a few cases, create from scratch. Close to a decade of major improvements in computer programming technology made software development for such a project feasible. At the beginning of the new century it seems needless to add that the Web and e-mail were crucial to getting much of the work done. Indeed, it is quite ironic that so much information technology should go into the creation of such an ancient and unchanged commodity—a book.

The book relies heavily on the output of our new TAIM^{ez} (Tax and Incentive Model—Enterprise Zones) hypothetical-firm model. Although in concept the model is similar to the TAIM model developed for our previous book on taxes and incentives, *Industrial Incentives* (Fisher and Peters 1998), TAIM^{ez} is entirely new and considerably bigger. We developed the basic code and many of the associated submodels using a series of grants from the Iowa Department of Economic Development (DED). Staff at Iowa DED—particularly Phil Dunshee, Allen Williams, and Harvey Siegleman—were crucial in guiding the development of the overall structure of the software and debugging the software and the tax models. In all this, the Director of Iowa DED, David Lyons, was a great supporter, as were David Forkenbrock, Director of the Public Policy Center at the University of Iowa, and John Lewis, Director of the Iowa Research Council. A large grant from the State of Ohio, to investigate the use of economic-development incentives in that state, provided us with an opportunity to apply the new software in a policy setting. We are grateful to Don Iannone, then at Cleveland State University, who directed this project; to a number of Ohio officials in the Department of Development, Statehouse and Treasury; and to the legislative committee (chaired by Senator Horn) that oversaw the research. The Ohio work was particularly important since it provided us with an opportunity to investigate and then firm up our ideas on the role of enterprise zones in economic-development policy (the first report we wrote as part of this project was on the Ohio enterprise zone program).

The completion of this book required pulling together a number of pieces beyond the TAIM^{ez} model. Two data sources were particularly important. The first, the SSEL (Standard Statistical Establishment List) ZIP-code database required three special runs by the Bureau of the Census. Melvin E. Cole III was our contact person there. He helped us decide that the SSEL was indeed the data source we needed and then helped us understand the data. Unfortunately, converting the data we received from the census into something useful for our analysis was a huge job. The other major data source, the *Census Transportation Planning Package* (CTPP), consisting of a mass of CD-ROMs, is provided free to researchers by the Bureau of Transportation Statistics.

The CTPP's main use is transportation planning at the local level but it is a wonderful—and little used—resource for commuting research. The CTPP is set up for use within TransCAD®, a commercial GIS (Geographic Information Systems) software package, which significantly aided ease of analysis.

John Engberg, at Carnegie-Mellon University, who also writes on enterprise zones, provided us with his valuable list of enterprise zones in the United States and then helped us think through some of our initial econometric ideas. His help and support were invaluable. Tim Bartik, this project's monitor at the Upjohn Institute for Employment Research, also provided enormous help and guidance. Indeed, our biggest scholarly debt is to Tim and we thank him. Johannes Ledolter furnished invaluable insight and help on our use of cross-sectional panel data. Randy Eberts, Director of the Upjohn Institute, was thankfully unconvinced by our first round of models on enterprise zones and growth. His skepticism forced us to reevaluate and better justify our econometric decisions. Kevin Hollenbeck at Upjohn guided the book through the editorial process. He provided enormous help, reviewing the manuscript not only for content but also for its readability and coherence. We owe Kevin a special debt. Upjohn then sent the manuscript out to two anonymous external reviewers; both wrote extensive and very helpful comments on the original manuscript. All along the way we endeavored to present our preliminary findings and methods at various academic and policy conferences. We thank all those who made comments on early drafts of our work.

Although we delivered the first full manuscript to the Upjohn Institute 19 months late (in February 2000), we still find it difficult to believe that we were able to do so much in so little time. We hope the book does not suffer too gravely from our expeditiousness. Certainly, we trust the results of our effort will be useful and worthwhile to both policy and academic audiences. It should be clear from this Preface that this book could not have been completed without the help, input, and support of a large number of people. Nevertheless, the errors and omissions the reader is bound to find are ours alone.

There are a number of other people at the Upjohn Institute to whom we owe a huge debt. David Nadziejka, the editorial manager, moved this book from manuscript to finished product. David had a way of making this transition as painless as possible for us. Elaine Goldberg, the primary editor for the manuscript, improved our writing and tables.

1
Introduction

Enterprise zones have been part of American urban policy for more than two decades. Between 1981 and 1991, 38 states and the District of Columbia passed enterprise zone legislation. As of 1995, 34 of those programs remained active, and in those states, 2,840 zones had been established (Wilder and Rubin 1996).[1] Two more states—Iowa and Michigan—have initiated enterprise zone programs since that time, and Pennsylvania has introduced a much more aggressive version of its enterprise zone. While thousands of state-sponsored enterprise zones now exist, there continues to be controversy about what enterprise zones should be designed to achieve, what incentive instruments are appropriate to enterprise zone goals, and whether these zones are likely to be more or less effective than the rest of the state and local economic-development effort. Moreover, the situation became even more confusing in 1993 with the passage of the Empowerment Zone and Enterprise Community Act. With this legislation the federal government jumped into the enterprise zone arena. The federal program initially added 11 empowerment zones and 99 enterprise communities to the list of state zones (Hambleton 1996). It also added a distinctive set of incentives and policy goals.

Given the public resources being dedicated to U.S. enterprise zones by the federal government and by states and cities, and given the small size of the literature on enterprise zones, we believe it is high time for a multistate evaluation of the effectiveness of enterprise zones. In this book we look at state and local zones only, and our sectoral focus is on manufacturing. We ignore federal zones because they are very different from state zones, making summary comparison figures difficult to construct, and because there are vastly more state zones than federal zones. We ignore retail and other services because state zones still tend to concentrate on new manufacturing investment. Erickson and Friedman (1990a) found in a study of 357 zones between 1982 and 1987 that manufacturing accounted for 73 percent of new jobs. In a more recent study, we found that 74 percent of enterprise zone agreements in Ohio have been with manufacturing firms (Peters and Fisher 1998). Here we examine seven policy issues that we believe should be the core of any serious evaluation of enterprise zones.

- What sort of business incentives are provided in state enterprise zones?
- What is the size of these incentives and what is their relative importance compared to other sorts of state and local business incentives?
- Do enterprise zone incentives encourage businesses to use more labor than would otherwise be the case? More generally, what sort of investment do the incentives favor?
- Do enterprise zones make sound fiscal sense? In other words, are enterprise zone incentives likely to produce revenue gains or losses for state and local government?
- How much business turnover is typical in enterprise zones?
- Is there a "causal" relationship between enterprise zone incentives and economic growth in enterprise zones? Do enterprise zones create growth?
- Do enterprise zones draw their labor from poorer, more depressed parts of metropolitan areas?

ENTERPRISE ZONES AND ECONOMIC-DEVELOPMENT POLICY

A central problem with almost all economic-development program evaluation is that, even after decades of research, we lack conclusive evidence on the effectiveness of policy. The problem is particularly acute in the case of enterprise zone incentives. Two difficulties bear special attention: proper measurement of incentives and assessing the impact of incentives on firm behavior.

At heart, almost all economic-development policy is a trade—government provides incentives that reduce the costs of doing business at a site; in return, business is meant to change its investment behavior in some way, by locating at one site rather than another or by employing more labor at a site than it otherwise would have, and so on. The problem we face is that, outside of a few geographically and temporally limited studies,[2] we do not have good measures of what government is giving away in enterprise zones; we don't know enough about the size of the public carrot being offered to the private sector. We need to know by how much zone incentives reduce the tax burden on business—thus increasing business profitability—since it is precisely this reduction in burden that is meant to give government its leverage over the firm's behavior.[3] To our minds, this is the fundamental hole in the enterprise zone literature. Our first tasks then are to find out what enterprise zone incentives are worth *to business* and to compare these to the size of other non-enterprise zone incentives routinely offered to industry (see Chapter 3). It turns out that these tasks have the useful side effect of allowing us to measure the true cost of incentives to government and to draw some conclusions about how incentive instruments could be designed to improve their overall cost-effectiveness (see Chapter 5).

The second issue is a variant on the first. A pressing policy question is whether enterprise zones actually work—whether they actually result in new local growth. Typically, econometric models are built to investigate whether a particular policy instrument has some "causal" influence on economic growth.[4] The problem is methodologically difficult because so many other factors could influence local growth, and all of these must be accounted for before the effect of enterprise zones *alone* can be properly measured. The existing econometric literature on enterprise zones reveals little regarding the impact of zone incentives on local economic growth, in part because the literature is so small and contradictory and in part because zone incentives have been measured so poorly. Some researchers, for instance, have simply counted enterprise zone programs to see whether places with more programs have more growth. This approach misses the fundamental economic point. It makes no economic or financial sense to expect a 100 percent property tax abatement over 10 years to have the same impact on growth as a 33 percent abatement over three years, or either of these to have the same impact as a sales-tax exemption on all machinery and equipment bought for use in the zone. Incentives lower the costs of operating at a particular site; the more they lower these costs, the more effective they are likely to be. If an econometric growth model treats all incentives as essentially homogenous, it ignores what makes a particular incentive "work." Other studies have looked at whether the geographical area covered by an enterprise zone experienced more economic growth after the designation of zone status than before designation. Again, what this misses is that designation alone does not alter the business operating environment; it is the incentives that come with designation that do that. At best, designation is a crude signaling mechanism to business of incentives to come. Our second major task, then, is to look at the impact of incentives on firm behavior.

In Chapter 7 we do finally develop econometric models investigating the relationship between incentives and local growth. Throughout the book, however, we look at the effect of incentives on firm behavior in various ways. In Chapter 3, for instance, we look at the size of incentives and compare them, using a wage-equivalency technique, to a factor widely seen as important in investment decisions, labor costs. This allows us to draw some conclusions about the likely impact of incentives on business decisions without having to rely on the results—and assumptions—of our econometric models. In Chapter 4 we look at whether zone incentives are likely to result in firms employing more labor than they otherwise would.

In this book, as in our previous book on economic-development competition, we use the "hypothetical firm" methodology to measure the value of enterprise zone incentives to business. The idea behind this method is quite simple. Construct a set of financial statements for reasonably typical firms, then apply the tax code and incentives to those firms. The extent to which a particular incentive increases the firm's returns on investment (calculated either as increased cash flow or an increased internal rate of return) is the measure of the incentive's worth to the firm. Underlying this approach are the principles of modern location theory—firms are profit maximizers and will therefore choose sites that maximize profits; government can influence firm location decisions by changing the after-tax profitability of operating at particular sites.

We use a new hypothetical firm model, TAIM^{ez} (the Tax and Incentive Model for Enterprise Zones), the building of which started in 1997. The new model is a direct descendant of the TAIM model that we used for much of our research in the mid 1990s. The TAIM^{ez} model, however, is larger, more flexible, and capable of tax simulations we were not able to perform in the original model. In order to encourage openness and transparency in this area of research, we feel it is imperative to discuss some of the methodological considerations involved in building this model *before* discussing our results. We include a short discussion of this model in Chapter 3 but leave almost all of the technical information for Appendix A. In Appendix B we also provide a comparison of results from TAIM^{ez} with results from the earlier TAIM model; this should aid comparability with past research.

The focus of most of the research reported in this book is on the enterprise zone programs in place in 13 states. These states were selected because they are the largest states (in terms of total manufacturing employment) that had significant enterprise zone programs in place by 1990. We examine the incentive packages available in a sample of 75 zones within those 13 states during the period 1990 through 1994, and the changes in manufacturing establishments within the zones from 1989 through 1995. A more complete discussion of the sample is provided later in this chapter.

THE ORGANIZATION AND ARGUMENTS OF THE BOOK

The book is organized into eight substantive chapters. In the first of these, Chapter 2, we provide the background to the other chapters in the book; it should be read by all readers. Here we examine the history of enterprise zones in the United States—in particular, what policymakers hoped to achieve with zones—and the arguments for and against an enterprise zone strategy. In Chapters 3 through 8 we cover our research results. In the first three of these we use TAIM^{ez} to measure the size and comparative worth of enterprise zone incentives sponsored by state and local governments. In these chapters we also look at the extent to which enterprise zone incentives are biased in favor of some industrial sectors and capital-intensive sorts of investment, and finally at the cost to government of these enterprise zone incentives. In Chapters 6 and 7 we utilize a new, very complete, business establishment database to analyze the growth that has occurred in enterprise zones. In Chapter 8 we focus on the labor markets that enterprise zones draw from. And finally, in Chapter 9 we summarize our results and consider alternative policies.

Needless to say, the organization of this book has posed some challenges. As we indicated above, our results often depend on fairly complex methodological procedures. The book is aimed at a broad policy audience, however, and we suspect that most readers will not want to wade through all the supporting methodological material. On the other hand, many readers will at some point wonder exactly how a particular number was calculated or conclusion reached. Our solution has been to segregate, wherever possible, the most technical material into appendices or endnotes. Moreover, by providing guides to our research and conclusions, both here and at the beginning of each chapter, we hope to direct readers to those places most appropriate to their individual interests. What follows is a brief summary of the content of each chapter and the conclusions we draw.

Chapter 2: Enterprise Zones and Economic-Development Policy

In Chapter 2 we present a history of enterprise zones in the United States and then critique the various rationales that have been put forward to justify geographically targeted approaches to economic development in general and enterprise zones in particular. The most notable of these rationales is the "spatial mismatch" hypothesis, which claims that inner-city residents face high rates of joblessness because they are spatially separated from suburban job opportunities. Enterprise zones can then be justified as a way of bringing jobs to depressed inner-city neighborhoods, thereby increasing employment rates of the urban poor. In this chapter we also review the major theoretical and policy criticisms that have been leveled at the enterprise zone idea. There is reason to be skeptical that spatial mismatch is the main cause of underemployment among inner-city minorities and that job proximity will necessarily produce higher rates of employment. Even if these claims were supported, it would be unclear that enterprise zones are the most cost-effective way to provide employment opportunities to those most in need of them. The primary conclusion of this chapter is that, even after decades of program experimentation, there is considerable confusion as to the goals of U.S. enterprise zone policy and the policy tools appropriate to attaining those goals.

Chapter 3: How Valuable Are Zone Incentives to Firms?

In this chapter we look at the sorts of incentives offered to firms locating in enterprise zones, estimate the true value of those incentives to business, and compare enterprise zone incentives to other (nontargeted) incentives available to firms. The typical package of incentives available to firms locating in an enterprise zone consists of an investment credit and a jobs credit, under the state corporate income tax, and local property-tax abatements. Looking at the 13 states that had substantial enterprise zone programs in place by 1990, we find that the average package among our 75 sampled cities was worth $5,048 per job in 1994, where the value of the package is measured by the increase in the present value of the 20-year cash flow attributable to investment in a new plant. Among the 75 cities, half had at least one sector for which the total incentive package exceeded $10,000 per job, and 14 cities would have granted at least one sector more than $20,000 per job. Incentives of this magnitude are equivalent to a gross undiscounted value in the range of $20,000 to $60,000 per job.

The total incentive-package values reported above included both incentives available only within enterprise zones in the 13 states and incentives available anywhere in the state. We also examined incentives available in a broader set of 20 of the most industrialized states and found that the average incentive package increased in value from $4,061 per job in 1990 to $5,338 per job in 1998. On average among the 20 states, the enterprise zone incentives per se accounted for 63 percent of the total package in 1990, but only 51 percent by 1998. Looking just at our 75-city sample, the enterprise zone share fell from 65 percent in 1990 to 57 percent in 1994. General incentives have been increasing more rapidly than enterprise zone incentives. Still, for the typical manufacturing firm, the incentive package more than doubles if the firm chooses an enterprise zone location over a non-zone location in the same state.

Competition among states and localities for manufacturing investment has led to reductions in basic state taxes as well as to increases in state and local incentives. The importance of these tax and incentive changes can best be measured by their effect on the overall state-local tax rate on new investment. The overall trend in the 1990s was overwhelmingly to reduce basic taxes on corporations. Among the 20 states, the median basic tax rate was reduced from 8.5 percent in 1990 to 7.9 percent in 1998. Larger reductions in the median effective tax rate occurred when general incentives were included (from 7.6 percent to 6.7 percent) and when targeted incentives were added (from 6.3 percent to 5.2 percent).

We found that tax rate and incentive competition continued through the 1990s with no indication that this is producing convergence in effective tax rates among the states; the process resembles a game of leapfrog, with no state apparently content to be merely average. The most striking evidence of this is the prevalence, by 1998, of *negative* tax rates on new investment: not only does the construction of a new plant, and the generation of sales and income from it, fail to generate additional tax liability to the state in which the plant is located, but the plant actually reduces the firm's tax liability to that state in many instances because new-plant credits exceed the entire new-plant tax.

Chapter 4: How Taxes and Incentives Favor One Industry over Another and Capital over Labor

Knowing how incentives increase business profitability is clearly key to evaluating enterprise zones, but we also need to have a sense of the firm's likely behavioral response to incentives. Do enterprise zone incentives change the relative prices of capital and labor, and should we expect to see some substitution of labor for capital, or capital for labor? This is an important issue. We argue in Chapter 2 that the central justification of the enterprise zone idea is the creation of employment in targeted areas. If the incentives we use "cause" a firm to locate in our zone, but at the same time cheapen the cost of capital relative to labor, the employment-creating effects of the investment may be much smaller than they otherwise would have been.

We found that 4 of our sample of 13 states provide, at the state level, a set of incentives to zone firms that clearly lowers the price of labor. Four other states have a clear capital bias. In the other 5 states, credits provide no clear reduction in labor or capital prices at the margin. When local incentives—property-tax abatements, primarily—are brought into the picture, however, the capital bias becomes much stronger.

The possible effects of incentives on a firm's choice of technology, and the relative use of capital and labor in the production process, depend not on the dollar amount of incentives but on changes in the prices of capital and labor. The effects of labor incentives on the price of labor are quite small. In only two states does the average price reduction exceed 1.0 percent, and the maximum price reduction among the 16

sectors we looked at never exceeds 3.0 percent in any state. Capital incentives, on the other hand, have substantial price effects in several of
the states. The average price reduction among sectors exceeds 5.0 percent in 8 of the 13 states, and in 6 states the maximum exceeds 20 percent for at least one sector. Indeed, there is a clear bias of incentive systems in favor of capital in all but 2 of the 13 states. Given the
significant substitutability between capital and labor in manufacturing
reported in empirical studies, it is likely that this capital bias in incentives will cause firms to adopt at least somewhat more capital-intensive
methods of production, which would partly offset—or possibly more
than offset—the employment gains from the location effects of incentives.

A related concern is the industrial policy implicit in enterprise zone
incentives. Incentives not only change the relative prices of capital and
labor, but also favor particular sorts of industrial firms. For instance,
the exemption of machinery and equipment from the local property tax
will benefit those firms that use relatively more machinery and equipment in their production processes. Sales-tax exemptions on energy
use will benefit those firms that use relatively more energy in their production processes, and so on. We find that the industrial-policy effects
of incentives are quite strong within our sample of 75 cities. It is quite
common for the most heavily taxed sector in a particular city to be facing a state-local tax rate two (or even three) times the rate on the least-
taxed sector. Thus, state and city taxes and incentives effectively dis-
criminate in favor of some sectors and against others. We believe it is
most unlikely that the industrial policy implicit in this pattern of sectoral preferences is intended, or even known, by state or local development officials or policymakers.

Chapter 5: The Fiscal Effects of Incentives

Even if enterprise zones do manage to encourage both new investment and new employment, they may still not be fiscally cost-effective
for government. There are a number of reasons for this, the most patent
being that expensive incentives may have a real but nevertheless small
total effect. The aim of this chapter is not to conduct a benefit-cost
analysis—we believe the benefits and costs of most economic-development policy still to be too ambiguous to be measured uncontroversial-

ly—but to analyze the direct fiscal impact of enterprise zone incentives. The analyses that we perform to look at this issue also permit us to evaluate the design of incentives and to recommend ways to structure them to increase the likelihood of generating a fiscal surplus.

Our research indicates that the direct revenue effects of enterprise zone incentives on state and local government combined are very likely to be negative, and rather strongly so. In the average enterprise zone city, among our sample of 75, each job that is actually induced by the zone incentives—in other words, jobs that would not exist there "but for" the incentives—would generate about $7,200 in net additional revenue to state government (in present-value terms over 20 years) and another $11,000 in local revenue. On the other hand, the state would lose about $4,600 for every new job that was not attributable to incentives (because some growth would have occurred anyway and that investment will receive the same incentive package), and localities would lose about $3,200 for each noninduced job. The key to determining whether government gains or loses from incentives is the ratio of induced to noninduced jobs. We find that in the average city, as long as this percentage of induced to total jobs was more than 30 percent, state and local government combined come out ahead. The problem is, research (ours and others) suggests that the percentage is likely to be considerably lower than 30 percent, if one defines an induced job as a job that would not have existed in that state but for the state-local incentive package. In fact, the current research consensus on the interstate or intermetropolitan effects of taxes on growth suggests the inducement percentage would be about 9 percent and the net annual state-local revenue loss would be about $7,130 per induced job in our average city. Total annual fiscal losses produced by an average-sized zone with an average incentive package could eventually be $1 to $2 million.

The purely local fiscal effects of a local zone tax incentive, on the other hand, are more difficult to estimate because of the paucity of intrametropolitan research studies, though positive effects are more likely since a move within the metropolitan area, while not representing a net gain for the state, will nonetheless produce a net gain for the receiving locale. Higher local inducement percentages are plausible and are supported by some research.

The work done for this chapter also allowed us to consider the design of incentive instruments. Contrary to conventional wisdom, we find that governments lose more revenue the more they front-load their incentives; other things being equal, a cost-effective incentive is a back-loaded one. Moreover, a permanent tax cut is more likely to produce positive revenues than a temporary cut with the same power to create jobs (i.e., with the same value to the firm over some decision-making time horizon).

Chapter 6: Manufacturing Growth and Decline in Enterprise Zones

In Chapters 3 through 5 we focus on zone incentives. In Chapter 6 we turn our attention to enterprise zones and growth. The analysis in Chapter 6 is descriptive and relies on special data runs undertaken for us by the Bureau of the Census. The data consist of establishment counts by industry and employment-size class. Our focus is on the composition of economic growth and decline in enterprise zones—the relative importance of establishment births, deaths, relocations into and out of zones, and employment expansions and contractions in zones.

When we examine the 13 sample states as a whole, we find that the six-year period 1989–1995 saw relative stability in the manufacturing sector, as measured by changes in the number of manufacturing establishments. The enterprise zones within those states, on the other hand, experienced a net loss of establishments. The average zone had 111 establishments in 1989; about 11 establishments were born or moved into the zone each year, but about 12.4 died or moved out. The net effect was a decline in establishments at a rate of about 1.2 percent per year, or a 7 percent net loss for the six-year period. Twenty-four zones experienced net declines of 15 percent or more over the period, however, while 11 experienced net *growth* of over 10 percent.

Establishments exiting the enterprise zones (through deaths or moves out) were, on average, just slightly larger than those entering. The percentage loss of manufacturing employment over the six-year period due to net loss in establishments was therefore likely to be a little more than the percentage loss of establishments. Zone employment was also greatly affected by the job expansions and contractions of firms that remain in the zone. Overall, of the establishments existing in these 64 zones at the beginning of a given period, about one in three expanded employment within the two-year period, and about one in three reduced employment. Larger establishments were much more likely to contract than smaller establishments, however, so it is likely that the net effect of expansions and contractions in these zones was further erosion in the job base, beyond the more than 9 percent attributable to net loss of establishments.

When we compared establishment growth and decline in zones with the states of which they were a part, we found that zones had a pronounced comparative disadvantage in attracting and retaining the more capital-intensive sectors of manufacturing. It is also clear that manufacturing in enterprise zones remains concentrated in "old economy" sectors, particularly printing and publishing and fabricated metal products. Zones appear to have a comparative disadvantage in electronic equipment, instruments, and chemicals.

When we examine expansions and contractions by time period we find a striking trend, however: the percent of establishments that remained in the zone and expanded increased with each two-year period, while the percentage that remained but reduced employment declined. Expansion rates exceeded contraction rates by a wide margin in the most recent period studied, 1993–1995, especially for the two smaller-size classes. It is quite possible that in the 1993–1995 period there was net employment growth in existing establishments in these zones sufficient to offset, or more than offset, the job losses due to exits exceeding entries. We think it likely that this trend persisted as the national economic expansion continued through the 1990s.

Chapter 7: Enterprise Zones, Incentives, and Local Economic Growth

In this chapter we make use of the same data set we employed in Chapter 6 and look again at the issue of growth, this time from an econometric point of view. Our aim here is to answer what is probably the key policy question: do enterprise zone incentives actually "cause" economic growth? We begin the chapter by looking at the various econometric models of enterprise zone impacts on growth developed by other researchers. Then we present results from our own analyses: one for our near-national sample of enterprise zones and another for enterprise zones in Ohio (Ohio has some of the best economic-development data in the nation). In essence, we develop models at two spatial scales and thus are able to measure both interstate enterprise zone impacts and intrastate impacts.

If zone incentives are to be effective, they must be sizeable enough to influence geographic investment decisions. We find that the average incentive packages for each of the sectors for the 13 states are equivalent to a 1.6 percent to 7.1 percent cut in wages. Thus, a relatively small wage premium would be sufficient in many locations to wipe out the advantages created by the incentive packages there. With the exception of some extreme cases, therefore, one would not expect incentives to have noticeably large effects on location decisions. Our statistical models of enterprise zone incentives and growth bear out this deduction. We find no evidence of a strong positive impact of enterprise zone incentives on growth: zones offering larger incentives (or a lower net tax rate) for firms in a given sector did not attract significantly more births and in-migrations of establishments in that sector than zones with a less attractive tax and incentive regime. While we do not claim that our research settles this matter, we do believe our results cast considerable doubt on the belief, widespread in economic-development policy circles, that incentives are crucial for growth in targeted areas. Our conclusions here are in line with much, but not all, of the recent econometric work on enterprise zones and growth. It is almost certain, then, that incentives have little impact on employment growth.

Chapter 8: Enterprise Zones and Access to Employment

All this leaves out an important issue: Who are the people who work in enterprise zones? Enterprise zones "may"—the results of Chapter 7 suggest that this is a big "may"—encourage new investment and employment, but we still need to know whether the zones provide jobs for residents of neighborhoods with less access to growing suburban labor markets. Merely creating local growth may not, in and of itself, be good enough. In Chapter 8 we assemble various data to give what are only preliminary answers to these questions. They are preliminary because the data we are able to use are both limited and not entirely appropriate to most of the questions we need to answer. We focus on the extent to which enterprise zones are able to attract more-disadvantaged workers and the extent to which they provide special work opportunities to those living in enterprise zones.

Tying the provision of business incentives to the requirement that recipient firms hire targeted workers appears not to have been a success. These requirements usually only apply to jobs credits and jobs credits are typically only a small part of the incentive packages provided. Moreover, it is possible that firms may avoid using incentives with strong "tying" provisions.

Improving the access of inner-city minorities and others to buoyant labor markets by locating zones in targeted areas also seems to be problematic. Enterprise zones attract workers from far and wide. In most of the enterprise zones we looked at, the majority of jobs were taken by commuters from outside the enterprise zone. Moreover, commute time of those working in enterprise zones appears to be longer than the average for those working elsewhere in the regions that contain the enterprise zones. This suggests that spatial proximity between home and work does not necessarily improve the accessibility of jobs.

Chapter 9: Conclusions and Policy Recommendations

In the final chapter we summarize our results and provide some broader thoughts on the role of enterprise zones, targeted incentives, and economic-development policy. Our overall assessment of enterprise zones is negative. There is great variability in what enterprise zones look like, what they are meant to achieve, and consequently what incentives are offered. Although our research has focused on those states in which enterprise zones are targeted at problem areas, enterprise zones in some other states look to be little more than delivery mechanisms for standard state and local economic-development policy. During the 1990s, in fact, non-spatially targeted incentives grew in importance relative to enterprise zone incentives, thus lessening the potential impact of enterprise zones. The zone incentives offered tend to favor capital rather than labor and appear to constitute a chaotic and unplanned industrial policy. Furthermore, these incentives usually cause losses to the public purse. Although there is a lot of business turnover in enterprise zones, zone incentives have only a minimal impact on new investment. Finally, enterprise zones do not seem to improve the spatial accessibility of employment to the disadvantaged. We end by proposing policy alternatives to enterprise zones.

There are many other policy questions about enterprise zones that need to be answered. For instance, we need to know the relationship between housing effects and economic-development effects in residential enterprise zones, whether zones can encourage minority entrepreneurship, and so on. We do not address these issues in this book, although we recognize that they are important to evaluating the overall effectiveness of the enterprise zone strategy. Because of how little we know about the basic employment effectiveness of enterprise zones, in this book we focus on a small set of basic economic questions: What are the incentives offered in enterprise zones and what are the employment growth effects of those incentives? Answering even this small set of questions has taken a huge research effort. We leave the other questions to other researchers.

STATES, CITIES, AND ENTERPRISE ZONES SAMPLED

The final issue to be dealt with in this chapter concerns our various state, city, and enterprise zone samples. The sample starts with the 20 states modeled in TAIM^{ez}—the largest industrial states, in terms of manufacturing employment. For these 20 states, we modeled taxes from 1990 through 1998. This sample provides us with our broadest historical view of enterprise zone policy in the United States and is the basis of the results in Chapter 3 comparing enterprise zone and nontargeted tax incentives. From these 20 states, we selected the 13 states with significant enterprise zone programs in place by 1990. (States with fewer than five enterprise zones were eliminated.) In each of these 13 states enterprise zone policy was "targeted" at distressed areas.[5] Within each state, we identified the enterprise zones located within cities of 25,000 population or more that were within a metropolitan statistical area (MSA or PMSA). The population cutoff was employed for two reasons: to facilitate data collection (since census data are readily available in much more detail for larger cities and for MSAs) and to avoid skewing the sample in favor of small cities in those states, such as Texas and Ohio, that have a very large number of zones in cities of all sizes. We then randomly selected six zones in each state, if possible (in a few states, there were only five zones in cities of 25,000 or more). This left us with a sample of 75 cities (see Table 1.1). It is a stratified sample, of course, based on states, in order to avoid having a sample made up largely of zones in the handful of states with 100 or more

Table 1.1 The 75 Enterprise Zones Sampled

State and zone name	Year started	City	City population	Included[a]
California				
Altadena/Pasadena (EZ)	1992	Pasadena	131,591	x
Los Angeles, NE Valley/Pacoima	1986	Los Angeles	3,485,398	x
Porterville (EZ)	1986	Porterville	29,563	x
Shasta Metro Redding/Anderson (EZ)	1991	Redding	66,462	
Sacramento: Northgate (EIA)	1986	Sacramento	369,365	
Stockton (EZ)	1993	Stockton	210,943	
Connecticut				
Hamden	1989	Hamden	52,434	x
Hartford	1982	Hartford	139,739	x
Meriden	1987	Meriden	59,479	x
New Britain	1982	New Britain	75,491	x
Norwalk	1982	Norwalk	78,331	x
Norwich	1987	Norwich	37,391	x
Florida				
Clearwater	1986	Clearwater	98,784	x
Fort Lauderdale	1986	Fort Lauderdale	149,377	x
Fort Myers	1986	Fort Myers	45,206	
Jacksonville	1986	Jacksonville	635,230	x
Miami Beach	1986	Miami Beach	92,639	x
Tampa	1986	Tampa	280,015	x
Illinois				
Champaign/Champaign County	1986	Champaign	63,502	x
Kankakee County (Manteno city)	1986	Kankakee	27,575	x
Maywood	1988	Maywood	27,139	x
Moline/Quad Cities	1988	Moline	43,202	x
Pekin/Tazewell County	1986	Pekin	32,254	x
Riverbend/Alton	1986	Alton	32,905	x
Indiana				
Evansville	1984	Evansville	126,272	x
Fort Wayne	1984	Fort Wayne	173,072	x

Table 1.1 (Continued)

State and zone name	Year started	City	City population	Included[a]
Indiana (continued)				
Hammond	1985	Hammond	84,236	x
Lafayette	1993	Lafayette	43,764	x
Muncie	1989	Muncie	71,035	x
South Bend	1984	South Bend	105,511	x
Kentucky				
Covington	1982	Covington	43,264	x
Hopkinsville	1982	Hopkinsville	29,818	
Lexington	1982	Lexington	225,366	x
Louisville	1982	Louisville	269,555	
Owensboro	1982	Owensboro	53,549	x
Missouri				
Joplin Area/Webb City	1985	Joplin	40,961	x
Kansas City Enterprise Zone	1985	Kansas City	435,146	x
Springfield Enterprise Zone	1984	Springfield	140,494	x
St. Joseph/Buchanan County	1985	St. Joseph	71,852	x
St. Louis Mid Town	1983	St. Louis	396,685	x
New York				
Auburn	1988	Auburn	31,258	x
New York City	1988	New York City	7,322,564	x
Niagara Falls	1988	Niagara Falls	61,840	x
Syracuse	1987	Syracuse	163,860	x
Troy	1987	Troy	54,269	x
Utica	1988	Utica	68,637	x
Ohio				
Canton	1986	Canton	84,161	x
Cincinnati 2 (#154)	1989	Cincinnati	364,040	x
Cleveland (#24)	1985	Cleveland	505,616	x
Elyria	1987	Elyria	56,746	x
Massillon	1986	Missillon	31,007	x
Warren (#111)	1988	Warren	50,793	x
Pennsylvania				
Chester	1983	Chester	41,856	x
Johnstown	1983	Johnstown	28,134	

Table 1.1 (Continued)

State and zone name	Year started	City	City population	Included[a]
Pennsylvania (continued)				
Lancaster	1988	Lancaster	55,551	x
Philadelphia-Hunting Park West	1983	Philadelphia	1,585,577	x
Pittsburgh: North Side	1983	Pittsburgh	369,879	x
Scranton	1988	Scranton	81,805	x
Texas				
Amarillo	1989	Amarillo	157,615	x
El Paso East	1993	El Paso	515,342	x
Fort Worth North	1988	Fort Worth	447,619	x
Pharr II	1991	Pharr	32,921	x
San Antonio: Eastside & Westside	1988	San Antonio	935,933	x
Waco Northwest	1991	Waco	103,590	
Virginia				
Danville	1984	Danville	53,056	
Lynchburg	1985	Lynchburg	66,049	
Newport News #1	1984	Newport News	170,045	x
Petersburg	1985	Petersburg	38,386	x
Portsmouth	1984	Portsmouth	103,907	x
Richmond #1 (south)	1993	Richmond	203,056	
Wisconsin				
Beloit	1989	Beloit	35,573	x
Fond Du Lac	1991	Fond Du Lac	37,757	x
Green Bay	1991	Green Bay	96,466	x
Milwaukee	1989	Milwaukee	628,088	x
Racine	1989	Racine	84,298	x

[a] x indicates that the zone was included in the final sample for the regression analyses.

zones each. There was no weighting applied; thus the results can be interpreted as comparisons of state enterprise zone policies, since each state receives approximately the same weighting in the sample. More detailed data on the sample can be found in Appendix E.

For the descriptive analyses of taxes and incentives in Chapter 3, we used the entire 75-city sample. The analyses in Chapters 6 and 7, on the other hand, were performed on a reduced sample of 65 zones, due to problems with the additional data required for these analyses, particularly the mapping of zone boundaries (see Appendix E for a discussion of the boundary issue). For the 13-state, 75-city sample and its derivatives, our concern was with taxes and incentives in 1990, 1992, and 1994. We also conducted a subsidiary analysis of enterprise zones in the state of Ohio. Because the state had readily available complete data on local taxes, including the actual property-tax-abatement schedules employed, as well as a complete set of computerized enterprise zone boundaries, it was feasible to do an additional analysis of all 104 Ohio cities with populations of 15,000 or more, with or without enterprise zones. Such a data set would be difficult or impossible to assemble for any of the other states we researched. The Ohio data set has an additional advantage: a number of new zones were created in these 104 cities during the period of our analysis, 1990–1994. This allows us to look directly at the impact of zone designation.

Finally, we have a small subsample of cities and zones (drawn from the original 75) for which we do further commuting analyses—these are described in Chapter 8. The reason for the reduction in sample size was that we needed to include a further set of conditions for zone specification in order to make sure that commuting patterns to and from zones were being measured appropriately. Thus, cities with fewer than 50 Traffic Analysis Zones (TAZs) were excluded as were cities that were part of very large, complex commuting regions (in essence, commuting regions with multiple, large, central cities). Also excluded were cities in which there were major changes to enterprise zone boundaries.

Notes

1. Of these zones, 2,083 were in just two states—Arkansas and Louisiana—and another 227 were in Ohio. At the other extreme, seven states had three or fewer zones. See Wilder and Rubin (1996).
2. See L. Papke (1994), Fisher and Peters (1997a), and Peters and Fisher (1998).
3. This assumes that differing tax burdens are not capitalized into land prices. We return to this issue in Chapter 2.
4. We put "causal" in quotation marks since econometric models by themselves are not evidence of truly causal relationships.
5. However, the degree of targeting varied, and some states had stricter targeting criteria than others. In Ohio, there were both targeted and nontargeted zones (see Table 2.1 in Chapter 2).

2
Enterprise Zones and
Economic-Development Policy

Enterprise zones have been on the American urban policy landscape for more than two decades. Indeed, there are many thousands of enterprise zones scattered across the United States. But there is still confusion as to exactly what enterprise zones are, what they are meant to achieve, and whether they are likely to be more effective than the rest of state and local economic-development efforts. The confusion is registered in the various names that states have given their enterprise zone programs: Renaissance Zones, Keystone Opportunity Zones, Development Zones, and Program Areas, for example.

In this chapter we attempt to bring some order to this confusion. We begin by looking at the early history of, and justification for, enterprise zones in the United States. We then focus on some of the more compelling arguments made in favor of enterprise zones: 1) the idea that targeting economic development at depressed areas is more effective and efficient than not so targeting; and 2) the claim that residents, particularly minority residents, of depressed inner-city neighborhoods are excluded from buoyant suburban labor markets and thus need targeted economic-development assistance. In the final section of the chapter we turn to the literature on the effectiveness of enterprise zones. We should point out that the issues highlighted in this chapter are important to understanding the arguments we make and conclusions we draw throughout the rest of the book.

WHAT IS AN ENTERPRISE ZONE?

With the passage of the Empowerment Zone and Enterprise Community Act in 1993, the federal government jumped into the enterprise zone arena, which until that time was exclusively a state and local policy domain in the United States. Between 1981 and 1991, 38 states and the District of Columbia passed enterprise zone legislation. As of

1995, 34 of those programs remained active, and in those states, 2,840 zones had been established (Wilder and Rubin 1996).[1] Two more states—Iowa and Michigan—have initiated enterprise zone programs since that time, and Pennsylvania has introduced a much more aggressive version of its enterprise zone. The federal program added 11 empowerment zones and 99 enterprise communities to this list in late 1994 (Hambleton 1996). These empowerment zones are located in eight major cities, each eligible for about $100 million in federal aid, and three multicounty rural areas, each eligible for $40 million. The enterprise communities are smaller cities and rural areas, each eligible for $3 million in federal assistance.[2]

It should not be surprising, then, that zones look different "on the ground." They vary widely in size, from sites smaller than 50 acres to entire counties (Rubin and Richards 1992). Louisiana has many thousands of zones, and more than one-third of Ohio is covered by the state's enterprise zones, whereas in many states there is a mere handful of zones and each zone is geographically small. Erickson and Friedman's (1990a) study of 357 zones found a median population of 4,500 and size of 1.8 square miles. In most states, zones are aimed at traditional industry (especially manufacturing), but some states encourage retail and service activity in their zones. Most zones have a residential component—in fact, many states have seen community and housing redevelopment as a crucial part of zone policy—but some do not. Probably the starkest difference concerns the incentives provided. States differ in what sorts of things they are prepared to subsidize with their enterprise zone legislation. Many have felt the need to cheapen the cost of labor in their zones in an attempt to increase labor demand for zone residents, but many others have adopted a strategy of cheapening the costs of capital, usually by utilizing some type of property-tax abatement or some type of tax credit for investment. Presumably, the capital-cheapening strategy has been pursued in the hope that the resulting new investment will create jobs.

Before moving on to more complicated questions we need a better understanding of what an enterprise zone is, or should be. In particular, we need to know how enterprise zones differ from other economic-development policy instruments and whether they have a unique set of goals that distinguishes them from other instruments. The words "enterprise," "empowerment," "renaissance," and so on, all point to the desire to revitalize or re-invigorate or regenerate targeted areas (zones) by relying on new private investment and entrepreneurship. In many states the criteria for zone designation suggest that they are antipoverty strategies as well. The implication—and it is no more than that—is that the enterprise zone strategy differs from most, but not all, other economic-development policy in that it is:

- geographically targeted;
- targeted at economically depressed (and probably older) areas, or areas in need of regeneration; and
- primarily reliant on investment by the private sector.

This is hardly a comprehensive definition.[3] In some states it would be controversial since it appears to imply that enterprise zones should not be located in new suburban greenfield locations. Nevertheless, we believe the definition goes to the crux of the original idea behind the enterprise zone movement in the United States and elsewhere. In the next section of this chapter we will briefly cover the history of enterprise zones in the United States. This will lead into a broader treatment of how enterprise zones differ from other economic-development policy instruments and the ideas behind the enterprise zone concept. In both these sections we will expand on and attempt to justify this definition (or understanding) of enterprise zones. This will provide us with some criteria for evaluating the effectiveness of state-level enterprise zones, criteria we will return to later in the book.

THE ENTERPRISE ZONE IDEA

In the United States, geographically targeted policy aimed at poor and economically declining areas has been around at least since the New Deal. After World War II the federal government became heavily involved in supporting the revitalization of older inner-city areas. First it was urban renewal; then came the various programs that were to become consolidated into the Community Development Block Grant (CDBG) program, and later Urban Development Action Grants (UDAGs) and several programs administered by the Economic Development Administration (EDA)—all meant to provide federal funding for the relief of blight and decay. Very often federal funds came in conjunction with state and local funding. For instance, Title IX (Special Adjustment Assistance) funding from the EDA provided flexible planning and program grants to help localities overcome sudden and severe job loss. In the case of the UDAGs, the focus was on leveraging private investment, usually in older inner-city or downtown areas, using relatively limited amounts of federal funds. Many of the other programs could be described in similar terms. Moreover, some states had funding mechanisms similar to the federal government's that targeted economically blighted or depressed areas.

Enterprise zones differ from all these programs in concept. The idea of the enterprise zone is usually attributed to a few British academics (particularly Peter Hall) and politicians who had become impressed, in the later 1970s, by the levels of local enterprise and entrepreneurship found in some east Asian economies, particularly Hong Kong (Hall 1977, 1982). In 1978, Sir Geoffrey Howe, then a conservative Member of Parliament and later a minister with various portfolios in Margaret Thatcher's Conservative government, coined the term. His belief was that government should lessen its hold over the more derelict parts of British cities. In effect, this would mean reducing government regulation (particularly land-use regulation) and taxation (Butler 1991). Underlying this proposal was the belief that east Asian economies were so vibrant precisely because the hand of government there was so light. The hope then was that a reduction in the burden of government in parts of British cities would stimulate local enterprise and investment that would otherwise be smothered.

Twenty years later it is still unclear whether there is a strong relationship between the burden of government and the level of entrepreneurship. Few today would see the earlier success of the Asian tigers as a result of the small burden of government in those countries. Nevertheless, the enterprise zone idea proved potent both in the United Kingdom—where by 1981 a dozen enterprise zones had been designated—and in the United States. Stuart Butler, an Anglo-American policy analyst at The Heritage Foundation, a conservative Washington think tank, is usually credited with popularizing the idea in U.S. policy circles.[4] The idea attracted bipartisan interest, in particular from Jack Kemp, then a Republican representative from New York, and from

Robert Garcia, a liberal Democrat from the South Bronx. Together, in 1981, they cosponsored the first U.S. enterprise zone legislation.

Three points need to be made about this legislation. The first is the wide range of groups who were attracted to the idea. The second is that the legislation failed, not only because of opposition from both left and right, but also because of opposition from some cabinet members in the Reagan administration, even though enterprise zones were part of the official Reagan administration policy as early as 1981.[5] The third is that the failure of the federal government to enact meaningful enterprise zone legislation created room for the states to pass their own enterprise zone bills.

Why did the enterprise zone idea attract bipartisan support? On the Republican side the answer is fairly clear: enterprise zones were different from traditional inner-city policy. They did not involve the federal government spending money on costly programs that seemed, at least from the Republican perspective, to have failed. They involved a reduction in taxes and regulation. They relied primarily on private initiative. Moreover, in 1979 David Birch came out with his very influential book—*The Job Generation Process*—which claimed that small firms were responsible for most job generation in the United States. Soon after, academics and policymakers began to argue for government policies to stimulate or facilitate the formation of new businesses. Enterprise zones seemed to fit directly with such a goal. It is also true that there were those on both the right and left who saw enterprise zones as a way of promoting indigenous inner-city entrepreneurship (locals creating local businesses employing local labor) instead of the more traditional way of dealing with urban blight (attracting big firms to depressed neighborhoods using the traditional array of economic-development incentives).

Reasons for early liberal Democrat support for enterprise zones are a little more difficult to discern—after all, enterprise zones involve a *reduction* of taxes and *deregulation*. Stuart Butler (1991) claimed that there were two important reasons. First, many inner-city politicians had come to the conclusion that traditional inner-city policy had failed their constituents. Most notoriously, urban renewal was widely credited with actually destroying inner-city neighborhoods. Second, enterprise zones were the only policy game in town—traditional inner-city programs were most unlikely to expand during the early Reagan years. But it is also true that many liberals supported enterprise zones because, at least in the U.S. version, they tied economic development to community development and they appeared to prefer small firms to large firms. They were pro big city (when some Democrats still saw this as an important part of their political base) and pro poor. Moreover, enterprise zones took an essentially optimistic view of the residents of depressed neighborhoods: given the opportunity, inner-city residents could be as entrepreneurial and hard working as the rest of Americans.

More than 20 years later, it is clear that many of these reasons for support were decidedly flimsy, possibly even misguided. The proposed federal enterprise zones would involve the federal government in very considerable tax-credit expenditures. It is difficult to maintain there is any substantive policy distinction between direct spending on program y to achieve goal x and indirect spending through some tax credit z revenue loss to achieve goal x. The Birch report massively exaggerated the role of small firms in job generation (Armington and Odle 1982; Brown, Hamilton, and Medoff 1990). The biggest obstacle to new business formation is unlikely to be taxes or regulation—most of the evidence suggests that factors such as access to capital are of much greater importance in the firm-formation decision.[6] The jobs provided by small firms are likely to pay less, have fewer benefits, and be less secure than those provided by big firms. Finally, using individual entrepreneurship as a way of dealing with individual unemployment is highly risky. New small firms, particularly those with little capital, tend to fail at an exceptionally high rate.

The early federal enterprise zone legislation failed partly because of bipartisan concerns over these and other issues,[7] and partly because of opposition from other federal departments, particularly the Treasury, which argued that the federal tax system should be as neutral as possible. In essence the Treasury view maintained that special tax treatments for targeted industries or places distorted the economy and thus made the United States poorer than it would otherwise be. The belief that the tax code was not the place to make industrial-policy or social-policy decisions won the day, in spite of the fact that the 1981 federal tax legislation was decidedly non-neutral (Fisher 1985).

State enterprise zones began as a result of federal activity. A few states passed enterprise zone legislation in the early 1980s in the hope that this would increase their chances of being chosen for federal enterprise zone status (Beaumont 1991). "Thus the eligibility criteria of most state measures mirrored those in the federal legislation . . . and the tax, regulatory and other measures included in the legislation and programs at the state level, broadly conformed to most people's best guess of a package likely to win applause from the federal officials administering an enterprise program" (Butler 1991, p. 39). The failure of the federal legislation changed this; states were now free to experiment—in fact, the states have dominated the enterprise zone debate from the failure of the early federal legislation to the passing of the Empowerment Zone/Enterprise Community legislation during the first Clinton administration. One result of this is that the enterprise zone idea has become much more nebulous than it was in the late 1970s and early 1980s. State zones differ on objectives, tools, and, thus, results. In some instances, enterprise zones are little more than geographically targeted versions of standard state and local economic-development programs.[8] They are a way of packaging and marketing traditional economic-development services to mainly suburban industrial parks. In many states, however, they are targeted in accordance with the original enterprise zone idea, though even here there is confusion as to whether the zone should be merely an industrial or commercial area needing revitalization or a low-income area with people needing jobs.

To what extent are zones targeted at more depressed areas? By design, all of the 13 states in our sample for this book target their enterprise zones at distressed areas, at least to a degree.[9] The criteria for zone designation in the 13 states are summarized in Table 2.1; clearly, there is considerable variation among the states. But does this targeting show up "on the ground"? In earlier research on state and local economic development, we found that enterprise zone incentives, unlike almost all other incentives, were more likely to be larger in higher-unemployment cities (Fisher and Peters 1998). This suggests that enterprise zone incentives, at least, are indeed targeted. However, probably the best evidence on this issue comes from Greenbaum (2001), who has examined zone siting decisions in the District of Columbia and nine states: California, Florida, Kentucky, Maryland, New Jersey, New York, Pennsylvania, Tennessee, and Virginia. He finds unequivocal evidence that zones are sited in distressed neighborhoods.

Table 2.1 State Enterprise Zone Eligibility Criteria as of 1992

State	Poverty, income, or unemployment criteria		Poverty rate	Income	Unemployment rate	Other criteria	Population	Area
	Must satisfy one	Not necessary						
California	Must meet both the income and the unemployment criteria (Waters zones)		1.5 times national average		1.5 times national average	UDAG program eligibility (Nolan zones)	At least 4,000	
Connecticut	Any of 3 criteria		25%		2 times state average	25% of population recipients of welfare		
Florida		Multiple criteria; 2 of 8 relate to income or unemployment						
Illinois	Any 1 of 5 criteria; 3 relate to income or unemployment		20%	70% of households less than 80% of city median income	1.2 times state average	Population decline of 20% 1970–80 or zone will result in investment of $100m. and 1,000 full-time jobs		

Indiana	Must meet either poverty or unemployment criterion	25% below 80% of poverty level		1.5 times state average	General distress	2,000 to 8,0000	0.75 to 3.0 square miles
Kentucky	Any 1 of 3 criteria; 2 relate to income or unemployment		70% of households less than 80% of city median income	1.5 times national average	Population decline of 10% 1980–90		
Missouri	Must meet both the income and the unemployment criteria		65% of households less than 80% of state median income	1.5 times state average	UDAG criteria, or pervasive poverty, unemployment, and general distress	4,000 to 32,000	
New York	Either zone or county must meet poverty and unemployment standards	20% (zone) 13% (county)		1.25 times state average		At least 2,000	Up to 1 square mile
Ohio (Distress Based)[a]	Any 1 or 2 of 6 criteria; 3 relate to income or unemployment		51% of residents less than 80% of city median income	1.25 times state average	Abandoned or demolished structures; 10% population loss 1970–90; low tax capacity school district	At least 4,000	

Table 2.1 (Continued)

State	Poverty, income, or unemployment criteria		Poverty rate	Income	Unemployment rate	Other criteria	Population	Area
	Must satisfy one	Not necessary						
Pennsylvania		City must be "financially disadvantaged"				Multiple criteria; some relate to income or unemployment		
Texas	Must meet the unemployment or the population-loss standard, and 1 other criterion		"low income poverty area"	70% of residents less than 80% of city or state median income	1.5 times local, state or national average	9% population loss for 6-year period or 3% for 3 years; UDAG eligible; property abandonment; tax delinquencies; disaster area		
Virginia	Any 1 of 3 criteria; 2 relate to income or unemployment			25% of residents less than 80% of city median income	1.5 times state average	Industrial or commercial vacancy rate of 20% or more		

| Wisconsin | Must meet 2 of 6 criteria; 5 relate to income or unemployment | 40% of residents less than 80% of state median income | 1.5 times state average | UDAG eligible; declining property values; rate of welfare recipiency 1.5 times state average; 5% of workforce permanently laid off | At least 4,000 |

SOURCE: U.S. Department of Housing and Urban Development, State Enterprise Zone Update, 1992; enterprise zone materials obtained from the states of New York, Ohio, Indiana, and Pennsylvania.

a Ohio also allowed zones to qualify without showing distress, but restricted somewhat the use of incentives in these zones. All 6 Ohio zones in our 13-state sample are distressed.

The typical state enterprise zone program includes investment tax credits (ITCs), job tax credits, sales-tax exemptions or credits, and property-tax abatements. In our 1998 study of incentives in 24 states in 1992, we found that 22 of those states had enterprise zone programs, 20 of them active (Fisher and Peters 1998). Five of the 24 states provided statewide ITCs, and 4 of these 5 provided more generous versions within enterprise zones. Another four states provided ITCs only in zones. Similarly, four of the states provided statewide jobs tax credits, and two of these provided more generous versions in enterprise zones. Another 14 states provided jobs credits exclusively to firms locating in zones. Seven states provided a full or partial exemption of income taxes on profits attributable to zone investment. Thus, state corporate income tax credits were in general much more prevalent and more generous in enterprise zones than statewide, and within enterprise zones, jobs credits were employed twice as often as investment credits.

Sales tax exemptions, on the other hand, were generally offered statewide. Exemptions for sales taxes on manufacturing machinery and equipment were permitted statewide in 19 of the 24 states; only 2 states restricted such exemptions to enterprise zones. The corresponding figures for fuel and electricity exemptions were 17 and 2. Four states exempted from sales taxation virtually all personal property purchased for business use in an enterprise zone. Of the 22 states with enterprise zone programs in our 1998 study, 19 permitted local property-tax abatements in the zones, though in 13 of those 19 states abatements were permitted outside zones as well. Of the 13 states that are the focus of this book, 4 did not allow abatements at all (or allowed them under such restrictive conditions that they were rarely used), 6 allowed them anywhere (and they were generally applied throughout a locality), and 3 permitted them only within an enterprise zone (though in 1 of these, Ohio, zones are so prevalent—there are over 300 in the state—that abatements cannot really be described as targeted to distressed areas). Local property-tax abatements, where they are allowed, are always applied to real property improvements—new buildings, additions to buildings, or site improvements such as access roads. They are not applied to land purchases. In states in which personal property such as inventories, vehicles, or machinery and equipment are subject to the property tax, abatements may apply to one or more categories of personal property as well. The typical abatement relieves a declining percentage of taxes each year for a number of years, usually 5 to 10.

In our 1992 sample of 112 cities, 44 contained enterprise zones. The total incentive package available in these zones was, on average, worth two to three times as much as the incentive package available in the average city without an enterprise zone. Within the zones, enterprise zone incentives accounted for 35 percent of the total incentive package on average, with substantial variation depending on firm characteristics. State incentives represented about two-thirds of the total enterprise zone package, the remainder consisting of local incentives (mostly property-tax abatements). It is significant that general incentives (available to non-enterprise zone firms) were two to three times as generous in the enterprise zone cities as in the non-enterprise zone cities. In other words, the cities that contained enterprise zones were providing larger incentives citywide than the average city. The average city with an enterprise zone had a 27 percent higher unemployment rate, a 45 percent higher poverty rate, and an 85 percent higher proportion of blacks in the population than the average city without zones.

The average effective state-local tax rate in the 20 states with active enterprise zones was measured by constructing a representative city for each state, with a property-tax rate equal to the average or the median for that state, and a property-tax-abatement program typical of the cities in our sample for that state.[10] The tax rate in these cities averaged 9.1 percent outside enterprise zones, but 7.3 percent within a zone. The average state enterprise zone program thus reduced the state and local tax burden on new investment by about 19 percent. Although effective tax rates differ dramatically depending on firm characteristics, zones had similar effects (in terms of the percentage reduction in the tax rate) among firms. There was considerable variation among the 20 cities, however. Outside enterprise zones, the effective tax rate was 5.6 percent in the lowest-tax city (averaged over the 16 firms we modeled) but 14.7 percent in the highest-tax city. With zone incentives included, the tax rates among the states ranged from 3.7 percent to 13.2 percent. Tax rates were lowered by enterprise zones, but the variation among states remained high. Some states with high average tax rates, such as California, had very generous enterprise zone incentives, while other high-tax states, such as Washington, had enterprise zone programs that did very little to offset these taxes.

Depending on how one looks at these things, this very brief history suggests either a certain amount of policy confusion or a certain level of policy experimentation. Nevertheless, excluding those cases in which enterprise zones are merely a way of packaging and marketing standard incentives, we can characterize enterprise zones as targeting incentives at particular geographical areas, originally as a way of encouraging local indigenous enterprise in depressed neighborhoods, but more recently as a way of encouraging new investment. The need to target is usually justified in terms of the need to provide better access to job opportunities for the un- and underemployed, though in many states defining exactly where access to job opportunities needs to be improved is politically controversial. It is to these issues we now turn.

DOES THE ENTERPRISE ZONE CONCEPT MAKE SENSE? SOME PRELIMINARY ISSUES

Are enterprise zones a good idea? It appears fairly straightforward that targeting economic-development policy at the places and people most in need of help must be the right way to do economic-development policy. Indeed, when we embarked on this project, that was our belief. As we attempted to develop the arguments that would justify this position, however, we found that the issues are anything but straightforward.

We begin the discussion of those issues here by placing enterprise zones in the wider context of economic-development policy, which has been the target of much criticism over the past two decades. Economic-development policy has been widely charged with corporate welfarism and fiscal irresponsibility, among other things. Moreover, it is commonly asserted that U.S. economic-development policy, when evaluated from a national perspective:

- is a zero-sum game (economic-development policy has not generated net new American investment; it merely moves investment around), or
- has a negative net impact on the national economy (economic-development policy distorts the workings of private location decisions),[11] or

- is fundamentally ineffective (incentives are too small to influence investment decisions).

Furthermore, many economists are doubtful that state and local development policies are effective even from a local perspective and even if they do influence investment decisions. Economic development tends to provide mainly place-based subsidies, encouraging investment in particular localities. Most economists argue, however, that because of the high level of mobility of U.S. workers, the localized (or place) effects of policy are lost through in-migration. Creating jobs in a particular place x, will not necessarily lower the unemployment rate in x, or even increase the labor-force participation rate there, because almost all the new jobs will be taken by better qualified in-migrants (Foster, Forkenbrock, and Pogue 1991; Marston 1985). These sorts of criticisms have been covered extensively in the literature—indeed, we dealt with many of them in the last book we wrote on economic-development policy.[12] Thus we will not review the literature here, except to make a few broad comments that have relevance to the enterprise zone issue.

Whether tax incentives amount to corporate welfare depends on how one defines the latter term. If by welfare one means that the firm receives more in government goods and services than it pays in taxes, the charge of welfarism is fairly easily dismissed. While there are clear fiscal differences among states and localities, the evidence suggests that, on the whole, business pays far more in state and local taxes than it receives in state and local services (Oakland and Testa 1996). Of course, the extreme economic-development deals and incentives that crop up in newspaper headlines fairly frequently may indeed amount to corporate welfare for particular firms. Furthermore, as we report later in this book, incentive packages can produce negative income tax rates on new investment, so that the new plant is clearly being subsidized, even if the firm as a whole is not.

Corporate welfare can, on the other hand, be defined more broadly—as tax expenditures benefitting business. The argument here is that a tax credit or exemption is a deviation from the base tax system and is therefore a tax expenditure, and so should be viewed in the same light as a direct expenditure program. Just as the homeowner deduction for mortgage interest can be characterized as one of the nation's largest "welfare" programs, and one disproportionately benefitting the rich (who nonetheless probably still pay more in taxes than they receive in benefits from government), so too can an investment tax credit be viewed as an economic-development subsidy to business, and hence as corporate welfare, even if corporations still pay more in taxes than they receive in benefits. The basis for this position is that the basic corporate income tax is part of the overall tax system based on the principle of ability to pay and should not be evaluated as a benefit tax in the first place, as is implied in the first definition of corporate welfare.

The issue of fiscal irresponsibility is more difficult to answer since it is dependent on the variable managerial abilities of state and local governments. Estimates we conducted for Ohio—one of the nation's better managed states—suggest that fiscal incentives, including enterprise zone incentives, nearly always cost states and cities more than they benefit firms (Peters and Fisher 1999a). In other words, the incentives have a value-to-firm/cost-to-government ratio of less than one.[13] Part of the reason for this is the interdependence of state and local taxes, on the one hand, and federal taxes on the other. A portion of the value of a state or local incentive will be captured by the federal Treasury and usually also by other state (and possibly local) governments. The much more extensive results we present in Chapter 5 confirm, for a wider set of states, our Ohio findings—enterprise zones are seldom fiscally cost-effective. But value-to-firm/cost-to-government ratios, or even the considerably more complex fiscal measures we develop in Chapter 5, do not take into account the full costs and benefits of incentives. It is possible for the value-to-firm/cost-to-government ratio to be less than one while the full benefit-cost ratio of the incentive is greater than one. The reason for this is that the benefits included in any benefit-cost calculation will cover more than just the income enhancement captured by the firm; they will also include the difference between the wages offered to those employees working in the new plant and the reservation wages of those workers, increases in the value of local property as a result of the new investment, and so on.[14]

Unfortunately, there are few reliable, applied, and broadly applicable benefit-cost estimates of economic-development incentives. With regard to enterprise zones, the benefit-cost studies that do exist suggest that zones are cost-efficient. Rubin and Armstrong's (1989) and Rubin's (1991) evaluations of New Jersey enterprise zones, Rubin,

Brooks, and Buxbaum's (1992) study of Indiana zones, and the more recent study of the Ohio program all indicated positive fiscal gains and positive benefit-cost ratios (once certain assumptions are met), although all show considerable variation among individual zones.[15] Less-formal estimates of the costliness of zones—attempts to calculate zone costs-per-job—suggested moderate costs, at least compared to other economic-development tools, although, again, there is evidence of wide variability among zones (J. Papke 1988, 1989; Rubin and Wilder 1989).

Unfortunately, all these studies are open to dispute. The results rely on questionable estimates of the extent to which the existence of the enterprise zones influences firm investment behavior. In the case of Rubin's (1991) important New Jersey study, Rubin was forced to survey firms to estimate the percentage of firms that actually responded to zone incentives. This estimate was then used to prorate the input-output derived-benefit calculation. For reasons that should become clearer later in this book, such survey-based estimates should be treated with some scepticism. Moreover, in all these studies, benefits and costs remain local—national consequences of zone incentives are essentially ignored. Thus it appears to us that, at this point, the most convincing benefit-cost analyses of economic development are purely hypothetical; they indicate the likely *national* benefit-cost situation, given a number of assumptions about economic-development subsidies.

Given the results of these hypothetical benefit-cost models, it seems that economic-development policy is neither necessarily cost-effective nor cost-ineffective. It all depends on how economic-development policy is managed. Bartik's (1991) hypothetical cost-benefit model has been widely quoted in the literature. If Bartik is correct, then one of the major determinants of policy effectiveness is the extent to which policy is targeted. He claims that economic-development policy is more likely to be cost-effective and efficient when it is pursued in economically depressed areas (measured by the unemployment rate) and less likely to be efficient when pursued in economically buoyant areas. One of the major reasons for this is a reservation wage differential between depressed and nondepressed areas. Typically the reservation wage—the lowest wage at which a person is willing to work—will be lower in more-depressed areas and higher in less-depressed areas. As a result, moving a $10.00-an-hour job from Omaha (a relatively

nondepressed low-unemployment area with individuals with a relatively high reservation wage) to Detroit (a relatively depressed high-unemployment area with a relatively low reservation wage), while not creating a net new job from the national perspective, does result in a net
increase in the benefits that the job provides. This is because the economic benefit of the job—$10.00 minus the reservation wage—is
greater in Detroit than it is in Omaha.[16] If this is true,

> The net national benefits of increasing job growth in one local area
> and reducing job growth in other areas thus depends on the rela-
> tive unemployment rate of the local area that enjoys increased job
> growth . . . from a national perspective, we should applaud eco-
> nomic development policies to increase job growth when these
> policies are pursued by high-unemployment local areas, and de-
> plore economic development policies to increase jobs when they
> are pursued by low-unemployment areas. (Bartik 1991, p. 192)

Bartik has made similar points in more recent papers on economic-
development policy. Two inferences are clear. First, economic-development policy need not be zero-sum even when no net new jobs are
created. It all depends on what the job-recipient region (the region receiving the plant) looks like compared to the job-donor region (the region losing the plant). Second, the targeting of economic-development
policy at depressed regions (regions with high unemployment rates) is
appropriate and, all else being equal, is likely to be beneficial to the national economy.

We believe Bartik's strong defense of targeting to be one of the
very best economic arguments in favor of the enterprise zone strategy.
However, this certainly does not mean that an enterprise zone strategy
focused on poor, high-unemployment, inner-city neighborhoods will
necessarily work or will necessarily be efficient economically. The
overall effectiveness and efficiency of a particular enterprise zone strategy will depend on a number of other factors, including such things as
how zones are designated, how many are allowed, the costliness of the
incentives used, the day-to-day management of the development strategy, whether incentives actually promote new investment, and so on.[17]
All Bartik's results allow us to conclude is that targeting may make
economic sense—that a place-based economic-development strategy
may be effective—provided that the right sort of area is targeted.

Part of the reason that Bartik's benefit-costs results are positive is that he is able to rebut that standard labor "mobility" argument. The traditional economic argument against place-based economic development is that the U.S. labor force is highly mobile. According to Marston (1985), over a typical four-year period, more than 13 percent of the population moves between metropolitan areas. The new people moving into an area are likely to swamp whatever new employment is created in that area. Thus the vast proportion of new jobs created (or locating) in an area will be taken by in-migrants. What is the effect of economic-development policies on the original inhabitants of the area who were unemployed? Not much! In fact, many have argued that place-based economic development merely provides incentives for people to move between areas and that it fails to resolve the employment needs of those who are un- or underemployed. The obvious conclusion is that employment-creating economic-development incentives will have little or no long-term impact on a local area's unemployment and labor-force participation rates. Thus, targeting economic-development policy at enterprise zones will not work because all it will do is attract labor from elsewhere. Economic-development policy needs to be people-based—if luring firms into an area will not help the economically disadvantaged, then the thing to do is directly improve the skills and mobility of the economically disadvantaged.

There is evidence that mobility rates are not homogenous across all demographic groups. Older people, people who have stayed in an area for longer periods of time, minorities, and women all tend to be less willing to move than the rest of the population and appear to be ready to forego significant amounts of income in order not to move. Moreover, the mobility of the rest of the population is anything but instant. People need time to hear of the opportunities available in other areas, and they then need to organize their move to those areas (selling their homes or arranging sublets, arranging for the transportation of household goods, arranging schooling for their children in the new area, finding a new home and so on). The result is that if 100 jobs are relocated to city z, it is most unlikely that all 100 jobs will be taken immediately by new in-migrants. Indeed, the delays involved in moving to a new labor market mean that when new jobs are created in city z, city z's un- and underemployed enjoy temporary but important labor advantages over potential new worker in-migrants. City z's un- and underemployed are where the jobs are! Consequently, they are more likely to become employed. Of course, if this temporary advantage does not translate into a longer-term labor effect, then the situation would still not be that hopeful for city z's un- and underemployed. If, say, after six or nine months the now newly employed locals were replaced by better-qualified labor streaming into city z, then the delays involved in migrating would only provide a fleeting advantage to the economically disadvantaged locals.

It appears from the empirical evidence that the job benefits conferred on some of the previously unemployed locals are long lasting. Bartik (1991) hypothesized that the reason for this was that by working, the newly employed locals increased their skills and human capital, thereby making themselves more attractive as employees in the future.[18] Clocking in on time and interacting with other employees and the public build the basic employment skills that employers believe the economically disadvantaged do not have. In fact, it appears that employment demand shocks have positive long-term employment, labor-force participation, and income effects. If all of this is true, enterprise zones seem to make a lot of theoretical sense. All else being equal, economically disadvantaged locals derive long-term benefits from local employment growth. The benefits of growth are not entirely taken by new in-migrants. Moreover, targeting at economically disadvantaged areas produces national economic benefits.

But why target enterprise zones? Or more specifically, why designate enterprise zones in older, inner-city neighborhoods? If metropolitan areas serve as single labor markets, why impose on business the extra costs of location in older inner-city neighborhoods? Why not have enterprise zones in the suburbs and encourage the economically disadvantaged to commute to these suburban employment sites? According to Dabney (1991), enterprise zones in older inner-city areas will nearly always be more expensive locations from which to operate than new greenfield sites. The reasons he offers are quite standard: inner-city locations have poorer infrastructure, are further removed from the non-congested parts of the federal highway system and from airports, have poorer agglomeration economies, have more crime, and are less accessible to suburban labor. If all this is true—and there is every reason to believe that it is—it may suggest a policy strategy of targeting economic-development incentives at depressed cities or metropolitan areas, but putting the enterprise zones in the most competitive part of those cities, probably the suburbs. Government could then be seen as having three separate roles: 1) making sure that these suburban areas are truly competitive for new investment; 2) developing policy instruments that encourage the economically disadvantaged to commute to the new jobs in the suburbs or to move their residences closer to these jobs; and 3) creating policy instruments that encourage business to employ the economically disadvantaged.

In many ways, this sort of criticism takes us full circle. It is to ask why those with fewer local employment opportunities do not commute to places with more opportunities. And it is to ask: If there is some hindrance to commuting to or hiring at these suburban work sites, why not deal with these problems directly (by increasing the accessibility of, or by removing skill or even racial barriers to, employment) rather than trying to resolve them only indirectly (by attempting to create jobs in inner cities)?

Unfortunately there are no clear answers to these questions. The most prominent theory of why un- or underemployed inner-city residents do not commute to buoyant suburban labor markets is the "spatial mismatch hypothesis." First developed by Kain (1968),[19] the hypothesis makes some fairly straightforward claims about urban labor and housing markets. Since the 1910s, but particularly after World War II, industry has been moving from inner-city locations to suburban greenfield sites. The reasons for this range from the development of the truck (making access to ports and railroad sidings less important), to the use of the modern land-consuming single-story factory, to the building of the interstate highway system (benefitting suburban sites served by the highway system), to the decentralization of labor to the suburbs, to the desire to escape unionized and minority workers (traditionally located in inner-city areas). Decentralization meant that inner-city areas lost employment opportunities. Moreover, the middle-class moved out from these areas, with the result that the inner cities developed concentrated populations of economically disadvantaged people, particularly racial minorities. Such individuals found working at suburban work sites difficult. Public transit was built, in the United States as elsewhere, on the basis of moving workers downtown. Serving scattered suburban work sites from inner-city origins (so-called reverse commuting) has proved difficult and costly to implement largely because of the low-density nature of suburban work sites. Moreover, the economically disadvantaged inner-city residents could not easily move to suburban homes because of the cost of those homes and because of long-standing racial discrimination in U.S. housing markets. Thus, economically disadvantaged inner-city residents are effectively cut off from buoyant suburban job markets. The results are lower levels of la- bor- force participation and higher levels of unemployment in inner- city neighborhoods. This suggests that insofar as enterprise zones di- rect jobs to the economically disadvantaged inner city, they may help overcome some of the constraints to employment experienced by inner- city residents. We believe that this sort of argument is the crux of the justification for traditional enterprise zones.

The problem with this argument is that it is not clear to what extent the spatial mismatch hypothesis explains the underemployment of mi- nority inner-city residents. A number of studies have shown that racial discrimination in job markets and lack of skills (the so-called skills mismatch) are much more important considerations than accessibili- ty—that "race not space" is the cause of un- or underemployment of the inner-city minority population. And even if it can be shown that space—that is, accessibility—is an important problem, it is still not clear that creating jobs in inner-city areas is the appropriate policy strat- egy. Transportation planners have for years been working on ways to make reverse commuting more efficient. Moreover, the federal govern- ment has engaged in various experiments involving moving the resi- dents of some disadvantaged inner-city neighborhoods to the suburbs. The earliest of these was the so-called Gautreaux experiment in Chica- go (Rosenbaum et al. 1991; Rosenbaum 1996). Behind this view is the belief that economic-development policy should be people based not place based—that it makes little sense to lure businesses to places they would rather not be, while it makes a lot of sense to expand the eco- nomic opportunities available to people. If it is indeed possible to pro- vide the inner-city minority population with full access—whatever this means—to suburban employment opportunities, then why bother creat- ing expensive inner-city jobs?

Defenders of enterprise zones have no easy answers to this ques- tion. Yes, even in those spatial mismatch studies which show that race and skill level are the predominant causes of inner-city underemploy- ment, accessibility to employment remains a non-negligible explanato- ry factor of underemployment. Yes, the Gautreaux experiment has had its problems (the children of those who were moved to the suburbs saw a large improvement in their long-term economic well-being but not their parents), and, because of political opposition, it has been very difficult to implement more widely.[20] Yes, public transit-based reverse commuting has not been a success and is likely always to be more expensive to operate than traditional transit. Yes, emptying out the inner city of employable adults is likely to worsen the situation of those left behind and further deprive inner-city neighborhoods of role models of employed adults actively participating in traditional labor markets. But it is not hard to think of policy alternatives that address these issues while still not relying on inner-city enterprise zones. With enough federal input and funding, reverse commuting may become viable. Gautreaux-type programs could be designed so as to overcome the objections of suburbanites and the reservations of inner-city residents. And so on. The point to make in favor of enterprise zones is that these possibilities require thought experiments. Successful people-based alternatives to enterprise zones (a place-based policy mechanism) do not exist outside of a few experiments. This is not to say that in the long run people-based strategies would not be better; we believe that the economics of the case suggest they would. But in the meantime taking jobs to people is one of the few politically feasible strategies available.

The upshot is that spatial targeting in the form of enterprise zones—where the zones are created in depressed inner-city neighborhoods—may be an appropriate economic-development strategy. This strategy is justified to the extent these two propositions are true: 1) the spatial mismatch hypothesis explains a fair amount of the underemployment of inner-city residents, and 2) creating jobs locally is a more viable strategy than expanding the journey-to-work mobility or access to suburban housing of inner-city residents. Obviously, this is not a strong defense of the enterprise zone strategy since it recognizes that many of the arguments made in favor of enterprise zones are partial or flawed, and that, at best, the enterprise zone strategy should be used to complement other employment strategies. One final point needs to be made here. We have been assuming that actual enterprise zones conform to this rationale—that they are in depressed neighborhoods in inner cities, in other words, that they are "targeted." In fact, as we indicated earlier, in this book we focus on those states that do target their enterprise zones.[21]

ENTERPRISE ZONES AND GROWTH:
ARE ZONES EFFECTIVE?

As we argued in Chapter 1, the incentives provided in enterprise zones are meant to increase the profitability of investing in a zone. This should tilt the spatial factor surface in favor of enterprise zones—provided that the incentives offered in the zones are not capitalized into land prices[22]—making them more desirable for investment and thus more likely to grow. Do enterprise zones actually result in new local economic growth?

As indicated earlier, a number of reviews of the enterprise zone literature have been conducted in recent years (Rubin and Richards 1992; L. Papke 1993; Wilder and Rubin 1996); we will not repeat the details of that work here. Instead, we will focus our attention on what appear to be the most important results and on those issues we address in this book. Studies of the effects of enterprise zones on investment or job growth fall into three categories. First, there are studies of one or a few enterprise zones, where measures of total gross or net employment growth in the zone since zone designation are compared either to growth rates in the zone area prior to designation or to growth rates during the same period of time in the metropolitan area as a whole or in a comparable, but non-zone, area.

Dabney (1991) looked at the effect of enterprise zone incentives on business location decisions, employing this growth-rate comparison approach. He argued that enterprise zone incentives were unlikely to make up for the significant locational disadvantages presented by inner-city enterprise zones. He argued that on most location factors—costs of transporting materials, commuting costs, access to airports, infrastructure, and building functionality—enterprise zones did poorly. Dabney then used analysis-of-variance procedures to determine whether zone designation had an impact on rates of change in the number of business establishments. The analysis covered eight enterprise zones in eight different states during three years prior and three years after zone designation. He found that there was no significant difference in the rate of growth in the zones versus the rest of the zone city.

Rubin and Wilder (1989) studied the Evansville, Indiana, zone, established in 1983. During its first three years, there was a net increase in employment of 1,878. Using a shift-share analysis to decompose the total job growth, Rubin and Wilder estimated that 325 of these jobs would have occurred if the enterprise zone had grown just at the average rate of growth for the entire metro area, and another 123 jobs could be attributed to the fact that the zone's industrial composition in 1983 would have produced above-average growth. The remaining 1,430 jobs (76 percent of the total) are attributed to the comparative advantage of the zone.

Prior to designation, the Evansville zone area grew more slowly than the metro area, yet it grew at more than five times the rate of the metro area in the first three years after designation. This dramatic change certainly begs for an explanation. Rubin and Wilder's conclusion that a large part of this shift can be attributed to zone designation is plausible, but, as they admit, cannot be established with any certainty using their method. Areas do sometimes reverse their fortunes after an extended period of decline; economic theory would tell us that capital may return to an area when that decline finally reduces factor costs (land and labor) to the point that the area is once again competitive. The zone may simply have arrived at a fortuitous moment.

The second approach to the study of enterprise zone effects involves the study of either one or a few zones, in which measures of investment or job growth (gross or net) are supplemented by questionnaires administered to zone firms to determine the extent to which zone incentives were perceived as important or decisive factors in their investment decisions. This literature has been extensively reviewed elsewhere (Wilder and Rubin 1996; Rubin and Richards 1992), and the conclusions are not surprising: other factors are consistently rated more important than zone incentives, but incentives may nonetheless make a difference at the margin, when other factors, such as access and labor costs, are equal. This, of course, begs the question that has been pursued by researchers for the past 20 years: just how large is the marginal effect of a tax or incentive difference?

Finally, there are studies using econometric methods to explain differences in zone growth rates, cross-sectionally or over time. Erickson and Friedman (1990b) studied 357 enterprise zones in 17 states. Average employment in these zones at time of designation was 4,776, and subsequent gross job growth averaged 232 jobs (about 5 percent) per year. These authors conducted a regression analysis to explain variation in investment growth rates and job growth rates across a subset of these zones. In their results, the number of zone incentives was positively and significantly related to both investment growth and gross job growth in models that included a variety of policy-related variables. In more complete regression models that also included other nonpolicy variables thought to affect zone growth rates, the incentive variable remained positive but was not statistically significant. Unfortunately, program counting is a very unsatisfactory method of measuring the value of an incentive package to a firm (Fisher and Peters 1997a). In addition, as Rubin and Wilder (1989) noted, the job data are imperfect since they come from zone coordinators (who have an incentive to exaggerate) and since the figures do not net out job losses. There are significant problems, in other words, with both the explanatory and the dependent variables.

In an interesting variation on the econometric approach, L. Papke (1994) studied the effects of enterprise zone incentives in Indiana on inventories, machinery and equipment purchases, and unemployment claims filed. This approach focuses on the presumed ultimate goal of enterprise zone incentives—the growth in investment and the reduction in unemployment. Papke found that enterprise zone designation reduced unemployment claims filed at the area office by about 19 percent to 25 percent, depending on the specification of the model. These are surprisingly large effects which appear to be permanent, as well.

The Indiana incentives consist of a jobs tax credit, the exemption of inventories from property taxation, and the exemption of profits attributable to new zone investment from the state income tax. The jobs credit is typical of credits provided elsewhere; it is equal to 10 percent of wages, but it has a ceiling of $1,500 per employee.[23] The capital incentive is peculiar, however. In most other states, enterprise zone capital incentives are directed at plant and equipment; moreover, most states exempt inventories from property taxation everywhere, thus rendering an inventory exemption in enterprise zones (as in Indiana) needless.[24] Thus, Papke's study provides a good test of the effects of jobs credits on unemployment,[25] but does not tell us much about the effects of more typical capital incentives, most of which clearly lower the price of capital goods and can be expected to have much larger substitution effects than an inventory exemption and, hence, to have potentially negative effects on employment.

In related research, Papke (1993) used census block-group data to compare the fortunes of zone residents between 1980 and 1990 with the fortunes of residents of a randomly selected set of non-zone urban census tracts in Indiana during the same period. Here she was able to identify the rates of unemployment of the actual zone population (or at least a close approximation) rather than for an entire unemployment claims office. Unemployment rates of zone residents did fall during the 1980s more than unemployment rates of non-zone areas did, but the difference was small. This suggests that new zone employment produces labor market benefits—measured by the reduction in areawide unemployment rates—but that much of the benefit accrues to non-zone residents, directly or indirectly. Population in zone areas declined more than in non-zones, and per capita incomes declined in zone areas but rose in non-zone areas. Papke concludes that enterprise zones apparently have not made zone residents appreciably better off.

Unfortunately, Boarnet and Bogart (1996), using methods similar to Papke's, found no evidence that the New Jersey enterprise zone program had a positive effect on local employment, employment in various sectors, or property values. They concluded that the New Jersey program was ineffective at improving the economic conditions around the zones. As the authors noted, their findings may have had as much to do with the nature of the New Jersey program compared to the Indiana program as with the reproducibility of Papke's findings.[26] Moreover, Greenbaum (1998), in a methodologically and empirically careful study, examined the impact of state enterprise zones on both business and housing market outcomes in six major states. The analysis was undertaken at the ZIP-code level, in part using the same SSEL data source (though not the same data) we use later in this book. Greenbaum found that while enterprise zones may create new business activity, these gains tend to be offset by shrinking business establishments in zones. The result is that overall zones have little impact on business outcomes. He found that zones have no impact on overall employment growth (but some impact on employment growth among new establishments). Two other recent papers are important to mention. Engberg and Greenbaum (1999) found no positive impact on housing market, income, or employment outcomes in six states. Bondonio and Engberg (2000)—using estimates of the monetary value of incentives as well as specific program features—found that neither the value of incentives nor program features matter, and that the zero impact on employment growth was robust to a wide range of sensitivity analyses.

In Chapter 7 we deal with some technical aspects of the econometric literature in greater detail. Here, however, all we feel able to conclude is that—aside from the last few studies mentioned[27]—there has been very little in the way of rigorous examination of the relationship between enterprise zones and growth. And while there is a large volume of work on the more general issues of the impact of state and local taxes and incentives on growth, even that research is not conclusive. Indeed, we still do not know if—even less, to what extent—state and local taxes in general affect growth. The problem with enterprise zones is much worse, in part because the methodological problems of measurement are much greater and data are much more difficult to come by. Given the paucity of enterprise zone studies, it seems highly unlikely that a broad research consensus on the impact of enterprise zones on growth will be possible for some time to come. The conclusions of the extant literature do point in quite contrary directions; however, the vast majority of the recent literature suggest that enterprise zones have little or no positive impact on growth.

CONCLUSIONS

Although there have been promoters of enterprise zones in both the Congress and the administration since the idea first took off, real federal involvement came late. This provided room for states to experiment with zones, resulting in considerable variation among states. Thus, we should expect some zones to work better than others. While many of the arguments initially used to justify enterprise zones—in particular, that they would become centers of entrepreneurship—seem decidedly flawed a quarter of a century later, a consensus has developed that targeting economic-development policy at depressed, high-unemployment neighborhoods is an "appropriate" and "good" state strategy.[28] Underlying this consensus are a number of theories about job search and commuting behavior and the geography of new investment, many of which we have discussed in this chapter. Probably the most important of the theories is the spatial mismatch hypothesis—the claim that, particularly minority, inner-city residents are spatially separated from suburban job opportunities. Enterprise zones geographically located in depressed inner-city neighborhoods can then be justified as a way of overcoming the spatial mismatch for the underemployed urban poor.

As we indicated earlier in this chapter, there is reason to be skeptical that spatial mismatch is the (main) cause of underemployment among inner-city minorities. And even if it were, it is unclear that enterprise zones are the best policy strategy. We return to these issues in Chapters 8 and 9. It is also unclear whether enterprise zones work—whether they have any discernible influence on business location decisions and thus on local employment. We return to this topic in Chapter 7. However, before we can deal with these broader issues we need a better understanding of the size and importance of enterprise zone incentives, the likelihood that zone incentives will encourage the use of labor, and the cost to government of zone incentives. It is to the first of these issues that the next chapter turns.

Notes

1. Of these zones, 2,083 were in just two states—Arkansas and Louisiana—and another 227 were in Ohio. At the other extreme, seven states had three or fewer zones. See Wilder and Rubin (1996).
2. There are also four "enhanced enterprise communities" in large cities, each eligible for $25 million in aid.
3. It leaves out many of the other goals of enterprise zones already mentioned, such as neighborhood revitalization and community development.
4. See, for instance, his *Enterprise Zones: Greenlining the Inner Cities*, 1981.
5. In fact, meaningful enterprise zone legislation passed only during the Clinton administration, even though Jack Kemp had been Secretary of the Department of Housing and Urban Development (HUD) during the Bush presidency.
6. Early versions of the federal enterprise zone legislation would have provided tax credits to investors who supplied capital to enterprise zone firms, which should have had the effect of lowering the cost of capital for entrepreneurs. Moreover, a jobs tax credit would have reduced the cost of labor, an important operating expense for start-ups.
7. Wilder and Rubin (1996) argued that there were five main academic or policy objections to enterprise zones. These arguments included 1) that incentives had little or no influence on business investment and location decisions; 2) that the incentives offered in enterprise zones would tend to benefit larger capital-intensive firms and not the smaller labor-intensive firms which are more likely to create

new employment; 3) that zones would result in a worrying increase in the tax burden on non-zone businesses and residents; 4) that enterprise zones would result in capital shifts into zones but not in new capital formation; and 5) that enterprise zones would draw resources away from more direct ways of helping to solve urban problems. See variously Birdsong (1989), Clarke (1982), Estes and Hammond (1992), Glickman (1984), Goldsmith (1982), Hawkins (1984), Humberger (1981), Jacobs and Wasylenko (1981), Ladd (1994), Levitan and Miller (1992), Massey (1982), Mier (1982), Mounts (1981), Pierce, Hagstrom, and Steinbach (1979), Rubin and Zorn (1985), Vaughn (1979), and Walton (1982). To these criticisms we would add those of the American Planning Association, which argued that since land-use regulation did not cause blight, the relaxation of land-use controls was unlikely to remove blight. It should be clear that many of these objections are contradictory to one another.

8. It is worth noting here that some researchers place considerable importance on the community-development component of zones, asserting that the more successful zones are those that are better managed and that involve close ties between the public and private sectors (Rubin and Richards 1992).

9. In Ohio, only a portion of state zones are truly targeted. We included only targeted zones in our national analysis—that is, zones that qualified due to economic distress.

10. Here the effective tax rate (sometimes we call this the "tax burden") is defined as the difference between the present value of the cash flow from a new plant investment after all federal, state, and local income, sales, and property taxes, and the present value of new plant cash flow in the absence of any taxes levied by the state and locality in which the plant is located, divided by the present value of before-tax income attributable to the new plant. The calculation of tax rates is discussed in detail in Chapter 3.

11. Economic-development policy is potentially negative-sum since it induces businesses to locate in places where they would otherwise not want to locate. Government interference in location decisions (through the tax code and incentives) results in firms' making location decisions which are inefficient from the viewpoint of the national economy.

12. See Fisher and Peters (1998). Bartik (1991) covered these issues in some detail.

13. This refers to the *average* value-to-firm/cost-to-government value for a particular tax incentive. However, at the margin (in other words, for a particular unit modification or extension of a tax credit program) it is quite possible to generate a positive value-to-firm/cost-to-government ratio.

14. It is also true that costs in the benefit-cost calculation will be broader than in the value-to-firm/cost-to-government calculation and will include the other costs of servicing the new plant and its employees.

15. See Iannone (1999) for the Ohio study. Both the New Jersey and Indiana studies relied on estimates from state input-output models for the benefit-cost calculations.

16. The evidence for these claims is fairly limited. See Fisher and Peters (1998).

17. Indirectly, Bartik's benefit-cost model does take these into account. See Wilder and Rubin (1996) for a review of the literature on what makes enterprise zones effective. Also see Elling and Sheldon (1991).

18. This is sometimes referred to as the hysteresis hypothesis. For a more complete treatment see Phelps (1972), but see Bartik (1991, pp. 76–78) for a treatment in this context.

19. See also a more recent restatement and evaluation by Kain (1992).

20. See, for instance, Briggs (1997) and Moberg (1995).

21. Where states have both targeted and essentially untargeted zones, we focus on those zones which are targeted.

22. In theory, locational advantages should be capitalized into the prices of immobile resources, which obviously means land prices. In central cities with a partly captive labor force, however, they should also be capitalized into wages to some extent. Industrial buildings are often not very mobile or adaptable either. Understood this way, the spatial mismatch hypothesis is the thesis that the locational disadvantages of central cities are "capitalized" into lower wages because labor is not perfectly mobile. Furthermore, there is an implied argument that wages cannot sink low enough to restore competitiveness, so inner cities remain in a disequilibrium depression. To conclude that capitalization will occur fully and will result in incentives having no effect seems to us erroneous, however. This would be true only if the effects were equal for all potential land uses, if markets were close to being perfectly competitive, and if all participants had nearly perfect information. None of these conditions is likely to hold. Our results (Fisher and Peters 1998 and Chapter 3 in this book) show widely varying tax rates and incentive values by industry in any given zone. Which of the tax rates is capitalized into land prices, assuming that buyers and sellers even know with much accuracy what those rates are? If it is the highest incentive rate or lowest tax rate, because land goes to the highest bidder, does this mean that other industries will no longer find it profitable to locate there because the sectoral bias of taxes and incentives has rendered land prices too high for any but the one favored sector? If this does not occur (and the wide range of sectors still moving into zones suggests that it does not), then even if land prices rise by some increment as a result of incentives, some sectors will still experience a net gain.

23. Fisher and Peters (1998) found that the Indiana jobs credit was worth a little less than the average jobs credit among 15 states with such credits; thus the size of the employment effects found by Papke cannot be attributed to an unusually generous jobs credit.

24. Among the 24 most industrialized states, only two fully tax inventories. Another four tax inventories in part or at a lower rate. The remaining 18 exempt inventories.

25. Given the way the data were gathered, though, we do not know how much of the reduction in unemployment occurred among zone residents rather than persons elsewhere in the labor market. Papke also found important effects on zone inventories, but again it is possible her results are a consequence of the way in which

inventory data were gathered. Firms may have an incentive to underestimate their inventories before—but not after—the provision of an inventory exemption.

26. But Papke (2000) has tried to reproduce her earlier results, using a more historically complete data set.

27. Sheldon and Elling (1989), which we have not reviewed in this section, should probably also be included in this group. In addition, we ignore analytical work using alternative, nonstandard approaches such as shift-share analysis—for example, Rubin and Wilder (1989) and Dowall, Beyeler, and Wong (1994)—since the methodology used there precludes analysis of the "causal" relationship between zones and growth.

28. See Anderson and Wassmer (2000) for a recent statement of this position.

3
How Valuable Are Zone
Incentives to Firms?

Any attempt to estimate the influence of economic-development incentives on firms' behavior must begin with an assessment of the value of those incentives to the firms. In this study we employ a computer simulation model, TAIM^{ez}, to measure how the actual incentives in place in each of the enterprise zones in our study would improve a firm's rate of return on an investment in a new manufacturing facility in that zone. We begin the chapter with a brief description of how that model works; a more technical discussion is presented in Appendix A.

By measuring the effect of taxes and incentives on a firm's bottom line, we are able to assess quantitatively the trends in economic-development policy in the 1990s and the differences among states and cities. Did incentive competition, which became a significant part of economic-development policy at the state and local level in the 1970s, continue through the 1990s? The answer is yes; among the 20 prominent manufacturing states that are included in TAIM^{ez}, the trend in the period 1990–1998 was overwhelmingly to reduce basic taxes on corporations and to enact or expand both general and targeted incentives for new business investment.

In the second section of this chapter we describe this trend in some detail, comparing the value of general incentives to target incentives, such as those available only within enterprise zones. While targeted incentives became more common during this period, there has been a weakening of the targeting effect in many of the states.

In the third section of this chapter we focus on the value of incentives in the 75 enterprise zone cities that are the major focus of this study. The trends in these cities during the period 1990–1994 mirrored the trends discussed above to a large extent: incentives became more generous, and nontargeted incentives grew more rapidly than targeted (enterprise zone) incentives, so that the competitive advantage of zones was weakened slightly. To put the magnitude of these incentives in perspective, we calculated the wage cut that would provide benefits to the firm's bottom line equivalent in value to the tax incentives available.

53

We found that the incentive packages were equivalent to a 1.6 percent to 7.1 percent cut in wages. One would probably not expect cost differentials of this magnitude to have large effects on location decisions.

In addition to the sample of 75 zones in 13 states, we also examine incentives available in all Ohio cities with populations of 15,000 or more, with and without enterprise zones. In the fourth section of this chapter describes the value of general state incentives and enterprise zone incentives in these Ohio cities.

HOW DOES ONE ACCURATELY MEASURE THE WORTH OF ENTERPRISE ZONE INCENTIVES?

The TAIM^{ez} computer model is an implementation of the hypothetical-firm method. This approach to measuring the effect of taxes on a firm's profitability was pioneered by Williams (1967) and the Wisconsin Department of Revenue (1973). The method was extended and substantially improved by Papke and Papke (1984), KPMG Peat Marwick (1994), and Fisher and Peters (1998), among others. The approach has been used fairly widely in the past decade's research on taxes, tax incentives, and even non-tax economic-development incentives.[1]

In essence, the hypothetical-firm method for measuring the value of a state's or city's taxes or fiscal incentives is based on the process by which firms make investment decisions. According to traditional location theory, a firm will evaluate alternative sites for new investment on the basis of the profitability of the marginal investment in each location. Our measure of this effect is the internal rate of return (IRR) or, alternatively, the long-term increment to cash flow, deriving from the investment.

The TAIM^{ez} model calculates the effective state-local tax rate on the income generated by new plant investment for a new plant in each of 16 manufacturing sectors in each of 20 states and in each of the cities within those states for which local tax data have been collected. We have modeled the tax systems for these 20 states. The effective tax rate in a particular state, say Indiana, is calculated by running the TAIM^{ez} model twice. The first run computes the net present value (NPV) of the incremental after-tax cash flow to the firm as a result of building a new plant in Indiana, but assuming that there are no state or local taxes on the new plant in Indiana. The hypothetical firm has existing operations in other states and pays state and federal income taxes on the income generated by the new plant.[2] The second run applies the Indiana state and local tax system to the new plant, including local income, sales, and property tax rates. The reduction in cash flow produced by Indiana taxes represents the tax bite. This amount divided by the before-tax income generated by the new plant represents the effective tax rate.

Note that this rate includes the effects of deductibility: the additional Indiana taxes are deductible against federal income and so are partly offset by lower federal income taxes. Furthermore, Indiana is one of a few states that allow a firm to deduct income taxes paid to other states, so the model's calculation of income taxes paid to other states is deducted from Indiana taxable income. Local property taxes, which are also deductible against Indiana income, further reduce Indiana income taxes.

The second run can include or exclude the various investment incentives offered in each state and property-tax abatements offered in localities in that state. State income tax incentives typically consist of investment tax credits (a percentage of the cost of buildings or machinery and equipment or both), jobs credits (a dollar amount per new job), training credits (a percentage of job-training expenses for new positions), or wage or payroll tax credits (a percentage of wages, or of payroll taxes withheld, for new positions). Tax incentives can also include income exclusions, where some portion of the income generated by a new facility in an enterprise zone is excluded from taxable income. Refunds of sales taxes on machinery and equipment or of local property taxes also exist. Where states permit localities to abate a portion of the property taxes on new manufacturing facilities or machinery, a typical abatement schedule for that state (or the typical abatement schedule employed in a particular city) is included in the model.

The value to the firm of a state and local incentive package, then, is the amount the package adds to the profitability of a new investment in that locality. The effect of the incentive package, as indeed the tax regime more generally, depends on the characteristics of the firm. Thus, it is important to construct various hypothetical firms, representing the characteristics of a typical firm in various manufacturing industries. Differences in the value of a given incentive are due to differences among firms in profitability, in the relative importance of certain kinds of assets, or in the ratios of jobs to assets. All else being equal, one would expect machinery-intensive firms to respond more vigorously to property-tax exemptions or abatements for machinery and equipment, profitable firms to reductions in the rate of income taxation, energy-intensive firms to exemptions of sales tax on fuel and electricity, and so on. The characteristics of the 16 manufacturing sectors included in our model are described in Appendix A.

A multiyear analysis is essential. Taxes and incentives affect the profitability of new investment not just in the initial investment year, but for many years thereafter. Credits sometimes must be used in the first year, but in other instances can be carried forward for up to 20 years. Property-tax abatements often provide the largest benefit the first year, but may continue at some level for 10 years or more. TAIM^{ez} employs a 20-year horizon, which is probably sufficient to capture all the significant differences in state policy. We assume, in other words, that the firm, in making a decision regarding investment in a new plant, evaluates the project over a 20-year period. This may in fact be longer than the typical firm actually employs. However, with a 10 percent discount rate, the project returns in later years are heavily discounted.

INCENTIVE COMPETITION IN THE 1990s

While this study focuses on incentive competition among enterprise zones during the period 1990–1994, this competition occurred within a broader context of state competition that has been going on for at least two decades and that continues unabated. Before examining the value of enterprise zone incentives in the 75 cities sampled for this study, we consider trends in the nature and magnitude of business tax incentives of all kinds. We have used the TAIM^{ez} model to measure the value of incentives and the effective tax rates on income from new plant investment in 20 states from 1990 to 1998. These 20 states include the 13 states that are the main focus of this study; all are among the 26 most industrialized states (in terms of manufacturing employment), including the top nine. These 20 states together accounted for

75 percent of the manufacturing employment in the United States in 1995 (U.S. Bureau of the Census 1997).

Table 3.1 shows the kinds of incentives available in each of the 20 states as of 1998. Twelve of the states had investment tax credits (ITCs) available statewide by 1998; another five offered ITCs only within enterprise zones or the equivalent. Investment tax credits typically allow firms to deduct from their state corporate income tax liability a credit equal to some percentage of the cost of new manufacturing facilities and machinery. Nine states offered a jobs credit statewide; another five offered jobs credits only in enterprise zones. The jobs credits also allow a credit against income taxes, equal to a dollar amount per new job created. Five states offered a credit for job-training expenses, and six allowed a credit for a percentage of wages paid, or payroll or income taxes withheld, for new jobs. Credits for sales taxes paid on goods purchased for the new plant, or for local property taxes paid on the new plant, were available in five states, and five states excluded all or a portion of income generated within a zone from corporate taxable income.

Many of these credits became effective after mid 1990, and many states also reduced corporate taxes across the board between 1990 and 1998. Table 3.2 shows the changes in basic tax systems and incentive programs that occurred during that eight-year period. Fifteen of the 20 states reduced basic taxes between 1990 and 1998. Most common was a movement toward greater reliance on the sales factor in state income tax apportionment formulas; this tends to reduce, often very substantially, the income taxes paid by firms exporting out-of-state. Five states moved from what was once the standard equal-weighted three-factor formula to double-weighted sales (50 percent sales, 25 percent each payroll and property), and—by increasing the sales fraction to 67 percent, 90 percent, or 100 percent—another three states moved closer to the single-factor formula that has made the income tax system in Iowa so attractive to manufacturing and other exporting firms. A firm with substantial facilities and employees in Iowa (a state with a 100 percent sales fraction), for example, could end up paying *no* Iowa corporate income taxes if all sales were destined for places outside the state, since profits would be apportioned to Iowa based on a sales factor equal to zero.

Fourteen states adopted new general incentive programs or made existing programs more attractive; eight states adopted new targeted

Table 3.1 Tax Incentives Available in 20 States, 1998

State	State incentives[a]	Local incentives
California	ITC, EZ jobs credit, EZ sales-tax credit	Abatements not allowed
Connecticut	ITC; training credit; EZ income exemption	Abatements allowed
Florida	ITC; EZ jobs and property-tax credits	Abatements little used
Illinois	2 ITCs; EZ ITC; EZ jobs credit	Abatements allowed but little used outside of EZs
Indiana	Credit for up to 3.1% of new employee payroll; EZ jobs credit	Abatements allowed in Economic Revitalization Areas
Iowa	ITC; jobs credit; EZ ITC	Abatements allowed
Kentucky	ITC; jobs credit; payroll credit; training credit; EZ jobs credit; EZ sales-tax exemption for M&E	Property-tax rate reduction allowed
Massachusetts	ITC; Econ. Opportunity Area ITC	Abatements not allowed
Michigan	Credits for corporate & personal income taxes attributable to new jobs; EZ exemption for all income and property taxes	Abatements allowed
Minnesota	Sales-tax exemption for M&E; very limited EZ credits	Abatements not allowed
Missouri	ITC & jobs credit; EZ income exemption; EZ ITC, training & jobs credits	Abatements allowed
New York	ITC; EZ ITC and wage tax credit	Abatements allowed
North Carolina	2 ITCs; jobs credit; training credit	Abatements not allowed
Ohio	ITC; jobs credit; EZ income exemption, training credit, and jobs credit	Abatements allowed in EZs
Pennsylvania	Jobs credit; wages credit; EZ ITC	Abatements allowed
South Carolina	Jobs credits; withholding tax credit; Economic Impact Zone ITC	Abatements allowed
Tennessee	ITC; jobs credit	Abatements not allowed

Table 3.1 (Continued)

State	State incentives[a]	Local incentives
Texas	EZ property-tax refund; EZ sales-tax refund; EZ property deduction	Abatements allowed
Virginia	Jobs credit; EZ income exemption; 2 EZ ITCs; EZ jobs credit	Very limited abatements allowed
Wisconsin	EZ ITC, jobs credit, & sales-tax credit	Abatements not allowed

[a] EZ = enterprise zone or equivalent; ITC = investment tax credit; M&E = machinery and equipment.

programs (enterprise zones in Iowa and Michigan) or made existing programs more generous. Only six states increased any basic tax rates and in three of these the increases were offset by other tax reductions. Only three states tightened or scaled back general incentive programs; another three discontinued their incentive programs but replaced them with others, typically more generous. Thus, the overall trend has been overwhelmingly to reduce basic taxes on corporations and to enact or expand both general and targeted incentives for new business investment.

The importance of these tax changes can best be measured by their effect on the overall state-local tax rate on new investment. Since enterprise zones are the focus of this study, we have calculated effective tax rates in each state for two different kinds of locations: one in which only the general statewide incentives are available, and one in which the firm qualifies for enterprise zone or other geographically targeted incentives.

Note that differences in state-local tax rates between 1990 and 1998 do not reflect differences in the average property-tax rate in each state because of the difficulty of identifying such statewide averages for 1990. Instead, we used the same property-tax rate for each year; this rate represents our best estimate of the average property-tax rate facing industry in that state in the most recent year for which data were available, which was generally 1996, 1997, or 1998.[3]

Table 3.3 shows the effective state-local tax rates on income from a new manufacturing facility in each of the 20 states in 1990 and 1998.

Table 3.2 Major Tax and Incentive Changes in 20 States, 1990–1998[a]

State	Changes[b]
California	Sales-tax rate increased; apportionment increased to 50% sales; jobs credit abolished; ITC enacted; sales-tax exemption for manufacturing M&E
Connecticut	Surcharge on income tax eliminated; tax rate lowered; old training credit and income exemption replaced with two ITCs and new training credit
Florida	EZ credits reduced; sales-tax exemption for electricity enacted
Illinois	Apportionment increased from 50% to 67% sales
Indiana	Payroll credit enacted; apportionment increased to 50% sales
Iowa	ITC and jobs credit enacted; enterprise zone program initiated; manufacturing M&E exempted from property tax
Kentucky	Sales-tax rate increased; ITC enacted and then expanded; payroll credit enacted and then reduced; EZ jobs credit enacted; training credit enacted
Massachusetts	ITC credit expanded; Economic Opportunity Area ITC enacted; apportionment changed to move from 50% to 100% sales over five years
Michigan	Sales-tax rate increased from 4% to 6%; apportionment increased to 50% sales and later to 90% sales, with throwback eliminated; statewide credits for corporate and personal income taxes, and renaissance zones (EZs) instituted
Minnesota	Sales tax on replacement manufacturing M&E reduced
Missouri	Sales-tax rate reduced; ITC and jobs credits tightened; training credit eliminated; income tax rate increased; deduction for federal taxes reduced from 100% to 50%
New York	Tax rate lowered; surcharge phased out; ITC reduced
North Carolina	Surtax eliminated; tax rate lowered; jobs credit expanded to statewide and benefits increased; ITCs and training credit enacted
Ohio	Property-tax credit ended; jobs credit and ITC enacted
Pennsylvania	Apportionment increased to 50% sales; capital stock tax rate increased and deductions increased; jobs credit enacted
South Carolina	Apportionment increased to 50% sales; jobs credit increased; withholding tax credit enacted; Economic Impact Zone ITC enacted
Tennessee	Apportionment increased to 50% sales; jobs credit enacted

Table 3.2 (Continued)

State	Changes[b]
Texas	Sales-tax rate increased from 6% to 6.25% but tax on manufacturing M&E eliminated; tax rate on capital reduced, tax on income instituted; EZ property tax-refund enacted
Virginia	EZ income exemption increased; jobs credit enacted; EZ ITCs enacted; EZ jobs credit enacted; EZ sales-tax refund ended
Wisconsin	Tax surcharge imposed; EZ program expanded

[a] Changes effective after June 1990 and before July 1998.
[b] EZ = enterprise zone or equivalent; ITC = investment tax credit; M&E = machinery and equipment.

Tax rates are shown with only the basic tax system included (no investment or jobs incentives), with the tax system plus general incentives only, and with all incentives available within an enterprise zone or the like. We also show the percentage reduction in taxes accomplished by the general incentives, and the further percentage reduction brought about by enterprise zone incentives (compared to the situation with general incentives only). All of the tax rates are weighted averages of the tax rates calculated for each of the 16 manufacturing sectors, where the weights are the sector shares of 1995 U.S. manufacturing employment.

There is striking variation in state and local tax rates among states, and striking variation in the magnitude of various kinds of incentives, as measured by the percentage reduction in tax rate accomplished by the incentive. In 1990, 8 of the 20 states offered statewide tax incentives that reduced the total state-local tax rate by more than 10 percent. By 1998, this number had increased to 13 states, with reductions of 20 percent or more in 9 of the 13. Targeted incentives were offered by 14 states in 1990 (and in 11 of the 14 these incentives further reduced tax rates by more than 10 percent); all but 1 offered such incentives by 1998, and in 11 states targeted incentives provided further reductions of 20 percent or more. The median basic tax rate was reduced from 8.5 percent in 1990 to 7.9 percent in 1998; larger reductions in the median

Table 3.3 Effective State-Local Tax Rate on Income from a New Manufacturing Plant in 20 States, 1990 and 1998[a]

State	1990 Effective tax rate (%)			1990 % reduction in rate		1998 Effective tax rate (%)			1998 % reduction in rate		% change in effective tax rate 1990–1998		
	After basic taxes	With general incentives	With general & targeted incentives	Due to general incentives	Due to targeted incentives	After basic taxes	With general incentives	With general & targeted incentives	Due to general incentives	Due to targeted incentives	After basic taxes	With general incentives	With general & targeted incentives
Calif.	9.3	9.3	8.7	0.3	6.8	9.0	8.0	7.1	11.1	10.9	-4.0	-14.5	-18.2
Conn.	9.5	9.5	6.1	0.0	36.3	8.1	7.2	4.5	11.0	37.9	-15.1	-24.4	-26.4
Fla.	8.0	8.0	6.4	0.0	19.8	7.6	7.6	6.1	0.0	19.4	-5.7	-5.7	-5.2
Iowa	5.3	4.0	4.0	24.2	0.0	2.9	2.0	2.0	28.6	2.0	-46.4	-49.5	-50.5
Ill.	5.9	5.5	4.4	6.5	20.0	5.5	5.1	4.0	6.9	21.4	-6.2	-6.6	-8.3
Ind.	13.8	13.8	8.9	0.0	35.6	13.6	10.8	5.9	20.0	45.5	-2.0	-21.6	-33.7
Ky.	7.7	6.7	-3.0	12.4	144.8	8.0	4.5	0.3	44.0	93.2	3.6	-33.7	nm[b]
Mass.	7.8	7.4	7.4	6.2	0.0	7.1	6.0	5.2	14.6	13.1	-10.1	-18.2	-28.8
Mich.	10.0	8.0	8.0	20.8	0.0	7.5	5.4	0.6	28.0	88.4	-25.4	-32.1	-92.1
Minn.	9.2	7.9	7.9	14.2	0.0	8.1	7.6	7.6	5.7	0.0	-12.0	-3.4	-3.4
Miss.	8.8	6.0	5.3	32.6	11.2	9.3	6.5	5.4	30.3	17.5	5.8	9.3	1.5
N.C.	7.1	6.0	5.9	15.3	1.8	7.0	5.9	5.8	15.3	1.1	-2.2	-2.1	-1.3
N.Y.	6.3	3.8	3.4	39.6	9.5	6.1	3.4	2.6	44.8	22.1	-2.4	-10.8	-23.3
Ohio	10.6	10.5	7.6	0.9	27.8	10.0	7.8	5.1	22.3	33.7	-5.5	-25.9	-31.9
Pa.	8.9	8.2	6.5	7.8	20.3	9.3	7.3	6.3	21.0	14.5	4.2	-10.7	-4.2
S.C.	8.9	5.5	5.5	37.7	0.0	8.4	0.8	0.1	90.3	83.9	-5.8	-85.3	-97.6
Tenn.	8.1	7.9	7.9	2.7	0.0	7.8	7.1	7.1	9.0	0.6	-4.0	-10.2	-10.7

Tex.	11.4	10.6	8.9	6.9	16.3	10.4	9.6	7.7	7.3	20.1	-8.7	-9.1	-13.2
Va.	7.1	7.1	6.2	0.0	12.1	7.1	7.0	4.5	1.6	35.6	0.0	-1.6	-27.9
Wis.	6.0	6.0	4.0	0.0	32.5	6.1	6.1	4.0	0.0	33.5	1.6	1.6[c]	-0.0[c]
Median	8.5	7.6	6.3	6.7	11.6	7.9	6.7	5.2	14.9	20.8	-4.8	-10.8	-18.2

[a] Effective tax rate is the reduction in the net present value (NPV) of the cash flow from a new plant due to state and local income, sales, and property taxes in the new plant state, divided by the NPV of the pre-tax income generated by the plant. Pre-tax income is measured before all federal, state, and local taxes; NPV is measured over 20 years. The reduction in cash flow is calculated by comparing project cash flow after actual taxes and incentives in the new plant state and after federal and other state taxes, with cash flow assuming the same plant location but with only federal taxes and taxes in other states. The tax rates shown are weighted averages of the tax rates calculated for firms representative of 16 two-digit SIC code sectors, where the weights are the sector shares of 1995 U.S. manufacturing employment.

[b] nm = not meaningful (because earlier tax rate was negative).

[c] Significant at the 5% level.

effective tax rate occurred when general incentives were included (from 7.6 percent to 6.7 percent) and when targeted incentives were added (from 6.3 percent to 5.2 percent). Both of the latter reductions are significant at the 5 percent level.

Has there been any convergence among these 20 states in terms of their tax rates on new investment, and what role have incentives played in reducing or increasing variability among states? In 1990, both general and targeted incentives actually increased the variability in tax rates among these 20 states, as measured by the variance in rates. In other words—and contrary to the claims of others (Eisinger 1988)—incentives were not by and large offsetting unusually high basic tax rates but were in fact reducing tax rates that were already below average. By 1998, the variability in basic tax rates among states had increased (although this increase was not statistically significant), but incentives no longer increased this variability. Thus, tax rate and incentive competition continued through the 1990s with no indication that this was producing convergence; the process resembled a game of leapfrog, with no state apparently content to be merely average.

Another way of examining the value of incentives to firms is to calculate the dollar value per job created. This is typically the way incentive package deals are reported in the press. This measure makes comparisons among industrial sectors more meaningful, since our assumed plant sizes vary across sectors. TAIM^{ez} calculates the present value of the increased cash flow produced by a given set of incentives over a 20-year period; this incentive value can then be divided by the number of employees in the new facility.

Table 3.4 shows the value of incentive packages per new job, averaged across the 16 industrial sectors as before. In half the states, general incentives were significantly increased (by $468 or more per job) between 1990 and 1998. In another eight states, general incentives were unchanged or changed only slightly (less than $100 per job in either direction). In only two states do we show a substantial reduction in incentives; and in both cases this is deceptive, being a matter of a tax rebate becoming less valuable because the underlying tax was reduced or eliminated.[4]

In 8 of the 20 states, targeted incentives were expanded between 1990 and 1998 by $440 per job or more, measured as the additional cash flow generated by targeted incentives, over and above the value of the generally available incentives. This was led by Michigan's extremely generous Renaissance Zone program, Massachusetts's new Economic Opportunity Area ITC, significant expansions of several zone credits in Virginia, and South Carolina's Economic Impact Zone ITC.[5] In another six states, there were very modest expansions ($113 per job or less) or no change at all.[6] In four states, there was a substantial reduction in the value of targeted incentives, and in another two, modest reductions.

The reductions in targeted incentives were most notable in Kentucky, where the very generous rural job credit was cut by about one-third and where the additional value of this rural targeted program was diminished by enactment of an urban counterpart (which we model as a general incentive because it applies in every county that does not qualify for the special rural tax break). Connecticut, Pennsylvania, and Ohio did not reduce enterprise zone incentives but did institute significant statewide investment and training credits. When states leave targeted programs unchanged but enact or expand general statewide incentives, they diminish the competitive advantage of enterprise zones, rural counties, or the like. This is because incentives are not usually strictly additive; the new statewide incentive may simply be a less generous version of the targeted one (so that a 10 percent EZ ITC, for example, then operates like a 6 percent add-on to a 4 percent statewide ITC) or because total credits cannot exceed state tax liability, so that the firm is unable to fully use the targeted credits on top of the new statewide credits. Our measure of the value of targeted incentives in Table 3.4, it must be remembered, measures the *additional* advantage the state has conferred on certain geographic areas.

What appear to have occurred in these 20 states in the 1990s are two contradictory trends: 1) some states have embarked on new enterprise zone programs, or increased the competitive advantage of existing zones or other targeted areas;[7] 2) other states have weakened the advantage of geographically targeted areas by reducing targeted incentives or, more commonly, by expanding nontargeted incentives. Perhaps more importantly, the trend in many states with long-standing enterprise zone programs (or the equivalent) has been to increase the maximum number of such zones allowed. This further weakens the targeting effect of zone programs, as a larger and larger portion of the state falls under the "targeted" program. Among 14 major manufacturing states with enterprise zone programs as of 1992, zone proliferation

Table 3.4 The Value per Job of Incentives to Manufacturing Firms in 20 States, 1990 and 1998 (in dollars)

State	Value of incentives per job, 1990			Value of incentives per job, 1998			Change in value 1990–1998		
	General incentives	General plus targeted incentives	Additional value of targeted incentives	General incentives	General plus targeted incentives	Additional value of targeted incentives	General incentives	General plus targeted incentives	Additional value of targeted incentives
Calif.	37	1,393	1,356	1,731	3,528	1,797	1,694	2,135	441
Conn.	0	5,785	5,785	1,479	6,027	4,549	1,479	242	-1,237
Fla.	0	2,294	2,294	0	2,188	2,188	0	-106	-106
Iowa	2,055	2,055	0	1,284	1,319	36	-772	-736	36
Ill.	661	2,461	1,800	659	2,459	1,801	-2	-2	1
Ind.	0	8,872	8,872	3,485	12,413	8,928	3,485	3,541	56
Ky.	1,654	15,580	13,926	5,640	11,575	5,936	3,986	-4,004	-7,990
Mass.	842	842	0	1,725	3,110	1,385	882	2,268	1,385
Mich.	3,566	3,566	0	3,582	10,553	6,971	16	6,987	6,971
Minn.	2,249	2,249	0	799	799	0	-1,450	-1,450	0
Mo.	4,760	5,998	1,238	4,683	6,748	2,065	-77	750	827
N.C.	1,910	2,069	159	1,897	1,940	43	-13	-129	-116
N.Y.	4,148	4,533	384	4,616	5,632	1,015	468	1,099	631
Ohio	164	5,361	5,197	3,417	8,103	4,686	3,253	2,742	-510
Pa.	1,059	3,990	2,931	3,117	5,092	1,975	2,058	1,103	-956
S.C.	5,571	5,571	0	11,487	12,391	904	5,915	6,820	904
Tenn.	378	378	0	1,166	1,281	115	789	903	115

Tex.	1,350	4,026	2,676	1,292	4,538	3,246	−59	511	570
Va.	0	1,045	1,045	98	3,809	3,710	98	2,763	2,665
Wis.	0	3,151	3,151	0	3,263	3,263	0	113	113
Median	951	3,358	1,297	1,728	4,173	2,020	283	827	84
Mean	1,520	4,061	2,541	2,608	5,338	2,731	1,087	1,278	190

NOTE: Figures represent the present value of the increased cash flow over 20 years accruing to the firm because of the package of tax incentives available in that state for a new manufacturing facility. All figures are weighted averages of the values for the 16 manufacturing sectors modeled. The table shows how 1992 manufacturing firms would have fared under 1990 versus 1998 tax law. For a discussion of how these numbers should be interpreted in light of inflation between 1990 and 1998, see Appendix A.

had occurred to some extent by the time of this study in 9: Connecticut (6 zones originally authorized in 1982, but the number had expanded to 20 by 1996), Indiana (expanded from 15 to 20 zones between 1992 and 1996), Missouri (33 authorized in the original 1982 legislation, but the limit was expanded to 62 in 1989–1991), New Jersey (number of zones expanded from 10 to 27 between 1992 and 1997), New York (from 19 in 1992 to 40 by 1997), Ohio (from 227 in 1992 to 317 by 1997), Pennsylvania (from 45 to 57 between 1992 and 1995), Texas (from 103 to 208 between 1992 and 1997), and Virginia (6 zones allowed in 1982 law, but authorization increased to 19 by 1989, and to 46 by 1997).[8] The number of zones was constant, or nearly so, during the 1990s in California, Florida, Illinois, Kentucky, and Wisconsin.

If we focus only on state corporate income taxes, we find another trend in the 1990s: it became increasingly possible for new investment to face negative income tax rates. Negative taxes can be produced in three ways. First, the state may allow new plant investment or jobs credits to be applied to a firm's total state income tax liability, not just the additional liability generated by the new plant. If the firm has a tax nexus and a tax liability in the state prior to building a new plant there, then credits that exceed the additional taxes caused by the plant can be applied to the firm's taxes on existing operations, so that the firm's total state tax bill is below what it would have been in the absence of the plant. The tax rate on new plant income is thus negative. Fourteen of the 20 states studied here had general credits with total state tax liability as the ceiling (usually with carryforward of unused credits); only 4 had credits where the ceiling was the tax attributable to the new facility. Ten of the 20 states had targeted incentives with a ceiling equal to the total state tax; 8 had targeted incentives limited by the state tax attributable to enterprise zone operations.[9]

Second, negative corporate rates can occur when the state corporate tax credits are based in part on the state personal income taxes paid by new employees, and these credits are refundable. This is the case with Ohio's Job Creation Tax Credit, Indiana's EDGE program, Michigan's certified credit under the Michigan Economic Growth Authority (MEGA) program, and South Carolina's Withholding Tax Credit. The firm can receive a payment from the state instead of a tax liability. Negative rates occur because we assume that employees pay 100 percent of their individual income taxes, so that when the *firm* receives a credit for the individual taxes paid by new employees, the credit offsets corporate income taxes.

Third, exporting firms in states with single-factor apportionment, or with apportionment formulas that approach 100 percent of sales, can experience negative tax rates on new investment. This is because the construction of a new plant may have very little effect on the firm's gross income tax liability since the additional in-state payroll and property do not affect the apportionment formula, and in-state sales may be unchanged. So a very low sales factor (we are assuming a firm that exports to national markets) would be applied to a somewhat larger total firm taxable income as a result of the new plant, producing a very modest increase in state tax, but the state's incentives for the new plant could easily exceed the additional tax.

In 1990, negative income tax rates were easily produced in Iowa (all 16 sectors) and Texas (12 sectors)—in both cases due to single-factor apportionment—and in Kentucky (16 sectors), due to generous credits combined with a statewide tax ceiling. They were less likely to occur in Florida, New York, and Wisconsin, and rarely or never in any of the other states (see Table 3.5). By 1998, negative tax rates were produced in 4 or more sectors in 11 of the 20 states. In addition to Iowa and Kentucky, negative taxes on new plant income occurred frequently (in at least 13 of the sectors) in Michigan, Ohio, and South Carolina, due to refundable withholding tax credits. In 6 states, 4 to 9 of the 16 sectors experienced negative tax rates, generally due to credits with statewide tax ceilings. If these trends continue, the corporate income tax, at least as it applies to new investment, is in danger of disappearing as a significant revenue source.

TAXES AND INCENTIVES IN 75 CITIES, 1990–1994

We turn our attention now to the 75 cities with enterprise zones, located in 13 states, that are the focus of this study. We computed the effective state-local tax rate on the income from a new plant for each zone and each of the 16 sectors in TAIM^{ez}. The model computes the before-tax cash flow generated by the new plant, and then measures the after-tax cash flow, both over 20 years. The tax rate is the state-local

**Table 3.5 Negative State Corporate Income Tax Rates on New
            Plant Investment[a]**

State	1990 Number of sectors with negative tax rate[b]	1990 Average rate in these sectors (%)	1998 Number of sectors with negative tax rate	1998 Average rate in these sectors (%)
Conn.	0	NA	2	−0.2
Fla.	7	−1.2	5	−0.9
Iowa	16	−0.3	16	−0.5
Ind.	0	NA	4	−1.0
Ky.	16	−8.7	15	−4.7
Mass.	0	NA	1	−0.1
Mich.	0	NA	16	−8.0
Mo.	1	−0.1	1	−0.1
N.Y.	5	−1.4	6	−2.8
Ohio	0	NA	13	−2.1
S.C.	0	NA	16	−5.0
Tex.	12	−0.9	9	−2.0
Va.	0	NA	5	−2.6
Wis.	3	−0.8	4	−0.6

NOTE: NA = not applicable.

[a] State average local property-tax rates and abatement terms were assumed. For each
state we used the most generous combination of incentives available. Negative tax
rates did not occur for any sector in either year for the six other states in the study:
Calif., Ill., Minn., N.C., Tenn., and Pa.

[b] The number of sectors is out of 16 possible.

tax bite as a percent of before-tax cash flow. In order to present an
overall picture of tax rates and incentives in these cities, we calculated
the weighted average tax rate among the 16 manufacturing sectors for
each city. We then calculated a simple average of the city tax rates for
each of the 13 states. (There were 6 cities in 10 of the states, 5 in the
other 3 states.) The average effective state-local tax rate on new manufacturing investment for each state, with and without incentives, is
shown for 1990 and 1994 in Table 3.6. The table also shows the highest and lowest rates among the 75 individual cities.

In 1990, the highest tax rate was about four to seven times the lowest tax rate among these cities (depending on which incentives were included). General incentives actually widened the gap between high and low and increased the variance among the 75 cities; enterprise zone incentives, on the other hand, reduced the disparity among cities. In 1994, the variance among cities had increased, either with basic taxes only or with general incentives included. However, zone incentives had an even larger effect in reducing disparities.

In 11 of the 13 states in 1990, zone incentives produced larger reductions in tax rates than did the general incentives available in those states. In 6 states, general incentives were trivial or non-existent; in only 4 did they provide more than a 10 percent reduction in taxes. Zone incentives, on the other hand, produced larger than 10 percent reductions in all but 2 of these states. By 1994, however, general incentives had become much more generous. Zone incentives had increased as well, but by then only 8 states provided larger percentage tax breaks with their zone incentives than with their general incentives. The zone advantage weakened somewhat on average.

In the 75-city analysis actual local property-tax rates are modeled for three years—1990, 1992, and 1994. These comparisons thus reflect changes in the total state-local tax burden, whereas our 20-state comparisons held average local property-tax rates constant and thus focused on changes in state policy. What we find in the city analysis is that the expanded state tax incentives were in part compensating for rising property taxes. Effective state-local tax rates without incentives increased, on average, in 11 of the 13 states between 1990 and 1994. With general incentives included, increases were produced in only 8 of the 13, and this number is further reduced to 6 when enterprise zone incentives are added. The average city saw about a 6.5 percent increase in basic taxes, no real change in taxes after general incentives, and a 3.6 percent reduction in tax rates with zone incentives included.

The pattern of increases in incentives can be seen more clearly in Table 3.7, where we show the dollar value of incentive packages per job created. The increases in just the four-year period 1990 to 1994 are very sizeable. The average general incentive package among the 75 cities rose from $1,276 to $2,199, a 72 percent increase. The additional value of zone incentives increased on average from $2,352 to $2,849, a 21 percent increase. General incentive packages increased measura-

Table 3.6 Effective Tax Rates on New Manufacturing Investment in 75 Cities (Weighted Average for 16 Manufacturing Sectors)[a]

| | 1990 | | | | | 1994 | | | | | Percent change, 1990–94 | | |
| | Effective tax rate[b] | | | % reduction in rate | | Effective tax rate | | | % reduction in rate | | Effective tax rate | | |
	After basic taxes	With general incentives	With general & zone incentives	Due to general incentives	Due to zone incentives	After basic taxes	With general incentives	With general & zone incentives	Due to general incentives	Due to zone incentives	After basic taxes	With general incentives	With general & zone incentives
Average by state[c]													
Calif.	9.2	9.2	8.9	0.3	3.4	8.9	7.4	6.8	17.3	7.7	-3.2	-19.7	-23.2
Conn.	7.6	6.1	4.8	20.1	21.9	8.9	6.8	5.7	23.5	16.6	17.5	12.4	20.1
Fla.	8.1	8.1	6.5	0.0	19.8	8.3	8.3	6.7	0.0	19.3	2.8	2.8	3.4
Ill.	6.1	5.7	4.7	6.3	18.1	6.2	5.8	4.7	6.2	17.9	0.9	1.0	1.2
Ind.	13.5	13.5	9.8	0.0	27.2	15.2	12.5	7.4	17.9	40.8	12.6	-7.6	-24.8
Ky.	7.7	6.5	5.5	15.1	16.1	8.1	5.1	4.0	37.6	19.9	5.2	-22.7	-26.2
Mo.	9.7	7.0	5.9	27.8	16.1	10.4	7.7	6.1	26.2	20.8	7.8	10.1	3.9
N.Y.	7.6	4.3	3.9	43.1	8.4	6.9	3.6	2.8	48.2	20.9	-8.4	-16.7	-28.1
Ohio	9.7	9.6	6.5	0.8	32.7	9.8	8.8	5.6	10.1	36.2	1.1	-8.3	-13.1
Pa.	9.0	8.5	6.8	5.5	19.6	10.6	10.1	8.2	4.8	18.8	18.0	18.8	20.0
Tex.	9.3	8.8	7.6	5.4	12.9	11.1	10.5	9.0	5.6	14.0	19.6	19.4	17.9
Va.	6.9	6.9	6.2	0.0	10.4	7.0	7.0	6.1	0.0	12.3	1.4	1.4	-0.7
Wis.	6.9	6.9	5.7	0.0	16.9	7.3	7.3	5.3	0.0	27.8	6.2	6.2	-7.8

Among the 75 cities

Highest	19.9	19.9	11.1	57.3	45.7	22.8	20.1	11.7	62.3	52.8	54.8	56.0	70.2
Mean	8.6	7.8	6.4	9.5	17.3	9.1	7.8	6.1	15.2	21.2	6.5	0.0	-3.6
Lowest	5.2	2.9	2.5	0.0	0.0	5.2	2.1	1.4	0.0	7.6	-15.8	-26.0	-50.5
Variance	0.05	0.07	0.04			0.08	0.07	0.04					

[a] Effective tax rate is the reduction in the net present value (NPV) of the cash flow from a new plant due to state and local income, sales, and property taxes in the new plant state, divided by the NPV of the pre-tax income generated by the plant. Pre-tax income is measured before all federal, state, and local taxes; NPV is measured over 20 years. The reduction in cash flow is calculated by comparing project cash flow after actual taxes and incentives in the new plant state and after federal and other state taxes, with cash flow assuming the same plant location but with only federal taxes and taxes in other states.

[b] The tax rates shown are weighted averages of the tax rates calculated for firms representative of 16 two-digit SIC code sectors, where the weights are the sector shares of 1995 U.S. manufacturing employment.

[c] There are either five or six cities in each state. The statistics for the 75 cities show the city with the effective tax rate averaged across the 16 sectors and the like, not the single sector with the highest rate.

Table 3.7 The Value of Incentives per Job Created to Manufacturing Firms in 75 Cities, 1990 and 1994 (in dollars)[a]

	Value of incentives per job, 1990			Value of incentives per job, 1994			Change in value 1990–94		
	General incentives	General plus zone incentives	Additional value of zone incentives	General incentives	General plus zone incentives	Additional value of zone incentives	General incentives	General plus zone incentives	Additional value of zone incentives
Average by state[b]									
Calif.	37	709	672	2,682	3,634	952	2,645	2,925	280
Conn.	2,644	4,787	2,143	3,547	5,370	1,822	903	583	–320
Fla.	0	2,297	2,297	0	2,301	2,301	0	4	4
Ill.	660	2,348	1,687	661	2,347	1,686	1	–1	–1
Ind.	0	6,681	6,681	3,485	12,769	9,284	3,485	6,088	2,603
Ky.	1,975	3,652	1,677	5,462	7,143	1,681	3,486	3,491	5
Mo.	4,562	6,445	1,883	4,635	7,346	2,710	73	900	827
N.Y.	5,419	5,803	384	5,597	6,615	1,017	178	811	633
Ohio	136	5,590	5,454	1,268	6,800	5,533	1,132	1,211	79
Pa.	744	3,674	2,929	782	4,019	3,238	37	345	308
Tex.	856	2,619	1,763	1,055	3,432	2,377	199	812	613
Va.	0	871	871	0	1,045	1,045	0	174	174
Wis.	0	1,867	1,867	0	3,237	3,237	0	1,370	1,370

Among the 75 cities[c]

Highest	7,285	15,930	15,930	7,359	22,678	19,193	3,576	10,758	7,273
Mean	1,276	3,628	2,352	2,199	5,048	2,849	924	1,420	497
Lowest	0	0	0	0	1,045	720	-278	-255	-461

[a] Figures represent the present value of the increased cash flow over 20 years accruing to the firm because of the package of tax incentives available in that state for a new manufacturing facility. All figures are weighted averages of the values for the 16 manufacturing sectors modeled.

[b] There are either five or six cities in each state.

[c] The statistics for the 75 cities show the city with the effective tax rate averaged across the 16 sectors and the like, not the single sector with the highest rate.

bly in 9 of the 13 states, as did zone incentives (though they were a different 9 states).

These average incentive values do not seem that large when compared to the incentive packages reported in the press. The average total package was just $3,628 per job in 1990 and $5,048 in 1994, though the highest award had risen to $22,678 per job by 1994. It is not uncommon to find reports of special deals for auto firms in excess of $100,000 per job (often including discretionary, non-tax incentives, which are not included in the TAIM^{ez} estimates). Such comparisons are not valid, however. Our figures represent the present value of an incentive package's effect on the firm's after-tax cash flow. Local incentives increase both state and federal income tax liability, and state incentives increase federal taxes. The combined effect is that the net value of a tax reduction in any one year is only around 60 percent of the gross value; it is invariably the gross value (the cost in lost revenues to state and local governments) that is reported in the press. Furthermore, the press reports the undiscounted sum of lost revenues over some period of years, whereas we discount future benefits at 10 percent. Both state tax credits and local property-tax abatements are spread over a number of years, sometimes up to 20 years, so that discounting has a large effect on the measured value of incentives.

If one-time incentive packages were put into an appropriate accounting framework, such as the TAIM^{ez} model, the value per job would be considerably less than what is reported. To illustrate these effects, we show in Table 3.8 the value of two incentive packages: one for an instruments plant in Hartford, Connecticut, the other for a chemicals plant in Utica, New York. We show the two major components, state income tax credits and local property-tax abatements, in three ways: 1) as a simple undiscounted sum of the gross incentive amounts for each of 20 years, 2) as a net present value (the gross amounts discounted at 10 percent), and 3) as the net discounted value to the firm, taking into account state and federal income tax effects. The real value of the incentive package to the firm was only 45 percent of the gross undiscounted sum in Hartford and only 33 percent in Utica.

Among the 75 cities, half had at least one sector for which the total incentive package exceeded $10,000 per job, and 14 cities would have granted at least one sector more than $20,000 per job. Incentives of this magnitude are equivalent to a gross undiscounted value in the range of

Table 3.8 Gross Cost of Incentives Versus Value to the Firm

Measure	Hartford, Conn. Instruments plant (100 employees)	Utica, N.Y. Chemicals plant (75 employees)
Dollars (000)		
State income tax credits		
Undiscounted sum	975.5	2,296.9
Gross NPV[a]	636.2	1,028.6
Value to firm	439.6	710.7
Property-tax abatements		
Undiscounted sum	704.4	437.4
Gross NPV	523.2	311.9
Value to firm	315.6	189.4
Total		
Undiscounted sum	1,679.9	2,734.3
Gross NPV	1,159.4	1,340.5
Value to firm	755.1	900.1
Percent of undiscounted sum		
State income tax credits		
Gross NPV	65	45
Value to firm	45	31
Property tax abatements		
Gross NPV	74	71
Value to firm	45	43
Total		
Gross NPV	69	49
Value to firm	45	33

[a] NPV = net present value.

$20,000 to $60,000 per job, which is not trivial in comparison to the reported packages offered to some firms in the past 10 years.

Another way of getting at the question of incentive size and importance is to consider the size of the wage premium that a given incentive package would just offset. Wages are a much larger component of costs than are taxes (about 14 times as large, on average), and wage rates can vary substantially from one place to another. Wages might be only slightly higher in a particular locale, but a large percentage reduction in taxes would be required to offset the wage disadvantage. To put it another way, if wage differentials of $1.00 an hour or more are common when manufacturers compare sites, then an incentive package that provides the equivalent of a 10-cent wage reduction is unlikely to exert a significant influence on location decisions; tax differences will be swamped by wage differences.

Again using TAIM^{ez}, we calculated the hourly wage differential at a new plant location that would provide the firm with the same present value of cost savings over 20 years as the incentives available at that location. These equivalent wage reductions were, for the most part, in the range of $0.10 to $1.50 per hour, with considerable variation both by state and by sector, as can be seen in Table 3.9. If we look at the average of all the 13 states for each of the sectors, we find that the incentive packages were equivalent to a 1.6 percent to 7.1 percent cut in wages. A relatively small wage premium would be sufficient in many locations to wipe out the advantages created by the incentive packages there. As a result we do not think it likely that incentives have much impact on the location of new business investment; other spatially variable factors, like labor and transportation costs, will tend to dominate location decisions. Indeed, our econometric analyses of this issue, presented in Chapter 7, confirm that enterprise zone incentives have little impact on the location of business investment.

TAXES AND INCENTIVES IN OHIO CITIES, 1990–1994

In addition to the analysis of five or six enterprise zones in each of 13 states, we have also analyzed incentives in all 104 cities in Ohio with a population of 15,000 or more. In the early 1990s, the state of Ohio was quite liberal in its rules permitting establishment of enterprise zones. As a result, many cities with little or no economic distress established zones, thereby being allowed to grant tax abatements to new industrial plants. These nondistressed zones increased substantially in number up until July of 1994, when new ones were no longer allowed. Between 1990 and 1994, 15 more cities (among the 104 total) created enterprise zones, but only one qualified under the distress criteria.

Table 3.9 Wage Equivalent of General and Zone Tax Incentives, 1994, Averaged by State for 75 Cities (The Hourly Wage Reduction That Is Equivalent in Value to the Total State-Local Incentive Package over 20 Years)

	Food SIC 20	Apparel & textiles SIC 23	Wood prod. SIC 24	Furniture SIC 25	Paper SIC 26	Printing SIC 27	Chemicals SIC 28	Rubber & plastic SIC 30	Leather SIC 31	Stone, clay & glass SIC 32	Primary metals SIC 33	Fabricated metals SIC 34	Indust. mach. SIC 35	Elect. equip. SIC 36	Transportation equip. SIC 37	Instruments SIC 38
Hourly wage ($)	10.89	6.69	9.59	9.32	15.19	11.60	16.80	10.86	7.49	12.82	15.96	12.59	13.85	11.73	18.22	13.65
Average wage reduction equivalent ($)																
Calif.	0.19	0.14	0.08	0.11	0.54	0.11	0.45	0.54	0.18	0.31	0.58	0.39	0.40	0.61	0.26	0.46
Conn.	0.28	0.27	0.28	0.24	0.62	0.19	0.89	0.65	0.33	0.49	0.65	0.58	0.60	0.91	0.33	0.87
Fla.	0.12	0.13	0.19	0.17	0.32	0.14	0.32	0.32	0.22	0.32	0.16	0.31	0.24	0.23	0.08	0.24
Ill.	0.15	0.09	0.07	0.11	0.31	0.07	0.33	0.31	0.08	0.18	0.31	0.26	0.21	0.36	0.13	0.34
Ind.	0.68	0.64	0.47	0.52	1.25	0.52	1.23	1.32	0.65	0.84	1.74	1.36	1.53	2.25	1.02	1.81
Ky.	0.32	0.31	0.22	0.24	0.95	0.22	1.07	0.93	0.34	0.59	0.96	0.69	0.80	1.35	0.44	1.14
Mo.	0.37	0.27	0.28	0.29	0.99	0.23	1.11	0.97	0.32	0.64	0.98	0.77	0.72	1.22	0.40	1.03
N.Y.	0.31	0.31	0.51	0.35	0.90	0.25	1.57	0.75	0.37	0.70	0.72	0.66	0.62	1.00	0.35	0.99
Ohio	0.42	0.38	0.24	0.30	0.86	0.25	0.85	0.88	0.38	0.57	1.01	0.71	0.74	1.11	0.48	1.00
Pa.	0.22	0.20	0.19	0.21	0.50	0.13	0.67	0.51	0.18	0.35	0.52	0.50	0.40	0.67	0.24	0.69
Tex.	0.23	0.15	0.09	0.14	0.41	0.11	0.39	0.45	0.15	0.29	0.49	0.35	0.36	0.52	0.19	0.47
Va.	0.10	0.07	0.10	0.10	0.10	0.10	0.10	0.10	0.10	0.10	0.10	0.10	0.10	0.10	0.05	0.10
Wis.	0.20	0.15	0.12	0.16	0.44	0.14	0.46	0.48	0.14	0.29	0.44	0.30	0.31	0.48	0.20	0.45
Mean	0.28	0.24	0.22	0.23	0.63	0.19	0.73	0.63	0.26	0.44	0.67	0.54	0.54	0.83	0.32	0.74
Percent[a]	2.5	3.6	2.3	2.4	4.1	1.6	4.3	5.8	3.5	3.4	4.2	4.3	3.9	7.1	1.8	5.4

[a] Mean wage reduction as a percent of hourly wage.

Table 3.10 Tax Rates and Incentive Value in 104 Ohio Cities, 1990 and 1994

| | City (population 15,000 or more) having | | | |
Variable	No enterprise zone	Non-distressed zone	Distressed zone	All cities
1990				
Number of cities	54	32	18	104
Average city characteristics				
Population	29,474	29,370	146,360	49,672
Property-tax rate (real property)[a] (%)	5.8	4.9	5.2	5.4
Local sales tax rate (%)	1.2	1.0	0.7	1.1
Local income tax rate (%)	1.5	1.6	1.8	1.6
Effective tax rate (%)				
Basic taxes only	10.68	9.54	9.85	10.19
With general state incentives	10.59	9.46	9.77	10.10
With all incentives	10.59	6.82	7.01	8.81
Value of incentive package per job ($)				
General state incentives	163	135	140	150
Local zone abatements	0	4,601	4,809	2,248
Total incentive package	163	4,737	4,949	2,399
1994				
Number of cities	39	46	19	104
Average city characteristics				
Population	26,326	27,863	150,395	49,672
Qualify for 13.5% ITC	4	11	13	28
Property-tax rate (real property)[a] (%)	5.9	5.4	5.6	5.6
Local sales tax rate (%)	1.3	1.1	0.9	1.1
Local income tax rate (%)	1.7	1.6	1.9	1.7
Effective tax rate (%)				
Basic taxes only	10.59	9.90	9.96	10.17
With general state incentives	9.54	8.91	8.97	9.16
With all incentives	9.54	6.06	6.20	7.39

Table 3.10 (Continued)

Variable	City (population 15,000 or more) having			
	No enterprise zone	Non-distressed zone	Distressed zone	All cities
Value of incentive package per job ($)				
General state incentives	1,336	1,268	1,268	1,293
Local zone abatements	0	4,963	4,824	3,076
Total incentive package	1,336	6,230	6,092	4,370

[a] Net tax rate (after various tax reduction factors are applied) as a percent of assessed value for commercial and industrial real property. Since assessment ratio is 35% for real property in Ohio, the effective rate as a percent of market value would be 35% of this rate.

Table 3.10 shows the incentives available in Ohio cities of 15,000 or more in 1990 and 1994 by three categories: cities without an enterprise zone, cities with a zone that did not meet distress criteria, and cities with zones established under the state's criteria for economic distress. The distressed-zone cities are much larger on average than the cities in the other two categories, but surprisingly the non-zone cities have the highest local tax rates (before and after incentives are taken into account). This is true considering both the simple local property, sales, and income tax rates, themselves, and the effective state-local tax rates calculated by our model. Tax rates in the distressed-zone cities were just slightly higher than tax rates in the nondistressed cities. Abatements had a dramatic effect in lowering effective overall tax rates in the enterprise zone cities.

The state of Ohio enacted much more generous state incentive programs after 1990, but these were available throughout the state rather than targeted at enterprise zones. (The state of Ohio does allow corporate income tax credits for enterprise zone firms, but these are so rarely used that we did not include them in our TAIM^{ez} simulations.) Because of the new statewide incentives, net effective tax rates in all categories of cities declined significantly between 1990 and 1994, despite slight increases in property-tax and local income tax rates overall. If one were to characterize Ohio's tax incentive strategy based on these numbers, it would be to use state tax relief to lower business taxes throughout the state and let localities, whether distressed or not, compete against one another using local property-tax abatements, which in fact are worth more than five times as much as the state tax credits.

CONCLUSIONS

Incentive competition within the sample of enterprise zone cities that are the focus of most of this book is part of a broader and continuing trend toward increased use of tax incentives by state and local governments. Among 20 prominent manufacturing states, the trend in the period 1990–1998 was overwhelmingly to reduce basic taxes on corporations and to enact or expand both general and targeted incentives for new business investment. In 1990, 8 of the 20 states offered statewide tax incentives that reduced the total state-local tax rate by more than 10 percent. By 1998, this number had increased to 13 states, with reductions of 20 percent or more in 9 of the 13. Fourteen states offered some kind of targeted incentives in 1990; 19 of the 20 offered such incentives by 1998, and in 11 states targeted incentives provided further reductions of 20 percent or more. The increasing generosity of incentives has led to the possibility of negative tax rates on new investment in a number of states. Furthermore, there is no indication that this tax and incentive competition is producing convergence in net tax rates; the process resembles a game of leapfrog, with no state apparently content to be merely average.

Two contradictory trends appear to have occurred in these 20 states in the 1990s: 1) some states have embarked on new enterprise zone programs, or increased the competitive advantage of existing zones or other targeted areas; 2) other states have weakened the advantage of geographically targeted areas by reducing targeted incentives or, more commonly, by expanding nontargeted incentives. Perhaps more importantly, the trend in many states with long-standing enterprise zone programs (or the equivalent) has been to increase the maximum number of such zones allowed. This further weakens the targeting effect of zone programs, as a larger and larger portion of the state falls under the targeted program. Among 14 major manufacturing states with enterprise zone programs as of 1992, zone proliferation has occurred to some extent in 9.

The 75 cities that were the focus of much of this book were located in 13 states from among the 20. The trends in these states during the period 1990–1994 mirrored the trends discussed above to a large extent: incentives became more generous, and nontargeted incentives grew more rapidly than targeted (enterprise zone) incentives, so that the competitive advantage of zones was weakened slightly. The average general incentive package among the 75 cities rose from $1,276 to $2,199 per job, a 72 percent increase. The additional value of zone incentives increased on average from $2,352 to $2,849 per job, a 21 percent increase. The expanded state tax incentives were in part compensating for rising property taxes. Effective state-local tax rates without incentives increased, on average, in 11 of the 13 states between 1990 and 1994.

Another way of putting the magnitude of these general and enterprise zone incentives into perspective is to calculate the hourly wage differential at a new plant location that would provide the firm with the same present value of cost savings over 20 years as the incentives available at that location. If we look at the average across the 13 states for each of the sectors, we find that the incentive packages were equivalent to a 1.6 percent to 7.1 percent cut in wages. A relatively small wage premium would be sufficient, in many locations, to wipe out the advantages created by the incentive packages there. Thus it is unlikely that incentives have much impact on the location of new business investment.

Notes

1. See, for instance, L. Papke (1987) and J. Papke (1988), both using the AFTAX model; Brooks et al. (1986); Laughlin (1993); Tannenwald (1996); and Peters and Fisher (1999a). For new applications of the method, also see Tannenwald, O'Leary, and Huang (1999).
2. In this instance, payments of taxes to other states are represented as payments to the "median state." See Appendix A and Chapter 3 of Fisher and Peters (1998).
3. Local tax rates for each enterprise zone city for 1990, 1992, and 1994 were ob-

tained, in many cases directly from each city; it was the statewide average rate that was difficult to determine several years after the fact since most states do not calculate such a rate.

4. The only general incentive in 1990 in Iowa was property-tax abatement, a large portion of which was for property taxes on machinery and equipment (M&E). By 1998, M&E had been exempted from property taxes altogether (which we considered a change in the basic tax system since it is not tied to new investment or job creation) so that the value of abatements was reduced, there being much less to abate. In Minnesota, a significant general incentive is the complete exemption of manufacturing M&E from sales tax when it is associated with new investment; but when the sales-tax rate on manufacturing M&E, including replacement equipment, was reduced from 6.5 percent to 2.0 percent, the value of the exemption was lessened because there was much less sales tax to exempt. An examination of Table 3.3 reveals that there was actually only one state, Missouri, where the effective tax rate after general incentives increased due to a tightening of incentive programs.

5. Table 3.4 shows a sizeable increase in the value of targeted incentive programs in Missouri. This occurred not because the parameters of the enterprise zone program were changed, but because basic income taxes were increased, so that the income exemption was more valuable and the credits were more likely to be fully used since the ceiling (Missouri income taxes) was raised.

6. Iowa's new enterprise zone program appears in our analyses to be of little value on average because it simply relaxes eligibility criteria for existing incentives for a firm locating in a zone; the principal effect is that small plants, and those with lower-paying jobs, are eligible only within zones. Most of our representative firms already qualified.

7. It should be noted that Pennsylvania has enacted the new Keystone Opportunity Zone Program, with very generous incentives, but that took effect in 1999, too late to be reflected in our 1998 effective tax rate comparisons.

8. These figures are from the U.S. Department of Housing and Urban Development 1992; database developed by John Engberg; and the Virginia and Texas state Web sites.

9. Three states appear on both lists since they have multiple credits with different ceilings.

4

How Taxes and Incentives Favor One Industry over Another and Capital over Labor

Enterprise zone incentives are invariably touted as a device to stimulate the creation of jobs, usually without regard to the industry providing those jobs. While localities do sometimes attempt to recruit plants in particular sectors, the incentives themselves are typically applied equally to all industrial facilities (certainly to all manufacturing plants, and perhaps to wholesale trade and other sectors as well). Implicit in those incentives, however, is an industrial policy of sorts. Tax systems and incentive programs always advantage some kinds of firms and disadvantage others. Economic-development professionals at the state or local level are probably unaware of biases embedded in state and local tax systems and in zone incentives in favor of certain industries. Furthermore, tax incentives may lower the cost of capital or of labor or of both or of neither. As a result, they may not provide strong incentives to expand employment, despite the stated program goals, but instead may encourage the substitution of capital for labor.

In this chapter we first explore how the zone incentive programs in the 75-city sample favor certain manufacturing industries. If localities are going to continue to offer tax incentives in the belief that they have a significant effect on firm decisions, they should do so in ways that are more likely to further their stated policy objectives. If the state tax system and local property taxes tend to discourage investment by firms in certain industries, that should be known so that the incentive system can be designed to counteract those effects, if that is appropriate. Overall, we found that the average city in our study imposed a tax rate on its most favored industry that was only 38 percent of the tax rate on its least favored industry. In many cities, the difference was extreme.

In the second section of this chapter we examine how enterprise zone incentives encourage the use of labor or of capital. If the goal of the enterprise zone program is to stimulate employment, incentives should unambiguously encourage firms to employ more, not fewer,

85

workers. What we find, however, is quite the opposite: there is a strong bias in favor of capital built into the incentive systems in most, but not all, states.

FAVORED INDUSTRIES

When we looked at the 75 enterprise zone cities in our sample, we found considerable variation in terms of the industrial sectors that were taxed most lightly and most heavily. It is quite common, in fact, for the most heavily taxed sector in a given city to be facing a state-local tax rate two or three times the tax rate on the least-taxed sector within that city. Furthermore, one does not find the same industries always being taxed more lightly or more heavily in different cities. In Illinois cities, for example, the paper industry tends to be taxed most lightly and the leather products industry most heavily. In California cities, on the other hand, rubber and plastics firms tend to face the lowest tax rates, while printing and publishing firms face the highest. It is doubtful that these differences are a desired outcome—the result of deliberate policy—in those two states.

The variation in effective tax rates is due primarily to differences among industries in terms of profitability, asset composition, and the relative importance of capital and labor, and to differences among localities in terms of the relative importance of income, sales, and property taxes, the makeup of the property-tax base, and the nature of tax incentives. More profitable firms are at more of a disadvantage in cities in which state (and occasionally local) taxes on corporate profits predominate. The relative importance of inventory, plant, and equipment in the firms asset structure can be very important; firms with a high proportion of real property (buildings and land) are disadvantaged in places with high property-tax rates or no tax abatements, while firms with substantial inventory are disadvantaged by states that subject inventories to the property tax. More-capital-intensive industries are advantaged by incentives tied to capital investment, while more-labor-intensive industries are advantaged by incentives tied to job creation.

To assess the magnitude of the variation in tax rates by industry within cities, we simply determined the state-local tax rate (after incen-

Table 4.1 Variation in Tax Rates within Cities in 13 States

State	Tax rate for the highest taxed sector (average among cities)	Tax rate for the lowest taxed sector (average among cities)	Lowest rate as a percent age of highest rate
California	9.7	4.8	50
Connecticut	8.7	3.5	40
Florida	11.4	2.7	24
Illinois	6.9	3.4	49
Indiana	12.2	3.4	28
Kentucky	6.1	2.9	47
Missouri	11.0	3.2	29
New York	5.2	–0.9	nm[a]
Ohio	8.0	3.7	46
Pennsylvania	10.6	6.8	64
Texas	13.1	5.9	45
Virginia	10.7	3.4	32
Wisconsin	7.9	3.7	47
Overall average	9.3	3.6	38

[a] nm = not meaningful.

tives) for each of the 16 industries for each city, and compared the highest rate with the lowest rate within each city. Table 4.1 shows the extent to which tax rates vary by industry within the same city; shown here are the average rates on the highest-taxed sector and the average rates on the lowest-taxed sector, averaged among the cities in each state. Overall, the average city imposed a tax rate of 3.6 percent on its most-favored industry, which was only two-fifths of the tax rate of 9.3 percent imposed on its least-favored industry. (Results for each of the 75 cities are shown in Appendix Table F.3.)

If tax rates do affect location decisions, then what determines the competitiveness of a particular city for a particular industry is not the absolute tax rate, but that city's tax rate compared to tax rates on that industry in other cities. A city could impose its lightest tax burden on the food industry but still have a high tax rate compared to how other cities tax food manufacturers. To examine the competitiveness issue, we ranked the 75 cities by tax rate for each of the 16 sectors. Then we identified, for each city, the sector that was most competitive (in other words, the one with the best ranking among the 75 cities by tax rate) and the sector that was least competitive (worst ranking). For example, in Fort Wayne, Indiana, printing and publishing firms faced a tax rate of 1.0 percent, which was low enough to rank that city 4th; only 3 cities among the 75 taxed that industry more lightly. Rubber and plastic products manufacturers, on the other hand, faced a tax rate of 6.7 percent in Fort Wayne (almost 7 times the rate on printing firms), which resulted in a ranking of 46th; approximately 60 percent of the 75 cities taxed rubber and plastics firms at a lower rate. The tax rates for the remaining 14 sectors resulted in Fort Wayne being ranked somewhere between 4th and 46th. Thus, a blanket assertion that a particular city is "very competitive in terms of taxes" may not mean much; it may be quite competitive for some sectors and out of the running for others.

The results of these ranking calculations are summarized by state in Table 4.2. In some states (Florida and Illinois, for example), the state tax system appears to dominate, there being little variation among the cities within the state in terms of the best- or worst-ranked sectors or in terms of city rankings. (This can also be due to similarity in local tax burdens, of course.) In most states, however, variation in local tax rates and property-tax abatement policies is substantial and plays a significant role in determining which sectors are taxed more or less heavily. We simply present the average of the cities in each state (Table 4.2); results for each of the 75 cities can be found in Appendix Table F.3.

There is sufficient variation within cities in most states that any city can be fairly competitive for at least one or a few sectors. As Appendix Table F.3 shows, in all states but California and Texas, there was at least one of our sample cities with a sector ranked in the top 20 percent (1–15). Altogether, 38 of the 75 cities had a sector ranked 15 or better, and 53 of the 75 had at least one sector ranked in the top 40 percent (30 or better). On the other hand, there were 11 cities (mostly in Pennsylvania and Texas) with all sectors ranked in the bottom 40 percent. Cities in those states simply do not have enough leverage on the overall state-local tax rate to overcome a disadvantageous state tax system. Property taxes are fairly high and cities are constrained in what they can do as far as abatements are concerned. All California cities have a best sector in the middle 20 percent; there is little variation in property-tax rates and no allowance for local abatements.

Given the implicit and probably unintended industrial policy implied by these varying tax rates, a state and city's average tax rate (for all sectors) may not be a particularly useful indicator of the citys tax climate for a specific industrial sector. A city might derive most of its growth from a small number of sectors, and it is possible that a city's growth is explained by the tax rates for the sectors in which that city has the greatest comparative advantage (at least in terms of ranking by taxes) rather than an overall average rate. For this reason, some of our analyses of the effects of tax rates on zone growth in Chapter 7 are conducted by sector—we investigate whether sectoral tax rates explain sectoral growth.

INCENTIVES TO EXPAND LABOR VERSUS CAPITAL

Much of the discussion of enterprise zones seems to assume that all incentives can be expected to stimulate the creation of jobs. As L. Papke (1993) points out, however, this is not the case. Incentives may affect factor prices, and incentives that lower the price of capital goods have both an output effect (whereby production and employment increase because costs are lowered) and a substitution effect (whereby capital is substituted for labor). If the substitution effect is stronger, a capital incentive could reduce employment.

To determine whether a particular incentive lowers the price of labor or of capital it is not enough to determine whether the incentive is nominally tied to one factor or the other. For example, a credit equal to $1,000 per job may or may not lower the price of labor, and a credit for investment in machinery may or may not lower the price of capital. In order to understand how this could be, we will start by categorizing tax incentives for business firms in the same way that one categorizes intergovernmental grants—that is, distinguishing lump-sum from matching grants. Tax incentives are, after all, functionally equivalent to grants to firms; they operate through the tax system instead of the expenditure system.

First, there are capital credits or abatements that operate as matching grants—incentives that lower the price of capital goods—such as sales-tax exemptions for the purchase of machinery and equipment, invest-

Table 4.2 Favored Industries

State	Most-competitive sectors			Least-competitive sectors		
	Sectors	Cities	Average rank	Sectors	Cities	Average rank
California	Rubber and plastics	3	41	Printing and publishing	6	61
	Primary metals	3	37			
Connecticut	Apparel	5	15	Printing and publishing	2	37
	Leather	1	31	Four others	4	45
Florida	Leather	6	11	Primary metals	6	61
Illinois	Paper	6	10	Leather	4	40
				Apparel	2	50
Indiana	Printing and publishing	6	27	Rubber and plastics	3	65
				Three others	3	65
Kentucky	Fabricated metals	2	10	Leather	2	22
	Electric equipment	2	10	Apparel	2	53
	Transportation equip.	1	1	Primary metals	1	19
Missouri	Leather	4	24	Paper	3	46
	Fabricated metals	1	2	Two others	2	60
New York	Lumber & wood	4	5	Food	4	9
	Food	1	1	Leather	1	59
	Apparel	1	2	Transportation equip.	1	2
Ohio	Food	5	17	Leather	4	58
	Transportation equip.	1	41	Apparel	2	57

State	Sector	Cities	Avg. rank	Sector	Cities	Avg. rank
Pennsylvania	Paper	3	51	Lumber and wood	2	73
	Primary metals	2	39	Leather	2	53
	Food	1	7	Two others	2	75
Texas	Chemicals	6	58	Apparel	2	72
				Primary metals	2	73
				Two others	2	70
Virginia	Apparel	4	22	Paper	4	50
	Leather	1	29	Stone, clay, and glass	2	59
	Food	1	5			
Wisconsin	Rubber and plastics	2	15	Lumber and wood	5	46
	Paper	2	21			
	Primary metals	1	25			

NOTE: For each state, table shows the number of cities for which the given sector was their most competitive sector, and the average rank for that sector among those cities. Cities were ranked within each sector based on the state-local tax rate after all incentives. A rank of 1 indicates the most competitive city for that sector (the lowest tax rate among the 75 cities).

ment tax credits, and property-tax abatements. Since the incentive is a percentage of the cost of capital, the larger the capital expenditure, the larger the total incentive. The public sector matches private capital spending—albeit through a "tax expenditure" rather than an outright grant. Second, there are jobs credits that operate as labor matching grants—incentives that lower the price of labor—such as corporate income tax credits equal to a dollar amount per job or a percentage of wages, and job-training programs that underwrite a portion of the initial cost of labor. Third, there are general incentives that also function as matching grants—incentives that simply reduce taxes and raise profits and therefore effectively reduce all factor prices proportionately—such as exemptions of all or a portion of the profits from operations in an enterprise zone from income taxation. Fourth, there are other incentives that are like lump-sum grants because they do not vary with plant size or employment levels or profits. Free access roads would be an example.

Table 4.3 shows the relative importance of the first three kinds of state and local tax incentives in our sample of 75 cities in 13 states as of 1994. State jobs and capital credits are credits against the firms state corporate income tax. Jobs credits are labor-matching grants (a percent of wages or dollar amount per job that increases with the number of jobs, or a share of job-training costs). State capital credits are typically an investment tax credit or a credit for sales or property taxes paid on purchases of machinery and equipment associated with new plant investment. Local property-tax abatements reduce the price of buildings and machinery. The state capital credits and local abatements together constitute the capital-matching grants. The category "other state incentives" consists of those that function as general matching grants—exemption of all or a portion of the income from a new plant from corporate income tax, for example.

California and Virginia are the exceptions among these 13 states in that 100 percent of their incentive packages in 1994 consisted of jobs credits. In the other 11 states, jobs credits represented less than one-third of the total package; in 10 of the 11, total capital credits made up at least two-thirds of the package. (Connecticut's largest incentive consisted of enterprise zone income exemptions; it was the only state with the majority of its package in the "other" category.) Thus, even within enterprise zones, where job creation is ostensibly the primary program objective, capital incentives dominate.

Table 4.3 State and Local Tax Incentives in 75 Cities, Averaged by State, 1994

State	Gross value to the firm of incentives, per job[a] ($)						Distribution of incentive package (%)				
	State jobs credits	State capital credits	Local abatements	Total capital incentives	Other state incentives	Total incentive package	State jobs credits	State capital credits	Local abatements	Total capital incentives	Other state incentives
Calif.	1,376	0	0	0	0	1,376	100.0	0.0	0.0	0.0	0.0
Conn.	574	0	2,988	2,988	4,581	8,143	7.4	0.0	33.6	33.6	59.0
Fla.	73	3,278	0	3,278	0	3,350	2.2	97.8	0.0	97.8	0.0
Ill.	113	1,559	1,969	3,529	0	3,641	3.5	47.8	48.7	96.5	0.0
Ind.	5,453	0	13,490	13,490	0	18,942	32.5	0.0	67.5	67.5	0.0
Ky.	157	4,548	566	5,114	424	5,694	2.8	82.1	9.3	91.3	5.9
Mo.	489	1,690	3,775	5,465	1,741	7,694	6.7	23.2	46.1	69.3	23.9
N.Y.	2,981	3,820	3,091	6,911	62	9,955	30.7	39.3	29.4	68.7	0.6
Ohio	1,852	0	9,122	9,122	0	10,974	17.6	0.0	82.4	82.4	0.0
Pa.	317	4,686	940	5,626	0	5,942	5.4	80.2	14.3	94.6	0.0
Tex.	0	2,126	1,702	3,827	0	3,827	0.0	62.9	37.1	100.0	0.0
Va.	1,513	0	0	0	0	1,513	100.0	0.0	0.0	0.0	0.0
Wis.	602	3,223	0	3,223	872	4,696	12.8	68.6	0.0	68.6	18.6

[a] Weighted average for 16 manufacturing sectors. Values are calculated including all tax incentives, available generally and only within enterprise zones. Gross value is the net present value of the credit or abatement without taking into account the effect on federal income taxes or other state income taxes.

This is not the end of the story, however. Many of the capital and labor matching grants are closed-ended. That is, they have a statutory ceiling on the total allowable credit. Firms bumping against that ceiling in effect receive a lump-sum grant rather than a matching grant because further increases in investment or employment produce no increase in the credit; there is no factor price effect at the margin. Typically, the credits are one-time credits taken in the year the new investment is placed in service; they are not refundable (though they may be carried forward) and the ceiling is therefore the firms tax liability before credits (or, in some instances, 50 percent of its tax liability).

This is not a trivial category. Table 4.4 shows the instances in which one of our representative firms was constrained by a job or capital credit ceiling. Here we distinguish between credits allowed generally and those available only for firms locating in an enterprise zone. We consider cities averaged by state and not as individual cities since we are dealing only with state income tax credits. A zero under "value of credits" indicates that a credit was available on paper, but the firm received no benefit from it either because the credit was substitutive rather than additive with another (more generous) credit or because another credit had consumed the entire sum available under the ceiling. A blank under "value of credits" indicates that no such credit existed in that state in 1994. When the average percent of credits used is less than 100 percent, then for at least some sectors, jobs credits there operate as lump-sum grants because wages are not reduced at the margin.

Among these 13 states, there were 17 job credit programs in operation in 1994. In 7 of the 13 states, there was at least one jobs credit program that operated as a true matching grant for all 16 firms. In 4 of the 7, these were enterprise zone, not general, incentive programs (Illinois, New York, Virginia, and Wisconsin). In 4 states (Connecticut, Florida, Kentucky, and Missouri), the jobs credits usually operated as lump-sum grants (in at least 11 of the 16 sectors). Texas had no job credit program, whereas Californias enterprise zone jobs credits were fully utilized in 10 of the 16 sectors. Clearly, it cannot be assumed that the mere existence of jobs tax credits implies employment-inducing effects. Among the 17 programs, 4 provided no benefits and another 5 operated as lump-sum grants for all or some of the sectors modeled.

Only 4 of the 13 states had true capital matching grants (Wisconsin, Illinois, Pennsylvania, and Texas). In all four cases, they were for en-

Table 4.4 Utilization of Capital and Labor Credits in 75 Cities: Firms Locating in an Enterprise Zone, Averaged by State, 1994

	Value of credits per job[a]				Percent of credits used[a]				Number of sectors with unused credits			
	Labor credits		Capital credits		Labor credits		Capital credits		Labor credits		Capital credits	
State	General	Zone	General	Zone	General	Zone	General	Zone	General	Zone	General	Zone
Calif.	0	1,376	—	0	0.0	84.1	—	0.0	16	6	—	16
Conn.	574	—	—	—	95.6	—	—	—	11	—	—	15
Fla.	—	73	—	3,278	—	6.4	—	44.0	—	14	—	0
Ill.	—	113	965	595	—	100.0	98.2	100.0	—	0	2	0
Ind.	5,044	409	—	—	100.0	100.0	—	—	0	0	—	—
Ky.	0	157	4,548	1,690	0.0	40.2	48.2	12.8	16	11	13	16
Mo.	0	489	0	—	0.0	12.8	0.0	—	16	16	16	14
N.Y.	—	2,981	141	3,680	—	100.0	7.9	48.6	—	0	15	—
Ohio	1,852	0	—	—	100.0	0.0	—	—	0	16	—	1
Pa.	317	—	—	4,686	100.0	—	—	96.1	0	—	—	0
Tex.	—	—	—	2,126	—	—	—	100.0	—	—	—	—
Va.	—	1,513	—	—	—	100.0	—	—	—	0	—	0
Wis.	—	602	—	3,223	—	100.0	—	100.0	—	0	—	0

NOTE: For these simulations, all available credits, inside and outside of enterprise zones, were applied.

[a] Weighted averages across 16 manufacturing sectors. A blank cell indicates that the incentive was not available; a zero indicates the credit was available but could not be used, either because other credits took precedence and used all of the credit available up to the ceiling (the gross tax before credits) or because the firm had to choose between credits and so took only the more generous one.

terprise zone firms only. Four states (Connecticut, Indiana, Ohio, and Virginia) offered no capital credit program, and a fifth (California) offered a program that could not be used by our firms. The remaining four states (Florida, Kentucky, Missouri, and New York) provided credits that operated as lump-sum grants for capital for at least 13 of the 16 sectors modeled.

In summary, 4 of the 13 states provide, at the state level, a set of incentives that clearly lowers the price of labor without an offsetting capital-matching grant: Indiana, New York, Ohio, and Virginia. In these four states, there is an open-ended labor matching grant worth $1,500 per job or more on average, and no capital grants (or, in the case of New York, only closed-ended capital grants). Three other states have a clear capital bias: Illinois, Pennsylvania, and Texas. In these states there is one or more capital grants that is open-ended for virtually all sectors and that provides $1,500 or more per job; the labor incentives are nonexistent or inconsequential (averaging $100 to $300 per job). Wisconsin has both labor and capital matching grants, but the latter are worth about five times as much per job. In the other 5 states, grants are lump-sum in form for many or all sectors, providing no clear reduction in labor or capital prices at the margin.

When local incentives are brought into the picture, the capital bias becomes clear, as we saw in Table 4.3. Property-tax abatements are not limited by a firms income tax liability and operate always as capital price-reducing grants. They are also very substantial in amount. In Illinois, Pennsylvania, and Texas they reinforce the capital bias; they neutralize or overwhelm the pro-labor state incentives in Indiana, New York, and Ohio; and they introduce a strong capital bias to the otherwise ambiguous incentive systems in Connecticut and Missouri. Thus, even within enterprise zones, the system of state and local incentives is more likely to favor the substitution of capital for labor than vice versa. Outside of zones, only two states (Ohio and Indiana) provide incentive systems favoring labor (both states reserve property-tax abatements for enterprise zones or urban revitalization areas). Connecticut, Illinois, Kentucky, Missouri, New York, and Texas provide capital incentives exclusively or predominantly.

The possible effects of incentives on a firms choice of technology, and the relative use of capital and labor in the production process, depend not on the dollar amount of incentives but on changes in the prices of capital and labor. We can estimate these price changes for each of the 16 manufacturing sectors and each of our 75 enterprise zone cities using the TAIM^{ez} model. To calculate the reduction in the price of capital, we first calculate the total cost of capital (plant and equipment) to the firm in the absence of incentives. We define this as the sum of the annual depreciation and interest expense associated with the new plant capital investment, plus property taxes paid on plant and equipment. We then take the present value of these capital expenses over the 20-year time horizon assumed in our model.[1]

Total capital expense is equal to the price of capital times the quantity of capital. The net present value of capital incentives represents a potential reduction in capital expense over 20 years. With quantity of capital held constant, the percentage reduction in capital expense is also the percentage reduction in the price of capital. Thus we need not measure price or quantity directly. Similarly, the total cost of labor is defined as the present value of annual new plant payroll. The percentage reduction in the price of labor is calculated by dividing the net present value of labor incentives by the net present value of total labor expense.

The results of these calculations are shown in Table 4.5. Since most of the variation is due to differences among states and sectors, we show the results averaged by state. That is, for each state we calculated the average price reduction for each sector among the five or six cities in that state. Table 4.5 shows the results in two ways: the weighted average for the 16 sectors, and the range of results—the sector with the smallest percentage reduction and the sector with the largest percentage reduction. Since all the incentives reduce the price of labor or capital, we show the percentages as positive numbers, representing the size of the reduction. In making these calculations, we included only those incentives that were fully utilized and that therefore lowered factor prices at the margin. That is, for each sector and city, if the firm could not use 100 percent of a given incentive, we in effect defined the incentive as a lump-sum grant instead of a labor or capital incentive.

The effects of labor incentives on the price of labor are quite small. In only 2 states does the average price reduction exceed 1.0 percent, and the maximum price reduction among the 16 sectors never exceeds 3.0 percent in any state. Capital incentives, on the other hand, have very substantial price effects in several of the states. The average price reduction among sectors exceeds 5.0 percent in 8 of the 13 states, and

Table 4.5 The Effect of Incentives on the Prices of Capital and Labor, 1994 (Averages by State for 75 Enterprise Zone Cities)

| | Reduction in price (%) | | | |
| | Average in 16 sectors | | Range for 16 sectors | |
State	Capital[a]	Labor[b]	Capital[a]	Labor[b]
Calif.	0.0	0.5	0.0–0.0	0.0–1.4
Conn.	4.5	0.1	2.9–6.7	0.0–0.3
Fla.	1.0	0.1	0.0–21.2	0.0–1.1
Ill.	5.7	0.1	3.9–8.9	0.0–0.1
Ind.	18.0	2.6	9.5–34.5	2.6–2.8
Ky.	3.2	0.0	0.4–21.7	0.0–0.4
Mo.	5.5	0.0	3.6–8.6	0.0–0.0
N.Y.	7.2	1.5	3.0–36.1	0.9–2.3
Ohio	13.4	0.9	8.5–29.5	0.9–0.9
Pa.	9.8	0.2	2.0–20.9	0.1–0.3
Tex.	5.5	0.0	3.6–10.1	0.0–0.0
Va.	0.0	0.8	0.0–0.0	0.3–1.3
Wis.	5.1	0.3	0.7–6.5	0.2–0.6

[a] Net present value (NPV) of fully utilized capital credits divided by NPV of the total cost of capital (annual depreciation, interest, and property taxes), all net of state, local, and federal income tax effects.

[b] NPV of fully utilized jobs credits divided by NPV of payroll, net of state, local, and federal income tax effects.

the maximum exceeds 20 percent for at least 1 sector in 6 states. The maximum exceeds 5.0 percent in all of the states except the 2—California and Virginia—where there are no capital incentives.

Empirical studies of manufacturing have generally shown a high degree of substitutability between capital and labor (for example, Berndt and Christensen 1973; Huang 1991). As the price of capital goods falls relative to wages, firms do indeed adopt more capital-intensive methods of production, substituting capital for labor. The effect of incentives, as we have shown, is precisely to lower the relative price of capital (in 11 of the 13 states studied). The output effect of cheaper capital (due to a lowering of costs and hence a lowering of product prices and increasing product demand) may be substantial, with the increased output leading to increased use of both capital and labor. The size of this effect will depend on the elasticity of demand—how much a price reduction increases sales. However, since the substitution effects are also likely to be substantial, the net effect of capital subsidies may be to *reduce* the demand for labor rather than increase it. Indeed, a study of the very large capital subsidies provided for manufacturers in Northern Ireland from 1955 to 1983 concluded that the substitution effect was larger than the output effect; capital subsidies led to higher investment but lower employment levels than would have existed in their absence (Harris 1991).

Why is this important? Surely if incentives do cause an increase in investment in zones, there will in fact be an increase in jobs there—perhaps not as large an increase as there would have been with incentives that clearly favored labor, but an increase nonetheless. The problem with this argument is that it ignores the fact that incentives go to firms that would have located or expanded in the zone even without incentives—noninduced investment—as well as to firms for whom the incentives were decisive. The substitution effect of incentives will operate on all firms; furthermore, as will be discussed in subsequent chapters, it is likely that incentives are not decisive for most firms. Thus even small job reductions in each noninduced firm through capital substitution could offset, or more than offset, the employment gains for the zone from those few firms induced to change location to the zone, because the noninduced firms are likely to be much more numerous.[2]

CONCLUSIONS

Among the 75 enterprise zone cities in our sample, we found considerable variation in terms of the industrial sectors that were taxed most lightly and most heavily. Overall, the average city imposed a tax rate on its most favored industry that was only 38 percent of the tax rate on its least favored industry. Furthermore, there is sufficient variation within cities in most states that any city can be fairly competitive for at least one or a few sectors. In all states but California and Texas, there was at least 1 of our sample cities with a sector ranked in the top 20 percent (1–15). On the other hand, there were 11 cities (mostly in California, Pennsylvania, and Texas) with all sectors ranked in the bottom 40 percent. Cities in those states simply do not have enough leverage on the overall state-local tax rate to overcome a disadvantageous state tax system.

All this amounts to implicit industrial policies, with states and cities providing favored tax treatment to a few industrial sectors. Our major concern here is that it is very likely that little or no thought has gone into the industrial policy consequences of most states' and cities' tax systems. Industrial policy has developed almost by default, as a by-product of decisions taken about other state and local policy issues. This is not to argue, however, that state and local tax policy can ever be entirely sector-neutral; it is hard to imagine how any change to a state or city's tax code would not favor some specific firms and disfavor others. But we doubt that it is wise for government—federal, state or local—to be in the business of picking industrial winners and losers "in the dark."

The tax incentives in place in the enterprise zones in our sample of 75 cities have a clear bias in favor of capital in all but 2 of the 13 states. The effects of labor incentives on the price of labor are quite small. In only 2 states does the average labor price reduction exceed 1.0 percent, and the maximum price reduction among the 16 sectors never exceeds 3.0 percent in any state. Capital incentives, on the other hand, have very substantial price effects in several of the states. The average capital price reduction among sectors exceeds 5.0 percent in 8 of the 13 states, and the maximum exceeds 20 percent for at least 1 sector in 6 states.

Given the significant substitutability between capital and labor in manufacturing reported in empirical studies, it is likely that this capital bias in incentives would cause firms to adopt more capital-intensive methods of production. This substitution of capital for labor would occur in all firms benefitting from the subsidies, including those for which location decisions were unaffected. If this substitution effect were large enough, it is possible that the net effect of zone incentives would be to lower employment rather than to increase it. Furthermore, labor incentives are usually expressed in terms of a fixed dollar amount per new job or as a percentage of wages up to a ceiling. The ceiling is generally below typical manufacturing wage rates so that the incentive is equivalent to a lump sum per job. Thus, the employment incentives that do exist do not encourage the creation of more-skilled or better-paid jobs. They encourage quantity rather than quality. The credit as a percent of payroll is maximized when employees are hired near the bottom of the wage scale.

If the principal objective of enterprise zone policy is to stimulate job creation, capital incentives should be replaced with pure labor "matching grants" that simply provide firms a percentage reduction in the wage rate. Any ceiling on wages eligible for such a credit should be high enough to retain incentives to hire more higher-wage skilled workers (where that is appropriate, given the targeted labor pool). Of course, part of the appeal of capital incentives may be that local government officials equate capital growth with an expansion of the local property-tax base. Whether capital incentives, or incentives generally, do in fact produce a net gain in local revenues is the focus of the next chapter.

Notes

1. We calculate capital costs as the present value of annual expenses rather than as the acquisition cost of plant and equipment because we want to compute after-tax costs, and it is these annual expenses for depreciation, interest, and property taxes that are dedicated for state and federal income tax purposes. Annual expenses also take into account the cost of replacement machinery and equipment during the 20-year horizon and permit a consistent treatment of labor and capital costs in terms of the time period, given the varying lives of different kinds of capital. That is, depreciation measures the capital actually "used up" during the period, if we assume that tax depreciation rates approximate economic depreciation.

2. One is tempted to ask: How could a capital subsidy be too small to affect a location decision but large enough to change the choice of technology? The answer is that capital costs are one among many factors that vary substantially by location and thus may be swamped by these other factors when firms make location decision. The choice between more or less capital-intensive technologies, on the other hand, is generally thought by economists to be made simply on the basis of the relative prices of capital and labor.

5
The Fiscal Effects of Incentives

Although the primary public justifications for business incentives generally, and enterprise zone incentives as well, are the attraction of capital investment and the creation of jobs, expansion of the property-tax base is an important secondary objective. The Ohio enterprise zone program, for example, specifies three separate objectives: 1) to expand employment in the state, 2) to increase business investment in the state, and 3) to increase the state and local tax base. As long as policymakers believe that incentive programs have positive effects, however small, on all three objectives, there is little reason for them to question whether such programs should continue. The programs appear to have no cost. Positive fiscal effects are routinely documented by development officials who assume (and for the most part honestly believe or at least prefer not to doubt) that all jobs benefitting from incentives would not have existed in the state but for those incentives. If the fiscal effects are negative, however, as some research suggests (Bartik 1994),[1] then policy analysts should assess whether or not the tax costs per job are outweighed by the benefits of increased employment.

In this chapter we investigate whether tax cuts—in the form of incentives tied to new investment—are likely to generate fiscal gains. We conclude that, in the majority of states that we modeled, it is unlikely that state and local governments will gain tax revenues from the incentive programs that they offer within enterprise zones. In some states, however, zone incentives consist entirely of state income tax credits; while these credits probably produce a revenue loss for the state, if they have any effect at all on job creation within enterprise zones, then local governments will gain tax base and revenue. At the other extreme are states in which the major zone incentives consist of local property-tax abatements; here the net fiscal effect is likely to be that local governments forego substantial revenue, though in so doing they may increase state corporate income tax receipts slightly.

We also examine the structure of incentives; many, but not all, places "front-load" their incentives, providing most of the benefits in the first few years after a new plant is built or an existing one is expanded. Is this a smart approach, or would back-loading generate more revenue? The answer, it turns out, is counterintuitive: a constant, permanent reduction in taxes on new zone establishments makes more fiscal and economic sense than larger initial tax breaks that are phased out over several years.

THE FISCAL EFFECTS OF TAX CUTS GENERALLY

Whether the fiscal effects of business tax cuts are positive or negative depends on how economic growth is affected by differences in state and local taxes. Economists measure the sensitivity of growth to tax changes by a ratio called the "elasticity," which is simply the percentage change in business activity (investment, employment) divided by the percentage change in taxes. The more business activity responds to differences in taxes, the larger will be the elasticity. Some researchers have concluded that the elasticity of investment with respect to interstate or intermetropolitan differences in taxation is between –0.2 and –0.4; in other words, the percentage change in business activity will be 20 percent to 40 percent of the percentage change in taxes.[2] A tax cut in one state or metropolitan region will not cause very much economic activity to shift to that state or region. Bartik (1994) takes the middle of this range, –0.3 , which implies that a 20 percent tax cut, for example, would produce a 6 percent increase in investment and jobs (6% / –20% = –0.3). He then notes that the revenue effect of a tax cut can be estimated from the following equation:

$$\text{Revenue change} = \frac{R}{J}\,(1 + 1/E),$$

where E is the elasticity of economic activity with respect to taxes and R/J is average revenue per job prior to the tax cut. (See Appendix C for a derivation of this formula.) With a national average business tax revenue per job of $1,620 and an elasticity of –0.3, a new job would generate on average about $3,780 in revenue *losses* as a result of tax cuts.

What would it take for localities to break even? The answer, from the above equation, is an elasticity of business activity with respect to tax cuts equal to 1. The right-hand side of the equation then becomes zero: there is no change in revenue, which means the incentive is fiscally neutral. If E is less than 1, the revenue change will be negative; if it is greater than 1, a tax cut will increase revenues. Since there is substantial evidence that the interstate or intermetropolitan elasticity is much less than 1 (Bartik (1991) puts the upper limit at 0.6), it is probably safe to conclude that these kinds of tax cuts will cost state and local governments revenue.

Why losses? Because it is, as a practical matter, impossible for one locality or state to successfully target tax cuts only at firms that would otherwise have located in another locality or state. As a result, tax cuts end up going to firms that would have made the same location decision without the tax cut, thus generating tax losses. Since location decisions are not greatly affected by the tax cuts, the revenue gains from firms that were induced to move or stay in the region will not be large and will be more than offset by the revenue losses from other firms that also had their taxes reduced.

Most of the research on the effects of taxes on growth has measured the effects of differences in the average level of taxation and therefore predicts the effects of across-the-board reductions in taxes. Nonetheless, we can conclude that, under certain conditions, the sensitivity of economic growth to tax *incentives* granted only for new investment will be in the same range of –0.2 to –0.4. This is a valid inference for the long-run effects of a certain class of incentives: those that are structured as a permanent tax cut on the income from new investment. An example of such an incentive would be a complete exemption of newly acquired (but not existing) machinery and equipment from the property tax. The incentives then represent constant and permanent cuts in taxes on the new investment. Eventually, all, or nearly all, business property in that locality will be "new" property benefitting from the tax incentive and the distinction between an across-the-board tax cut (such as, immediately exempting all machinery and equipment, old and new) and an incentive will have disappeared. Thus, in the long run the incentive will have the same effect on growth, and the same effect on state and local revenue, as the immediate across-the-board tax cut.

Our research enables us to estimate the average long-run fiscal effect of tax cuts among the 75 enterprise zone cities in our sample. The average direct state and local tax revenue (before incentives) across the 16 manufacturing sectors and 75 cities was about $3,050 per job per year. This implies a net state-local revenue loss of about $7,120 per year for each new job attributable to the tax cut, if we apply Bartik's formula and assume the interstate or intermetropolitan elasticity for incentives is –0.3. This will be a reasonable estimate for an across-the-board tax cut or a permanent incentive that will eventually become the equivalent. Our estimate is higher than Bartik's earlier estimate because our research shows a substantially higher gross revenue per job in manufacturing than Bartik's national average revenue per job across all business sectors of $1,620.

Thus far we have confined our analysis to the effects of taxes or incentives on the redistribution of business activity among states or metropolitan regions. This is the question that most research has addressed, and it is arguably the appropriate policy question as well. Enterprise zones are a state policy for solving the problems of distressed areas of certain cities within the state; it makes sense to evaluate the policy from the perspective of the collective cost of the tax incentives to the state and to local governments. There will be net revenue gains, then, only if the zone incentives succeed in attracting sufficient jobs from outside the state; interstate or intermetropolitan elasticities are thus appropriate.

One could, however, pose the local policy question as well: Are there *local* revenue gains from a reduction in *local* taxes? Such gains could come about from a redirection of investment within a metropolitan area or within the state, as well as from the attraction of capital from out of state. As for the elasticity of investment with respect to differences in tax rates *within* a metropolitan area, we have much less evidence to go on. Bartik (1991) reviewed seven intrametropolitan studies, but three of the seven studies compared suburban sites only and thus may tell us nothing about the effects of taxes on the competitive position of a central city relative to its suburbs.[3] Among the remaining four, the tax elasticities ranged from –0.8 to –2.5. Few relevant articles have been published since 1991. Luce (1994) studied 340 municipalities in the Philadelphia region and found an average elasticity of sectoral employment with respect to property taxes of –0.6, and to wage taxes of –0.4. Luce also argues that the elasticities of –1.5 to –2.0 reported in the earlier studies are substantially overstated. Mark, McGuire, and Papke

(2000), on the other hand, found elasticities of a little over –2.1, relating total employment growth in the Washington, D.C., region with sales tax rates and personal property tax rates, but found no significant relation to real property taxes or corporate income taxes.

There is thus only limited, inconsistent, and disputed evidence of the magnitude of tax effects among places within a metropolitan area, though in general the elasticities seem to be larger than those found between states or regions. It is true that these larger elasticities are consistent with location theory, which would predict that tax differences will be more important in determining location choice when other factors such as wage rates, energy costs, and access to markets and inputs are similar across localities, as they are likely to be within a metropolitan region. Still, there are only these six intrametropolitan studies to rely on, and none of them looked at enterprise zone sites per se or measured the effects of tax incentives (as opposed to overall tax levels or simply average tax rates).

MODEL ESTIMATES OF THE FISCAL EFFECTS OF INCENTIVES

The conclusion drawn above—that on average among our 75 enterprise zone cities, state and local governments collectively stand to lose in the long run about $6,750 per year per new job from tax incentives—is of limited applicability for a variety of reasons. We will consider each of these qualifications in some detail and then provide results from simulations of incentives using TAIM^{ez} that provide a more accurate picture of the actual workings of incentives.

First of all, the annual fiscal effects of incentives are the same as the annual fiscal effects of across the board tax cuts only in the long run. Eventually all investment will be new investment, but in the meantime there will be a period of many years during which incentives will be less costly because much of the existing industrial activity will be paying its full freight in taxes. This will be true even for incentives in the form of permanent tax cuts for new firms or new investment.

Second, most tax incentives are neither constant from year to year nor permanent. Property taxes on new capital are almost always abated for a limited number of years (typically 3 to 10) and at a declining rate. Income tax credits are granted for the year in which investment or job creation takes place, with unused credits (which may be a small or a large share of initial credits) carried forward for a limited period—typically not more than 10 years.

Third, there is some reason to believe that incentives have different effects on net growth than across-the-board tax cuts of the same magnitude. Incentives that are tied to new establishments or expansions of existing establishments will have no effect on existing firms' decisions to remain in the community without expanding (in many instances the site will not permit expansion, and the firm may not need more capacity anyway) versus building a new lower-cost facility elsewhere. Across-the-board cuts, on the other hand, do improve the competitive position of the locality vis-à-vis greenfield sites elsewhere and so could plausibly reduce exit rates. It may be the case that actual firm deaths have little or nothing to do with taxes, but the loss of business activity is driven to a major extent not by firm deaths but by branch plant closings (which may be accompanied by branch plant births elsewhere) and plant relocations. Furthermore, symmetry requires that if tax differences induce plant relocations they must affect out-migration rates and in-migration rates equally, since every migration is a move out as well as a move in.

We will return to the question of how taxes or incentives might affect establishment exit rates (and therefore job-loss rates) in the discussion of policy alternatives at the end of this chapter. For now, we want to investigate in detail the other question raised above: how the time pattern of tax incentives matters. The timing of state and local enterprise zone incentives is complex and varies greatly from place to place. This suggests that a detailed simulation of their effects may produce useful insights. The TAIM^{ez} model developed for this research does simulate actual incentives year by year and thus can be used to illustrate the fiscal effects on state and local government, as well as the effects on a firm's rate of return on new investment.

The TAIM^{ez} model calculates, for each representative firm and each locality, the gross property taxes that the firm would pay each year for the first 20 years after a new plant is built, based on the value of its taxable property each year and a constant local property-tax rate. It then calculates the size of the abatement it would receive each year from the local government being modeled. The model also measures the increased state and local sales taxes paid on purchases of machinery and equipment for the new plant and on purchases of fuel and electricity for the new plant, taking into account any special exemptions or credits for enterprise zone firms. Finally, it calculates the increase in state and local income taxes paid by the firm as a result of the increased taxable income generated by the new plant (including the effects of deducting from taxable income the net local property taxes on the new plant), and then deducts all state credits resulting from the new plant investment. The result is an estimate, year by year for 20 years, of the increase in state and local taxes, with and without tax incentives, as a result of the representative firm's investment.

The model's fiscal results do not include any secondary effects, such as increased personal taxes paid by in-migrants taking jobs at the new facility or by the previously unemployed, or increased taxes paid by other businesses that may experience a growth in sales and employment as a result of the new economic activity generated by the new plant. Nor does the model take into account any of the increased state and local public service costs that would follow from such secondary effects, as well as directly from the new plant itself, that could offset much of the revenue gains.[4] It thus measures only the direct revenues from the firm itself.

Since taxes and incentives will vary from year to year, we present our results by collapsing the 20-year stream of revenues into one figure: the present value of that stream (discounted at 10 percent). For the average state and city in our sample, the tax system—without incentives—would result in about $26,000 in additional state and local tax revenue over a 20-year period for every new job that arrives in the zone. The package of state and local incentives available in the average enterprise zone, on the other hand, is worth about $7,800 per job. The net gain in state-local revenue for each job that was induced by the incentives would be the $26,000 in gross taxes less the incentive package, or $18,200. Each new job that was not incentive-induced would cost the state and local governments the $7,800 in wasted incentives.

These average revenue gains and losses conceal considerable variation across states and cities. In Table 5.1 we show more detailed results of our simulations. These results are averaged in two ways: First,

Table 5.1 State and Local Direct Revenue Gains per New Job for Investment Induced by Incentives

	State taxes			Local taxes		
	Corporate income	Sales	Total	Property	Sales and corporate income	Total
Average by state						
Calif.	9,396	2,383	11,778	6,948	695	7,643
Conn.	5,039	1,493	6,532	9,700	0	9,700
Fla.	1,207	2,670	3,876	15,474	185	15,659
Ill.	6,924	1,224	8,148	4,856	131	4,987
Ind.	5,748	1,244	6,992	14,997	0	14,997
Ky.	4,249	1,766	6,015	5,016	1,347	6,363
Mo.	2,273	2,921	5,195	10,547	2,164	12,711
N.Y.	2,522	995	3,517	4,354	881	5,235
Ohio	7,055	979	8,034	8,168	2,071	10,239
Pa.	15,495	1,493	16,988	4,621	7,125	11,746
Tex.	1,535	2,504	4,039	21,556	770	22,327
Va.	5,184	685	5,870	11,524	196	11,720
Wis.	3,070	2,451	5,521	9,361	49	9,410
Among the 75 cities						
Highest	21,543	2,921	23,036	22,776	13,153	23,590
Mean	5,448	1,729	7,177	9,837	1,202	11,039
Lowest	912	685	1,907	2,226	0	2,973

NOTE: These figures represent the present value of revenues gained with 1994 taxes and incentives over the first 20 years after the firm's investment that triggers the incentives; they represent the weighted average across 16 sectors and the discount rate is 10 percent.

for each of the 75 cities we computed a weighted average of the 16 manufacturing sectors; then, for each state, we computed a simple average of the weighted averages for five or six cities in the state. To illustrate the range of results, Table 5.1 also shows the highest, the mean, and the lowest weighted average among the 75 cities. (Appendix Table F.4 shows the sectoral, as well as city, variation.) The highest net revenue per induced job among all 16 sectors and 75 cities was

$86,675, while the lowest was –$2,045 (see Appendix Table F.4). (In Chapter 3 we explain how incentives can create negative tax rates for the firm, which is also how they produce negative net revenue for state and local governments.)

The net revenue gains from induced investment are only half of the picture. Some plants would have located or expanded in the city in question even in the absence of incentives, and for every noninduced job there is a loss of revenue measured by the cost of the state and local incentives. Table 5.2 summarizes the fiscal effects. The revenue losses consist of the state income tax revenues foregone due to investment and jobs credits, and local property-tax abatements. The average incentive package among the 75 cities was $7,793 per job, but in the most generous city the average package among the 16 sectors was $35,036. Appendix Table F.4 shows the sectoral as well as city variation: the maximum revenue loss across all sectors and cities was $70,423 per job, while the smallest loss was $656. These revenue loss figures represent the gross value of the incentive package (before the effects of income tax deductibility) but still discount the benefits at 10 percent over 20 years. Without discounting, the largest packages would rival those publicized for some of the major auto plant competitions.

At first glance, our fiscal results as summarized in Table 5.2 appear to indicate that a fiscal surplus is quite plausible. The average induced job produces a substantial revenue gain of approximately $18,200, and this will be offset by a revenue loss of only about $7,800 for each noninduced job. Whether the states or cities come out ahead by offering incentives depends, however, on the proportion of all new manufacturing jobs that are actually induced by the incentives. For example, using these average figures for gain and loss per job, the fiscal effect on state and local government would be negative if there were three noninduced jobs for every induced job—and losses would equal three times $7,800, which exceeds the $18,200 gain.

Can we estimate the net fiscal effect for the average city among the 75 by applying the "consensus" elasticity of –0.3 as we did earlier? We have previously argued that this is an appropriate elasticity for measuring the long-run annual effect of incentives in the form of permanent tax cuts on new investment. But here we have estimates of the short-run revenue effects (over the first 20 years) of incentive programs that

Table 5.2 Summary of State and Local Fiscal Effects per New Job in 75 Cities

	Induced investment: Revenue gained per job			Non-induced investment: Revenue lost per job			Incentives as % of gross taxes		
	State	Local	Total	State	Local	Total	State	Local	Total
Average by state									
Calif.	11,778	7,643	19,421	10,771	6,067	6,948	176,947	1,683,786	871,785
Conn.	6,532	9,700	16,231	10,194	1,493	12,687	0	1,168,690	1,268,715
Fla.	3,876	15,659	19,535	4,557	2,670	15,474	18,481	722,677	1,565,862
Ill.	8,148	4,987	13,134	8,596	1,224	6,825	13,055	982,003	695,567
Ind.	6,992	14,997	21,989	11,201	1,244	28,487	0	1,244,488	2,848,673
Ky.	6,015	6,363	12,378	9,377	7,833	5,582	133,915	1,720,988	692,139
Mo.	5,195	12,711	17,905	6,192	5,516	14,322	352,775	1,170,778	1,784,998
N.Y.	3,517	5,235	8,753	9,385	995	7,445	88,117	1,038,043	832,666
Ohio	8,034	10,239	18,273	8,907	979	17,290	204,619	988,623	1,933,591
Pa.	16,988	11,746	28,734	20,498	1,493	5,561	712,477	2,199,054	1,268,548
Tex.	4,039	22,327	26,365	3,660	3,724	23,258	114,419	738,454	2,440,196
Va.	5,870	11,720	17,590	6,697	685	11,524	19,582	738,257	1,172,009
Wis.	5,521	9,410	14,931	7,767	2,451	9,361	4,902	1,021,735	940,959
Among the 75 cities									
Highest	23,036	23,590	43,476	12,803	29,583	35,036	78.2	65.8	68.2
Mean	7,177	11,039	18,216	4,635	3,158	7,793	40.1	19.5	29.6
Lowest	1,907	2,973	4,902	1,513	-8	1,513	17.0	-0.1	6.5

NOTE: These figures represent the present value of revenues gained and lost per new job with 1994 taxes and incentives over the first 20 years after the firm's investment that triggers the incentives; they represent the weighted average across 16 sectors and the discount rate is 10%. Weighted average new plant employment across 16 sectors is 127.

provide benefits that are generally concentrated in the first 10 years. The elasticity is nonetheless useful, provided we are willing to accept the following—quite reasonable—assumption: that firms making plant investment decisions employ a limited time horizon and a discount rate reflecting the cost of capital. We assume a time horizon of 20 years and a 10 percent discount rate. An incentive that reduces the present value of the firm's tax burden on the income from the new plant over this time horizon by 25 percent, then, will have the same effect on the firm's investment decision as a permanent reduction in annual taxes of 25 percent.

The elasticity of –0.3, which measures the sensitivity of new investment to a cut in business taxes, can be used to estimate the proportion of new jobs induced by the tax cuts versus those that are not. It can be shown that the percent of new jobs that are induced is equal to the elasticity times the percentage cut in taxes (see Appendix C). What we find is that, for the average industry in the average city in our sample of 75, incentives represented an approximated 30 percent tax cut (see Table 5.2); therefore, new jobs that were induced by incentives would equal only about 9 percent (0.3 times 30 percent). For every 100 gross new jobs each year, there would be just 9 that were induced by incentives. Over the next 20 years, these 9 jobs would generate a revenue gain of $163,800 (9 times the average $18,200 gain per job). The remaining 91 jobs created the same year would produce a revenue loss of $709,800 over that same time period (91 times the average $7,800 loss per noninduced job). The net state-local revenue loss is therefore $546,000, or about $60,700 per new induced manufacturing job. Converting this to an annual flow, state and local governments would lose about $7,130 each year for each job gained.[5] Interestingly, this is quite close to our earlier estimate of the long-run effect of permanent incentives: $7,120 per year per new job.

But do state and local governments also use a 20-year horizon and a 10 percent discount rate? What is the appropriate way for them to evaluate the decision to adopt an incentive program—its long-term annual effect in equilibrium, the present value over a fairly long time horizon like 20 years, or a shorter-term annual effect? This becomes a particularly important issue when we realize that the decision for the community or state is quite different from the decision for the firm.

While it makes sense to assume that a firm applies standard capital budgeting techniques to a single plant-location decision, the city is making a decision about the long-run consequences of a policy change that is going to affect the capital budgeting decisions of many firms over a period of many years, and for each firm there are multiyear fiscal effects. Thus, for the community we must model not only the time pattern of the revenue and incentive flows per firm, but the time pattern of firm arrivals and departures, births, and deaths.

To learn more about the fiscal effects of incentives, we developed a simple simulation model. We assume that each locality is initially in a steady state with 10 percent birth and death rates; that is, for every 100 initial establishments, 10 establishments are born or move in each year, and 10 die or move out.[6] We also make an assumption about the distribution of establishment lives, because some establishments will generate revenue gains or losses longer that others. A death rate of 10 percent implies an average life expectancy of 10 years; we assume that deaths are approximately normally distributed around the tenth year after birth, and that by the fifteenth year all establishments have died. (We are using the term "death" here as a short cut for both actual establishment deaths and establishment relocations out of the community.)

Under these assumptions about births and deaths, revenue gains and losses will have reached a plateau by year 15 after incentives are adopted. This is because, by this year, the level of employment will have reached its new equilibrium level, and the distribution of establishments in their first, second, or third year since birth (and so on) will remain constant thereafter. As a result, the distribution of establishments receiving various incentive amounts appropriate to the year since the investment was made will also be constant: the same number of new establishments arrives each year receiving first-year incentives, while the same number disappears each year after receiving year-15 incentives. This assumption does affect the results; the longer the assumed life span, the longer it takes to reach establishment equilibrium, which will affect the distribution of fiscal gains and losses over time.

To illustrate how fiscal losses and gains approach a plateau over time, we constructed Figure 5.1, which shows the year-by-year fiscal gains and losses for a Texas city with typical local property-tax rates and with typical tax abatements in its enterprise zone. In this example, we assumed that all new establishments arriving in this city after adoption of the incentives are fabricated metals plants. We also assumed that establishment births are, in fact, quite sensitive to tax rates; that is, we assumed an elasticity of –1.0, so that the 23 percent tax cut produced by state and local incentives in this Texas enterprise zone would increase economic activity by 23 percent. Even with this assumption, the state and local incentives produce a net loss of state and local revenue every year after incentive adoption. The net fiscal effect would settle at an annual loss of $431 per induced job by year 15, and the net present value of the fiscal effects over the first 20 years would amount to a loss of $7,227 per induced job. For state and local governments to break even over the first 20 years in this scenario, establishment births would have to increase by more than the 23 percent cut in tax rates, on new investment. In all likelihood, establishment births would increase by much less.

The time pattern of incentives depicted in Figure 5.1 is fairly typical for the states and sectors we modeled. Table 5.3 shows the break-even elasticity (in absolute value) for the 13 states and for 8 sectors (the 8 that accounted for most of the establishments in our enterprise zone sample). Again, break-even is defined not on an annual basis but in

Figure 5.1 Annual Fiscal Effects of Incentives for a Fabricated Metals Plants in a Texas City

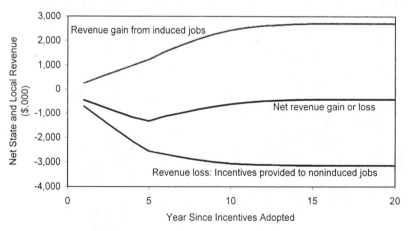

Table 5.3. Elasticity of Establishment Growth Required for Fiscal Break-Even for Selected Manufacturing Sectors in the Thirteen States, 1998 Taxes and Incentives

SIC	Sector	Calif.	Conn.	Fla.	Ill.	Ind.	Ky.	Mo.	N.Y.	Ohio	Pa.	Tex.	Va.	Wis.
20	Food and kindred products	1.25	1.48	1.20	1.35	1.29	1.24	1.30	1.08	1.32	1.43	1.30	1.18	1.25
23	Apparel and other textile prod.	1.16	1.45	1.25	1.41	1.20	1.34	1.31	1.06	1.35	1.47	1.31	1.27	1.33
27	Printing and publishing	1.28	1.53	1.25	1.36	1.30	1.23	1.30	1.05	1.33	1.45	1.31	1.31	1.33
28	Chemicals and allied products	1.26	1.46	1.27	1.35	1.31	1.20	1.30	—[a]	1.34	1.46	1.34	1.18	1.21
30	Rubber and misc. plastics prod.	1.26	1.49	1.20	1.35	1.28	1.19	1.30	1.06	1.32	1.44	1.30	1.06	1.19
34	Fabricated metal products	1.18	1.49	1.23	1.40	1.23	1.21	1.30	1.08	1.34	1.45	1.33	1.12	1.27
35	Industrial machinery	1.18	1.49	1.27	1.39	1.19	1.23	1.30	1.06	1.36	1.46	1.31	1.20	1.27
36	Electric & electronic equipment	1.36	1.50	1.27	1.39	1.19	1.22	1.30	1.07	1.37	1.47	1.29	1.20	1.26
	Average elasticity	1.24	1.49	1.24	1.38	1.25	1.23	1.30	1.07	1.34	1.45	1.31	1.19	1.26
	Front-loading of incentives[b]	0.69	0.78	0.66	0.78	0.64	0.65	0.76	0.53	0.71	0.81	0.67	0.75	0.67

NOTE: Elasticity is defined as the percentage increase in annual establishment births (induced births over total births) divided by the percentage decrease in taxes attributable to the average state and local incentive package. Fiscal break-even occurs when the present value of state-local revenue gains from growth induced by incentives over the first 20 years after incentives are enacted equals the present value of state-local revenue losses from granting incentives to establishments that would have located there anyway, over the same 20 years. Estimates are based on average local property tax rates and tax abatements by state, with all general and enterprise zone incentives applied.

[a] Unable to calculate.

[b] Front-loading of incentives is the ratio of the present value of the incentive package over 20 years to the undiscounted sum of those incentives over 20 years; the index ranges from a value of 0.16 (all incentives received in year 20) to 1.00 (all incentives received the first year).

terms of the present value of revenue over the first 20 years after adoption of incentives. The overall average break-even elasticity was 1.29; thus a 20 percent tax cut would, for example, have to produce a 25.8 percent increase in economic activity. The higher the break-even elasticity, the less likely it is that the real sensitivity of economic activity to taxes exceeds that break-even level. The lowest average break-even elasticity was 1.07 in New York, which is also the state with the least front-loaded incentives. We will explore in the next section why front-loading makes break-even less likely.

WHY FRONT-LOADING INCENTIVES
IS A COSTLY STRATEGY

The conventional wisdom appears to be that incentives should be front loaded—more generous in early years and eventually phased out. By granting temporary abatements or one-time credits rather than permanent reductions in taxes, governments appear to believe that they are minimizing their revenue losses. Eventually, the argument goes, these firms we have attracted will be paying the full freight in local taxes, and it will be worth the temporary loss in revenue to get the permanent gain.

To test the conventional wisdom, we created a measure of the degree of front loading: the ratio of the discounted value of incentives over 20 years to the undiscounted value. Where incentives are provided entirely in the first year, the front-loading measure is equal to 1.0, which is its maximum value. Were incentives provided entirely in year 20 (entirely backloaded), discounting at 10 percent would produce a ratio of 0.16, which is the lowest value the front-loading index can assume. Incentives equal in value each year for 20 years would produce an index value of 0.47. The front-loading measure ranged from 0.53 in New York (only slightly front-loaded) to 0.81 in Pennsylvania. Our simulations show that the states with more front-loaded incentives tended to require a *higher* elasticity to produce fiscal break-even. The break-even elasticity for a sector and the front-loading of incentives for that sector are, in fact, highly correlated. Overall, the correlation is 0.82. In other words, the more incentives are front-loaded, the greater must be the response of investment to tax cuts if the locality is to break even, and the more likely the incentives will generate a net loss of revenue.

What is it about New York's incentives that makes them less front-loaded? First of all, there is a ceiling on investment tax credits equal to the firm's total state tax liability. Second, the general investment tax credit is sizeable but could rarely be used fully in the early years, so that many firms took full advantage of the 15-year carryforward. The additional enterprise zone credits have a lower ceiling (50 percent of state tax liability), but an unlimited carryforward. Thus, the generous incentives combined with long carryforwards and a low ceiling on annual use (for zone credits) means that incentives are, in effect, spread over the entire 20-year period.

Why do our simulations of the fiscal effects of incentives yield a wide range of break-even elasticities, unlike the results of Bartik's equation, which indicates a break-even elasticity of -1.0 regardless of the magnitude of the tax cuts (see our Appendix C)? To understand this, consider first what the simulation produces if we model a constant and permanent reduction in taxes on new investment. Here we find that the break-even elasticity calculated in our model simulation is exactly equal to the theoretical value of -1.0, and that government exactly breaks even in year one and in every year after that. But when we simulate real-world incentives in which the percentage tax reduction varies from year to year, we find that most incentive systems are front-loaded and that this tends to generate fiscal losses in the first years after incentives are adopted. This is because we assume gross establishment growth in the absence of incentives (which accords with the real world, even in enterprise zones), and this non-induced growth begins to produce losses immediately. Furthermore, the net revenue gains from induced jobs may be minimal, or even negative, in the early years. As a result, the net fiscal effect is negative in most states early on. Since the positive net benefits come only later, they are more heavily discounted when we employ a present value decision criterion.

Why is the conventional wisdom about the front-loading of incentives wrong? The problem is that the conventional view ignores the fact that establishments do not live forever. By front-loading, one is increasing the odds that a given establishment will get most or all of the potential incentives but will pay full freight for only a few years, or none at all; by the time the incentives are phased out, many establishments will have died or moved on to start the incentive pattern over again in another community. As we will see in Chapter 6, there is a large amount of establishment turnover in the enterprise zones we studied. The average death rate was actually a little higher than the 10 percent assumed in our fiscal simulation model.

The conventional view makes the mistake of focusing on the life cycle of one establishment instead of looking at the annual flows of establishments—induced and noninduced—into and out of the community. Every year, those businesses that arrived in previous years are paying more and more in taxes as the incentives phase out. But every year new establishments arrive, and existing ones expand—paying very little taxes. When one considers the community as a whole rather than a single business, it is clear that the large up-front costs are not one-time "investments," but continuing drains on resources.

To further reinforce this point, suppose a community were considering a choice between two incentive strategies: 1) a permanent exemption of 25 percent of the taxable income attributable to new enterprise zone operations, or 2) a 34.6 percent tax abatement each year for only the first 10 years. The net present value of these two incentives over 20 years is identical at a discount rate of 10 percent: both represent a 25 percent reduction in taxes over that period. In our simulation model, which assumes that firms make project decisions based on a 20-year horizon, both incentives would produce the same increase in jobs. With an assumed elasticity of -1.0—so that the 25 percent tax cut in both instances generates a 25 percent increase in the annual flow of new establishments—the first alternative just breaks even for the community, while the front-loaded version generates net fiscal losses every year following the adoption of incentives. For the 20-year period, the community loses $3,446 per induced job, in present value. Interestingly, the annual fiscal effect in equilibrium (by year 15) for the temporary 34.6 percent abatement is also negative: $508 per induced job. In other words, it is not just discounting that accounts for the negative fiscal consequences of front-loading; it is also the continual arrival of new establishments taking the full benefit of early incentives, combined with the continual exit of older firms that had been paying the full tax, or close to it. Because the average firm in our simulation remains in the community only 10 years, though, the average firm never ends up paying the full property-tax rate.

THE TOTAL FISCAL EFFECTS FOR A ZONE

To better appreciate the significance of the fiscal effects of tax incentive policy, it is useful to consider the likely magnitude of *total* revenue losses for an average enterprise zone. To estimate these losses, we simulated a zone that grants front-loaded incentives in the form of a 34.6 percent tax cut each year for 10 years, with no further incentives after that. As we noted earlier, such a tax incentive is equivalent, in present value terms, to a 25 percent permanent tax cut, approximately the size of the tax reduction in the average enterprise zone in our study. We assumed a zone initially containing 100 manufacturing establishments, each employing 30 people on average, and annual establishment birth and death rates of 10 percent. These numbers are also fairly representative of the sample zones, as we will see in the next chapter.[7] If we then assume an elasticity of –0.3, there would be approximately 24 jobs, out of the 324 gross jobs created annually, that would be induced by the incentives.

In the first year after adoption, with 324 new jobs appearing that year, the incentives would produce about $176,000 in lost state-local tax revenue. In the second year, those same 324 jobs would produce the same net losses again, and an additional 324 jobs would appear and generate a like amount. Thus the annual losses would continue to increase, since incentives provided to jobs created in one year continue to generate losses as long as those jobs remain in the community and remain qualified for the incentives (which, in our example, means for 10 years), and each year incentives are provided to a fresh batch of new jobs as well (mostly noninduced). By the time equilibrium in employment is attained in year 15—at a level 243 jobs greater than would have existed without incentives (about 8 percent of the 3,000 initial jobs)— the annual revenue losses for the zone total about $1.5 million, and they continue at that level indefinitely. This represents a great deal of money to be spent annually on economic development in a single zone, a point to which we will return in the book's concluding chapter.

CONCLUSIONS

In the majority of states that we modeled, it is unlikely that state and local governments collectively will gain tax revenues from the incentive programs they offer within enterprise zones. This conclusion is based on previous research showing that business activity is simply not sufficiently influenced by tax differences, that other location factors are more important. As a result, much of the cost of incentives is wasted; incentives end up subsidizing investment that would have occurred anyway because it was driven by non-tax location considerations. The tax revenues lost on these noninduced investments are likely to exceed the revenue gains from the few establishments for which the incentives do in fact tip the balance in favor of the zone location. The magnitude of these revenue losses could be very sizeable; in an average zone in our study, state-local government would lose in the neighborhood of $1.5 million per year as a result of offering a typical incentive package, under a reasonable assumption about the sensitivity of growth to taxes (though we argue later that even this assumption is probably too generous, and the losses would be even greater).

The fiscal effect can be quite different for the state as a whole than for the cities with enterprise zones. Let's consider, first, the four states in which the state provides tax credits to zone firms but the localities do not offer property-tax abatements in zones, or where such abatements are very limited or rarely used—California, Florida, Virginia, and Wisconsin. Due to their front-loaded incentives, it is not likely that these states (with the possible exception of California) will gain revenues from offering zone credits. This is particularly true given that the credits are not statewide, but are quite localized. Thus, even where the incentives are effective in drawing establishments into a zone, these establishments might otherwise have located elsewhere in the same state; if so, there will be no gain in the tax base for the state. For the localities, on the other hand, the incentives have no tax cost since they are entirely state-financed. Furthermore, the zones benefit from any investment drawn to the zone, whether from out of state or from a neighboring city. In these four states, therefore, the state is financing a program that cannot produce local fiscal losses, but would produce local gains if incentives were to have any effect on local activity.

At the other extreme, consider Indiana and Ohio, states in which there are both state and local zone incentives, but in which the local property-tax abatements cost two to five times as much, on average, as the state tax credits. Here, state enterprise zone policy is to encourage local governments to engage in costly competition with one another for jobs and tax base. The local abatements are not only costly but heavily front-loaded, which increases the likelihood that they produce a net fiscal drain on local government. When the local incentives do succeed in attracting capital to the zone (by which we mean that the state incentives alone would not have been sufficient), they also succeed in generating new tax revenue for the state, if that capital was attracted from out of state. The latter effect is more likely to occur in Ohio, where there are over 300 "zones," and in any state where local tax abatements are allowed with or without an enterprise zone and have thus become commonplace. In such states, it is likely that local abatements simply lower the property-tax rate on industry in that state in general, making the state a more attractive location and possibly producing an increase in state revenue, but at considerable local expense.

In this chapter we also found, surprisingly, that the conventional preference for temporary and front-loaded incentives, on the grounds that this is the way to increase the fiscal benefits in the long run, actually makes the situation worse. The more front-loaded the incentives, the less likely the state or locality is to gain revenue by offering incentives. There is one further policy implication: the cheapest way for state and local governments to induce a given percentage increase in the gross rate of growth of establishments or jobs in an enterprise zone is to provide a simple, constant, permanent reduction in taxes on new zone operations. The state could, for example, simply exempt from income taxation some fraction of the taxable income attributable to a firm's new operations in a zone.[8] While the prospect of a fiscal surplus is still dim, this strategy will at least minimize drains on the state treasury.

Eventually, such a permanent exemption on new zone income will become equivalent to an across-the-board tax cut on all zone businesses. An across-the-board cut has an advantage over tax relief to investment or jobs: the exemption benefits existing establishments as well as new ones. Surely job retention should be an important part of any strategy for maintaining and expanding the economies of depressed areas, at least as important as the attraction of new plants. The exemption should help lower exit rates as well as increase birth rates and, as such, should be more effective than an investment incentive.

Some states do recognize the importance of retaining existing businesses and grant incentives for job retention as well as job creation. It is difficult for a locality to target such incentives at firms that really would not stay but for the incentives, however which weakens the argument that such an approach is cheaper than an across-the-board cut because it is never wasted. Furthermore, a strict job-retention incentive sends rather perverse signals to firms: the locality is offering a financial reward for firms to think seriously about moving somewhere else, and in fact to come up with alternative locations that are more favorable for their business.

To the extent that the quality of local public services is also a factor in location decisions, it would be better state policy to provide tax incentives through the state corporate income tax system rather than encouraging (or requiring) financially strapped cities to compete with one another (and in larger cities, for zones to compete with other zones and non-zones in the same city) by adopting property-tax abatements that will in all likelihood produce a net drain on the local treasury. This is another argument for a state enterprise zone policy that takes the form of a state corporate income tax exemption for zone income and disallows local abatements altogether.

In the next chapter we shift focus and look at the economic performance of zones, particularly establishment turnover. We find that actual turnover has not been that different from what we assumed in this chapter. We also compare zone performance to that of our 13 sample states. Once this has been done we are finally in a position to generate our own estimate of the elasticity of growth with respect to enterprise zone incentives (Chapter 7). We find this to be much smaller than what we assumed in this chapter. Thus, the fiscal losses described in this chapter should be taken very much as best-case estimates—actual fiscal losses are likely to be much greater.

Notes

1. There is some research which shows positive fiscal effects. See, for instance, Rubin (1991).
2. These represent Wasylenko's (1997) estimate and about the middle of Bartik's (1991) range, both figures cited earlier. It should be noted that in his 1991 book Bartik argued that there is some reason to believe that these elasticities are too high, given the kinds of wage elasticities researchers have found and the relative importance of wages versus taxes in a firm's cost structure. In Chapter 7 we develop our own taxes/growth elasticities which suggest that the Bartik-Wasylenko consensus elasticities are much too optimistic.
3. Bartik's 1991 review included seven other studies that did not allow for the calculation of elasticities; most of these found only marginally significant tax coefficients or dropped the tax variable because its effect appeared to be nil. Of the three suburb-only studies, elasticities ranged from +0.62 to –4.43.
4. These secondary effects are notoriously difficult to measure. The conventional wisdom, supported by some research but still controversial, is that industrial and commercial development generates direct fiscal surpluses and residential development generates direct fiscal losses, because the majority of service costs are attributable to residents rather than property, whereas it is the property that pays the taxes. In the long run, of course, we know that growth in the aggregate "pays for itself" in the trivial sense that local budgets remain balanced, and this comes about as job growth begets population growth, and the tax base grows with service demands. But the long-run fiscal consequences of growth must also take into account changing demands for services and changing cost conditions (economies or diseconomies of scale, changing factor prices) associated with the growth of tax base and population. Whether a particular industrial project should be charged with a share of all of the consequences following from its small contribution to the future growth of the community, and how these consequences should be measured and apportioned, is not at all clear. What is clear is that, to the extent that communities count on direct fiscal surpluses from nonresidential property to cover the "deficits" associated with most residential development (all but high end), tax incentives that turn fiscal surpluses into deficits for manufacturing property represent a reduction in the community's ability to finance growth in general. In other words, it is important to focus on the direct revenue gains or losses because the indirect effects (from induced population growth) are likely to be negative, as are the direct public service costs.
5. The irregular annual flow is first converted to a present value by discounting the 20-year stream at 10 percent. We then calculate the equivalent annuity—the equal

annual payment over 20 years at 10 percent that is equivalent to the present value amount.

6. These assumptions about birth and death rates are close to the reality of zones. See the establishment turnover results in Chapter 6.

7. The average employment size was calculated by using the average distribution of establishments across the three employment-size classes for the sample zones, and assuming 10 employees for firms in the 1–19 employment-size class, 50 in the 20–99 class, and 200 in the 100+ size class.

8. Connecticut, Missouri, and Virginia do exempt a portion of zone income from state income taxation, but they do so only for 10 years. Michigan exempts 100 percent of income and property taxes for as long as the renaissance zone exists, but these zones are scheduled to expire between 2006 and 2011.

6

Manufacturing Growth and Decline in Enterprise Zones

One is tempted to think of enterprise zones as narrowly drawn areas of concentrated poverty and unemployment within large older cities, areas with an industrial base that has been declining for decades and continues to erode year by year. It is a struggle to get new establishments to locate in such places, and incentives are employed in an attempt to overcome the inherent locational disadvantages—aging infrastructure, crime, and an unskilled workforce. The economy is stagnant at best, with little going on save the predictable announcements of yet another firm shutting down or heading for greener pastures. In this chapter we investigate whether one aspect of this image—industrial stagnation—of enterprise zones squares with reality. This allows us to draw some preliminary conclusions about the economic growth consequences of the enterprise zone strategy. This latter issue is then pursued in greater methodological detail in the next chapter.

In order to conduct the analyses for this chapter and the next, we obtained data on the number of manufacturing establishments by sector, ZIP code, and employment size and matched ZIP codes with zone boundaries as best we could. We were then able to estimate the growth or decline in the number of manufacturing establishments in our sample of enterprise zones from 1989 to 1995, considering births and deaths, and moves into and out of the zones. We found a surprisingly large amount of activity in both directions. While the zones did exhibit net declines in the number of establishments, these declines were modest (at an average rate of about 1.2 percent per year) and came about because the very substantial rates of entry of new establishments were offset by slightly larger rates of exit.

We also found a fairly high degree of sectoral diversity within most of the enterprise zones. Most were not dependent on just one or two manufacturing sectors at the beginning of the study period, and in most the new establishments arriving during the six-year period represented a variety of sectors.

A second question addressed in this chapter is whether or not zones fared significantly worse than the state economies of which they were a part, and whether they appeared to have a comparative disadvantage in attracting or retaining establishments in more capital-intensive and higher-wage sectors. We compared establishment turnover in the zones with establishment change in the 13 states in our study during the same period. We found that zones do, indeed, exhibit larger rates of net decline than the states as a whole, but the difference is not dramatic on average. There were clearly identifiable sectors in which the zones did relatively better or worse than the states; the zones did suffer greater declines in the more capital-intensive sectors, though not necessarily in higher-wage sectors.

Finally, an examination of trends over time indicates that the economic expansion that began in the early 1990s left its mark on enterprise zones. The number of establishments expanding employment, relative to the number reducing jobs, increased noticeably during the latter part of the time period (1993–1995), and may well have continued to increase in the latter 1990s.

THE MANUFACTURING ESTABLISHMENT DATA

The data used to examine the patterns of manufacturing growth and decline consist of establishment counts from the U.S. Bureau of the Census's Standard Statistical Establishment List (SSEL). This list is an integral part of the economic censuses, such as the five-year census of manufactures, and is the primary source of the summary statistics on establishments, employment, and payroll published in *County Business Patterns* (e.g., U.S. Bureau of the Census 1997). The database covers establishments of all domestic employer and non-employer business firms and is updated annually. Prior to 1994, however, non-employers (many proprietorships and partnerships) were represented in the database only for economic census years (those ending in 2 or 7). Thus our data for the two-year periods between 1989 and 1995 include only establishments with employees. The number of omitted establishments is unlikely to be significant in the case of manufacturing, which is the focus of our study. In Appendix D we discuss the SSEL data in detail.

In order to obtain a finer geographic scale than the usual county level of reporting, we ordered a special run by ZIP code. Employment or payroll data at such a scale would be largely unreportable due to disclosure problems; since we asked only for establishment counts, however, there were no disclosure problems—we have 100 percent of the establishments. This is one of the central advantages of the SSEL database for our analyses. Establishments were categorized by three employment-size classes: 0–19, 20–99, and 100 or more. The data were obtained by two-digit SIC code; within the manufacturing division, there are 20 industries represented. There are three data sets, one for each of three time periods: 1989–1991, 1991–1993, and 1993–1995. At the time of analysis, 1989 was the first year the linked SSEL data were available and 1995 was the last year for which data could be computed.

Within each ZIP code, industry, size class, and time period, each establishment was classified in one of seven status groups; these are defined below, using 1989–1991 for illustrative purposes. These status groups are based in part on a determination of whether or not the establishment existed in the ZIP code in the first year and/or the last year of the period. The existence of an establishment in a particular ZIP code is defined by the presence of payroll *at any time* during the year. For establishments that existed in the ZIP code at the beginning *and* the end, three groups are defined depending upon the change in employment during the period. The seven status groups are as follows:

Births: Establishments that had no payroll in that ZIP code or any other ZIP code at any time during 1989 but that did have payroll in that ZIP code at some time during 1991.

Deaths: Establishments that had payroll in that ZIP code at some time during 1989 but had no payroll in that ZIP code (or anywhere else) at any time during 1991.

In-movers: Establishments that had payroll in that ZIP code at some time during 1991 but that were located in a different ZIP code in 1989.

Out-movers: Establishments that had payroll in that ZIP code at some time during 1989 but that were located in a different ZIP code in 1991.

Expansions: Establishments that had payroll in that ZIP code at some time during both 1989 and 1991 and that had more employees in March 1991 than in March 1989.

Contractions: Establishments that had payroll in that ZIP code at some time during both 1989 and 1991 and that had fewer employees in March 1991 than in March 1989.

Constant: Establishments that had payroll in that ZIP code at some time during both 1989 and 1991 and that had the same number of employees in March 1991 as in March 1989.

The seven categories are mutually exclusive. Establishments in the expansion and contraction categories are not counted in any of the other categories, for example. For in-movers and out-movers, we do not determine whether their employment expanded or contracted during the two-year period. In all cases except births, the employment-size category is based on employment as of March 1989; for births it is March 1991.

For analysis purposes, we usually combine births and in-movers into one category. For multi-establishment firms, the census distinction between a new establishment and one that has changed location is somewhat arbitrary. If an old establishment closes and a new one is built elsewhere, the firm decides whether the new plant will be reported to the Census Bureau as a new establishment or as the same establishment in a new location. The same considerations argue for combining deaths and out-movers into a single category. Conceptually, the factors influencing new branch plants and relocated branch plants should be the same. Though we would expect a different set of factors to explain firm (as opposed to branch plant) births, we cannot identify from this dataset the new establishments that are also new firms.

The existence of an establishment in a particular ZIP code at the beginning and/or the end of a period determines the status categorization, and existence is defined as the presence of payroll *at any time* during the year. As a result, births and moves in for the first period, 1989–1991, are establishments that were not present in 1989 but were born or moved in some time during the 24 months of 1990 and 1991. Similarly, the births and moves in for the second period are those that occurred during 1992 and 1993, and for the third period, during 1994 and 1995. Deaths and moves out by period, on the other hand, are those that occurred during the years 1989 and 1990 (since a firm that exited in 1991 would still have been counted as present at some time during that year), 1991 and 1992, and 1993 and 1994. This must be kept in mind when interpreting tables comparing gross gains and losses in establishments; the time periods do not exactly coincide.

Expansions and contractions are determined by comparing establishment employment in March 1989 to March 1991; in March 1991 to March 1993; and in March 1993 to March 1995. They are slightly overcounted since they include some establishments that should properly be classified as births or deaths instead. The reasons for this problem and the procedure used to adjust expansion and contraction rates are discussed in Appendix D. The data presented in this chapter are the adjusted rates. Finally, enterprise zones are never coterminous with ZIP boundaries. Our method for translating enterprise zones into ZIP regions is discussed in Appendix E.

ESTABLISHMENT DIVERSITY AND TURNOVER IN THE ENTERPRISE ZONES

The 64 zones in our study exhibited surprisingly large rates of gross establishment growth, as can be seen in Table 6.1. In this table we have computed averages in two ways: for all zones and for all except the two largest, Cleveland and Milwaukee, which skew the averages. The average number of manufacturing establishments in a zone by the second measure was 111 at the beginning of the period, and the average number of establishments moving into or being born in the zones during the six-year period 1990–1995 was 67, which represents a 60 percent gross growth in establishments. This represents a growth of about 11 establishments per year for the average zone, or about a 10 percent annual growth rate.

As would be expected, the deaths and out-migrations exceeded the births and in-migrations in the majority of zones (41 of the 64). The average number of deaths and moves out was 75 (again considering all zones except the two largest), and this amounted to a 67 percent rate of gross decline over the six years, 1989–1994. This translates into a loss of 12.4 establishments per year for the average zone, or about an 11

Table 6.1 Sectoral Diversity and Gross Rates of Establishment Growth and Decline in 64 Enterprise Zones, by Zone, 1989–1995

City (zone)[a]	Establishments in mid 1989		Births and moves in 1990–1995			Deaths and moves out 1989–1994		Net change
	Number	Sectors[b]	Number	Sectors[b]	Rate[c]	Number	Rate[c]	Rate[c]
Pharr, Tex.	12	10	22	6	191.3	12	104.3	87.0
Evansville, Ind.	67	7	65	7	96.7	43	63.9	32.7
Porterville, Calif.	32	9	23	7	72.4	14	44.1	28.3
El Paso, Tex.	140	8	190	9	136.0	153	109.5	26.5
Fort Wayne, Ind.	158	5	121	6	76.6	83	52.5	24.1
Massillon, Ohio	66	8	64	7	97.3	50	76.0	21.3
Newport News, Va.	57	9	53	6	93.0	43	75.4	17.5
Beloit, Wis.	64	6	30	5	47.1	21	32.9	14.1
South Bend, Ind.	163	4	116	6	71.1	95	58.2	12.9
Owensboro, Ky.	65	7	59	9	90.4	51	78.2	12.3
Fort Worth, Tex.	144	7	124	9	86.1	108	75.0	11.1
Pekin, Ill.	29	7	18	8	61.5	16	54.7	6.8
Elyria, Ohio	187	7	113	8	60.6	104	55.8	4.8
St. Joseph, Mo.	86	7	50	10	58.5	46	53.8	4.7
Joplin, Mo.	105	6	82	7	77.9	78	74.1	3.8
Hammond, Ind.	81	6	41	8	50.8	38	47.1	3.7
Springfield, Mo.	241	7	137	8	56.9	129	53.6	3.3
Kankakee, Ill.	74	8	32	11	43.4	30	40.7	2.7

City								
Norwich, Conn.	44	9	26	5	58.8	25	56.5	2.3
Lexington, Ky.	152	4	123	4	81.2	122	80.5	0.7
Kansas City, Mo. (#2)	142	5	65	8	45.9	65	45.9	0.0
Petersburg, Va.	37	10	28	7	75.7	28	75.7	0.0
Portsmouth, Va.	45	8	27	6	60.7	27	60.7	0.0
Racine, Wis.	227	5	102	8	44.9	105	46.2	−1.3
Lafayette, Ind.	61	8	40	6	65.3	42	68.6	−3.3
Cincinnati, Ohio (#2)	163	5	99	8	60.9	106	65.2	−4.3
Lancaster, Pa.	244	6	149	5	61.1	161	66.1	−4.9
Canton, Ohio	220	6	97	9	44.1	108	49.1	−5.0
Alton, Ill.	70	7	34	5	48.4	38	54.1	−5.7
Los Angeles (Pacoima), Calif.	254	8	184	10	72.5	201	79.2	−6.7
Auburn, N.Y.	57	9	17	8	29.8	21	36.8	−7.0
Amarillo, Tex.	104	8	68	7	65.4	76	73.1	−7.7
San Antonio, Tex.	205	6	123	10	60.1	140	68.4	−8.3
Utica, N.Y.	84	7	45	6	53.7	52	62.1	−8.4
Fond Du Lac, Wis.	82	6	57	4	69.5	64	78.0	−8.5
Muncie, Ind.	119	4	57	8	47.9	69	58.0	−10.1
Warren, Ohio	82	5	56	5	68.1	65	79.0	−10.9
New Britain, Conn.	126	5	55	8	43.8	70	55.8	−12.0
Moline, Ill.	96	5	44	5	45.8	57	59.4	−13.5
Cleveland, Ohio	1,583	5	588	7	37.2	820	51.8	−14.7
Green Bay, Wis.	155	7	105	5	68.0	129	83.5	−15.5
Troy, N.Y.	51	6	28	8	54.9	36	70.6	−15.7
Milwaukee, Wis.	624	6	270	8	43.3	369	59.1	−15.9

Table 6.1 (Continued)

City (zone)[a]	Establishments in mid 1989		Births and moves in 1990–1995			Deaths and moves out 1989–1994		Net change
	Number	Sectors[b]	Number	Sectors[b]	Rate[c]	Number	Rate[c]	Rate[c]
Pittsburgh, Pa.	87	7	45	6	51.6	59	67.6	−16.0
Philadelphia, Pa.	43	5	26	6	60.1	33	76.3	−16.2
Covington, Ky.	61	5	30	7	49.2	40	65.6	−16.4
Hartford, Conn.	24	6	11	9	45.4	15	61.9	−16.5
Fort Lauderdale, Fla.	145	5	117	7	80.8	141	97.4	−16.6
Syracuse, N.Y.	207	5	104	6	50.3	139	67.2	−16.9
Clearwater, Fla.	70	6	63	6	90.0	78	111.4	−21.4
Pasadena, Calif.	75	8	58	5	77.9	74	99.3	−21.5
Scranton, Pa.	156	5	62	7	39.7	96	61.5	−21.8
Maywood, Ill.	135	7	37	6	27.5	75	55.7	−28.2
Hamden, Conn.	198	8	90	9	45.5	148	74.7	−29.3
Jacksonville, Fla.	303	9	129	6	42.6	221	72.9	−30.4
New York (Harlem), N.Y.	26	5	16	3	62.1	25	97.1	−35.0
Meriden, Conn.	111	6	40	8	36.0	79	71.2	−35.1
Chester, Pa.	58	10	15	7	25.8	36	61.8	−36.1

Average[d]							
All zones	142	7	78	7	55.0	91	63.9	-9.0
Excluding two largest zones[e]	111	7	67	7	60.2	75	67.2	-7.0

[a] Listed in descending order by rate of net change.

[b] The number of sectors significantly represented, defined as a sector with at least 5% of the total number of establishments in that zone in 1989, or 5% of the total number of establishment births and moves in, 1990–1995. There are 16 total sectors.

[c] Rate = percent of establishments in mid 1989.

[d] This is a weighted average, which is the same as a simple average except in the case of the rates. For example, the average rate of "births and moves in" is calculated by dividing total births and moves in for all zones by total number of establishments in 1989.

[e] Cleveland and Milwaukee were much larger than any of the other zones and together accounted for 24% of the establishments in 1989, 17% of the births and moves in, and 21% of the deaths and moves out. They were dropped from this average to avoid their skewing the results.

percent annual rate of shrinkage for the median zone. But since the number of new establishments was almost as large, the average zone saw a net loss of only about 8 establishments over the six-year period, representing an annual rate of net decline of about 1.2 percent. There was enormous variation among zones, however: 20 of the 64 zones actually experienced a net gain in manufacturing establishments, and in 6 of these cases the gain was in excess of 20 percent over the six-year period. At the other extreme, 10 zones suffered net losses of 20 percent or more.

Most enterprise zones in our sample exhibited a substantial degree of diversity in terms of the number of different manufacturing industries with a presence in the zone. Table 6.1 shows the number of different manufacturing sectors (at the two-digit SIC code level) with a significant representation in each zone.[1] A sector was considered to have a significant presence if it accounted for at least 5 percent of the total number of establishments in the zone. In all but 4 of the zones, there were at least 5 of the 16 sectors represented, and in 19 of the zones, there were 8 or more sectors. Furthermore, if instead we counted all sectors with at least one establishment, we would find that in all but 10 zones at least 13 of the 16 sectors were present. This reflects a surprising degree of diversity. It also reflects the fact that some zones are quite large, drawn to include a major portion—if not all—of the city's industrial land.

Sectoral diversity was also present among the new establishments. The median number of sectors significantly represented among the births and moves in (accounting for at least 5 percent of the total) was seven; all but five zones saw new establishments representing five or more different sectors.

Looking at the 64 zones as a whole, was the growth or decline in establishments concentrated in certain industrial sectors, and were the new establishments of the same employment-size classes as the exiting establishments? If the entrants were small and the departures large, the employment effects of the net decline would be much larger than the average 7 percent reduction in establishments shown in Table 6.1. Establishment entries and exits by manufacturing sector and by establishment employment size are shown in Table 6.2. The number of births and moves in during these six years was quite large relative to the initial size of the manufacturing sector, particularly for the smallest-size

Table 6.2 Establishment Turnover by Employment Size and Sector in 64 Enterprise Zones, 1989–1995

SIC	Sector description	Total establishments in mid 1989			Births and moves in 1990–1995			Deaths and moves out 1989–1994			Net change		
		0–19	20–99	100+	0–19	20–99	100+	0–19	20–99	100+	0–19	20–99	100+
20	Food and kindred products	241	177	155	167	79	30	184	100	53	−17	−21	−24
23	Apparel and other textile prod.	215	105	47	200	75	19	243	100	18	−43	−25	0
24	Lumber and wood products	228	76	12	222	23	4	224	32	6	−2	−9	−2
25	Furniture and fixtures	183	60	24	145	34	6	171	42	6	−26	−8	−1
26	Paper and allied products	58	111	58	50	38	6	47	41	12	4	−3	−5
27	Printing and publishing	1,148	302	107	719	114	25	894	154	31	−175	−41	−6
28	Chemicals and allied products	211	125	61	149	41	12	159	41	10	−11	−1	1
30	Rubber and misc. plastics prod.	194	147	47	150	61	21	157	91	19	−7	−30	2
31	Leather and leather products	27	18	13	26	8	8	19	7	14	7	1	−6
32	Stone, clay and glass products	198	102	20	147	32	4	158	43	5	−10	−11	−2
33	Primary metal industries	126	105	79	69	40	25	86	41	20	−17	−1	4
34	Fabricated metal products	718	461	160	394	146	30	495	181	46	−101	−35	−16
35	Industrial machinery	1,079	373	141	661	136	34	710	162	49	−49	−26	−15
36	Electric & electronic equipment	173	114	90	123	78	34	150	68	34	−28	10	−0
37	Transportation equipment	110	49	52	93	59	20	102	32	16	−8	26	4
38	Instruments and related prod.	137	65	40	81	20	12	106	28	23	−24	−8	−11
	All sectors												
	No. of establishments	5,046	2,390	1,107	3,398	981	288	3,904	1,165	363	−506	−184	−75
	Distribution (%)	59.1	28.0	13.0	72.8	21.0	6.2	71.9	21.4	6.7	66.2	24.0	9.8

class. The number of deaths and moves out exceeded the number of births and moves in, in 14 of the 16 sectors (all but SIC codes 31 and 37), but not by that much. (These rates are not strictly comparable since gross gains are for 1990–1995 and gross losses for 1989–1994.) Clearly, though, if one focuses only on the net loss or net gain in number of establishments one misses most of what is going on: new plants are constantly emerging to replace older ones that disappear, and the gross changes in both directions are five to eight times as large as the net change in most sectors.

Can we infer that the percentage loss of employment due to establishments entering and exiting the zones was similar to the net percentage loss of establishments? The last row of Table 6.2 shows the percentage distribution of establishments by establishment employment size. While the smallest establishments accounted for 59 percent of all establishments in 1989, they accounted for a much larger portion of the entering and exiting firms. Of the new establishments, 72.8 percent were in the smallest class, compared to 71.9 percent of the exiting establishments. The largest employment-size class accounted for 6.2 percent of the gross growth, but 6.7 percent of the gross shrinkage. Thus, exiting establishments were on average slightly larger than entering establishments. The loss of manufacturing employment from entries and exits over the six-year period (excluding expansions and contractions of firms with a continual presence), therefore, was likely to be a little more than the median 8 percent net loss of establishments.[2]

Overall gains or losses in jobs will be determined not only by establishments entering and exiting the zones, but also by those that remain in the zones and expand or contract employment. Table 6.3 shows the number of establishments expanding or contracting employment over each two-year period as a percentage of the total number of establishments that were in the zone at the beginning of the period, by SIC code. The smallest establishments were much less likely to expand or contract than those in the two larger-size classes, in part because they were much more likely to die or move out, instead (as shown in Table 6.2). But the smallest establishments expanded a little more often than they contracted. For the large-size classes (particularly the 100+ category), the percent contracting exceeded the percent expanding. Overall, of the establishments existing at the beginning of a two-year period in these 64 zones, about one in three expanded employment within two years, and about one in three reduced employment. About one in five died or moved out.

Clearly the behavior of establishments remaining in a zone has a great deal to do with whether jobs in the zone increase or decrease. Without knowing the magnitude of the job expansions and contractions, however, we do not know whether these job changes are more or less important than the job changes resulting from establishments' exiting and entering. However, given the substantially higher rates of contraction among the larger firm sizes, it is likely that the net effect of expansions and contractions in these zones has been further erosion in the job base, beyond the more than 8 percent attributable to net loss of establishments.

SECTORAL CHANGE AND THE COMPARATIVE ADVANTAGE OF ZONES

Which sectors accounted for the largest share of establishments in these enterprise zones, and which ones accounted for the largest share of establishment growth or shrinkage? It turns out that three sectors— printing and publishing (27), fabricated metal products (34), and industrial machinery (35)—accounted for 52.5 percent of the manufacturing establishments in these zones in 1989, as shown in Table 6.4. These same sectors accounted for about half of the births and moves in as well, and about half of the deaths and moves out. These same three sectors also accounted for the bulk of the net decline in establishments; the net loss of 222 establishments in printing and publishing alone represented 29 percent of the overall net loss of 765 establishments in these 64 zones.

Which were the fastest growing or most rapidly declining sectors? Table 6.4 also shows gross annual rates of growth (births and moves in), rates of decline (deaths and moves out), and rates of net decline in establishments for each sector. The three sectors that dominated the initial set of establishments in 1989 were among the seven *slowest* growing in percentage terms.   The sectors experiencing the highest percentage rates of birth and in-migration were 23 (apparel), 24 (wood products), 25 (furniture), 31 (leather), and 37 (transportation equip-

Table 6.3 Average Percent of Establishments Expanding or Contracting Employment per Two-Year Period in 64 Enterprise Zones, 1989–1995

SIC	Expansion rates by employment size				Contraction rates by employment size			
	0–19	20–99	100+	All	0–19	20–99	100+	All
20	27.6	40.9	40.6	35.3	26.7	36.3	45.6	34.8
23	23.2	29.0	40.3	26.8	22.0	36.8	46.4	29.1
24	27.6	32.6	33.7	28.6	22.9	48.4	41.2	29.4
25	26.5	29.0	34.0	27.7	26.2	47.7	57.6	34.0
26	36.6	43.8	45.2	42.2	21.1	40.5	46.9	37.4
27	24.2	34.9	39.6	27.3	26.7	42.7	48.4	31.3
28	28.4	39.4	39.9	33.8	22.7	45.1	52.8	34.5
30	34.1	43.7	31.3	37.8	23.2	35.9	53.8	31.8
31	33.5	34.6	21.5	31.8	22.4	46.0	22.5	30.6
32	29.4	37.2	37.9	32.2	24.2	43.2	51.2	31.5
33	32.4	41.4	38.8	37.1	26.1	41.3	49.8	37.2
34	32.4	41.3	38.0	36.0	28.3	42.3	50.9	35.7
35	30.7	38.8	39.9	33.3	27.1	41.8	46.3	32.0
36	28.8	35.9	32.6	31.7	25.5	40.4	54.4	36.7
37	31.1	34.1	35.0	32.9	24.6	46.3	54.2	36.7
38	29.6	42.3	35.5	33.9	26.9	40.6	38.9	32.5

| All | 28.7 | 38.6 | 38.1 | 32.6 | 26.0 | 41.5 | 49.0 | 33.2 |

NOTE: These rates are adjusted to eliminate estimated overcounting of expansions and contractions. Rates are calculated using a denominator equal to the estimated number of establishments in existence as of mid March of the first year of the period (1989, 1991, or 1993). These cannot be converted to annual rates. Suppose, for example, that out of 10 establishments at the beginning, 2 expanded the first year and a different 2 the second year; the two-year rate would be 40 percent at most (if the first 2 did not revert to their original size the second year). But if it was the same 2 establishments that expanded both years, then the two-year rate would be 20 percent. So all we can infer from the two-year rate is that the percent expanding in an average year would be somewhere between the two-year rate and half of the two-year rate.

142   Chapter 6

Table 6.4 Sectoral Composition of Establishment Growth and Shrinkage in 64 Enterprise Zones, 1989–1995

SIC	Sector description	Establishments in mid 1989		Births and moves in 1990–1995			Deaths and moves out 1989–1994			Net change 1989–1995		
		Number	Percent of total	Number	Percent of total	Average annual rate[a]	Number	Percent of total	Average annual rate[b]	Number	Percent of total	Average annual rate[c]
20	Food and kindred products	573	6.7	276	5.9	8.3	337	6.2	10.0	−61	8.0	−1.7
23	Apparel and other textile prod.	368	4.3	293	6.3	13.4	361	6.6	16.3	−68	8.9	−2.8
24	Lumber and wood products	315	3.7	249	5.3	13.5	262	4.8	14.1	−13	1.7	−0.6
25	Furniture and fixtures	268	3.1	185	4.0	12.0	220	4.1	14.1	−35	4.6	−2.2
26	Paper and allied products	227	2.7	94	2.0	6.5	99	1.8	6.9	−5	0.7	−0.4
27	Printing and publishing	1,557	18.2	857	18.4	9.4	1,079	19.9	11.7	−222	29.0	−2.3
28	Chemicals and allied products	398	4.7	201	4.3	8.4	211	3.9	8.9	−10	1.3	−0.4
30	Rubber and misc. plastics prod.	388	4.5	232	5.0	10.1	267	4.9	11.6	−35	4.6	−1.5
31	Leather and leather products	57	0.7	42	0.9	12.8	40	0.7	12.2	2	−0.3	0.6
32	Stone, clay and glass products	320	3.7	183	3.9	9.2	206	3.8	10.2	−23	3.0	−1.1
33	Primary metal industries	310	3.6	133	2.8	7.3	147	2.7	8.0	−14	1.8	−0.7
34	Fabricated metal products	1,339	15.7	570	12.2	7.2	722	13.3	9.1	−152	19.9	−1.8
35	Industrial machinery	1,593	18.6	831	17.8	8.8	921		9.7	−90	11.8	−0.9
36	Electric & electronic equipment	378	4.4	235	5.0	10.2	253	4.7	11.0	−18	2.4	−0.8
37	Transportation equipment	211	2.5	172	3.7	12.6	150	2.8	11.1	22	−2.9	1.5
38	Instruments and related prod.	242	2.8	114	2.4	8.4	157	2.9	11.3	−43	5.6	−2.9

| All sectors | 8,543 | 100.0 | 4,667 | 100.0 | 9.2 | 5,432 | 100.0 | 10.7 | -765 | 100.0 | -1.5 |

[a] Growth rates are calculated by dividing the number of births and moves in during a two-year period by the estimated number of establishments in existence at the end of the first year of the period (1989, 1991, or 1993), dividing by two (to get an annual rate), and averaging over the three periods.

[b] Shrinkage rates are calculated by dividing the number of deaths or moves out during a two-year period by the estimated number of establishments in existence at the beginning of the first year of the period (1989, 1991, or 1993), dividing by two (to get an annual rate), and averaging over the three periods.

[c] For the net change in number of establishments, the rate is simply the average growth rate minus the average death rate.

ment). These are "traditional" low-technology sectors. They—with the exception of 37—also displayed the highest rates of gross decline (deaths and moves out as a percentage of initial establishments). Leather products and transportation equipment were the only sectors showing a net gain.

If we consider the net change in number of establishments (births plus moves in minus deaths and moves out), we find that five sectors accounted for 78 percent of the total net loss of 765 establishments in these 64 enterprise zones from 1989 to 1995: 20 (food), 23 (apparel), 27 (printing), 34 (fabricated metal products), and 35 (industrial machinery). As shown in Table 6.4, the sectors that showed the highest overall *rates* of net loss (net change in establishments as a percent of the number in 1989) were 38 (instruments), 23 (apparel), 27 (printing), and 25 (furniture), in that order. The sectors that grew over this period, 31 (leather) and 37 (transportation equipment), did not account for many establishments to begin with and produced a net gain of only 24 establishments between them. Sectors 26 (paper) and 28 (chemicals) also had a modest presence but only a very slight decline (15 establishments total). Overall, the net rate of decline was about 1.5 percent per year. Over the six years, this represented a net loss of about 9 percent of the establishments that existed at the beginning of the period.

How did the enterprise zones fare compared to the states in which they were located? Table 6.5 compares the gross birth and death rates in the 64 enterprise zones with birth and death rates for the 13 states as a whole (minus the sampled enterprise zones). Overall, the birth rates in zones were significantly smaller than in the state economies generally—5.8 percent per year versus 8.5 percent per year—and this was true for each sector except 31 and 37.[3] The states as a whole also experienced somewhat higher death rates than did the zones, and this was the case in all but one of the 16 sectors. This is probably because higher birth rates are strongly associated with higher death rates, perhaps in part because some sectors are simply more volatile and hence generate higher birth *and* death rates, but no doubt also in part due to the simple fact that higher birth rates produce more potential corpses and thus higher death rates.

For the 13 states as a whole, there was a net loss of only 2.4 percent of the establishments over the six-year period. Three of the 16 sectors experienced net growth, and just 2 sectors experienced a net decline in excess of 1.0 percent per year: 25 (furniture) and 31 (leather), both small sectors to begin with (see Table 6.5). In the zones, 8 of the 16 sectors declined by more than 1.0 percent per year. This six-year period, in other words, saw relative stability in the manufacturing sector in the 13 states that we examined, with small rates of growth in some sectors offset by small rates of decline in other sectors. On the other hand, enterprise zones within these states experienced relatively pervasive decline, though not at a particularly high rate; this net decline was produced through very substantial growth rates being offset by slightly larger rates of shrinkage.

One might expect that the sectoral composition of births in the zones would differ significantly from that of the states as a whole. Given that enterprise zones are thought to contain concentrations of lower-skilled workers, and given that zone incentives are more skewed toward labor than capital, one would expect to see relatively more activity in labor-intensive and low-wage sectors in the zones. To explore this issue, we determined how each sector contributed to the overall net loss of establishments in the 64 zones and in the 13 states over the six-year period 1989–1995. For example, sector 25 (furniture) experienced a net loss of 35 establishments in the enterprise zones in the aggregate, taking into account the net effect of births, moves in and out, and deaths (see Table 6.4). These 35 represented 4.6 percent of the total net loss of 765 establishments in the zones. In the remaining portions of the 13 states, on the other hand, sector 25 accounted for 695 of the 4,133 total net decline in establishments, or 16.8 percent.[4] Thus the zones fared much better than the states as a whole in attracting new establishments or preventing the closing of existing establishments in this sector, at least relative to other sectors.

The sectors were then ranked by the difference between the zone and state percentage shares (see Table 6.6); a positive number indicates that the zones did better than the states as a whole, while a negative number indicates that the zones performed less well than the states. (Note that where a sector experienced a net gain instead of a loss, the percentage contribution to the overall loss is negative.) The six sectors shown in the top portion of Table 6.6 together accounted for 96 percent of the total shrinkage of establishments in the 13 states, but only 53 per-

Table 6.5 Births, Deaths and Net Change in Number of Establishments by Sector in 64 Enterprise Zones and 13 States, 1989–1995

SIC	Sector description	For the 64 enterprise zones			For remainder of the states[a]		
		Average annual birth rate	Average annual death rate	Annual net change rate	Average annual birth rate	Average annual death rate	Annual net change rate
20	Food and kindred products	5.5	6.4	-1.8	7.7	7.7	-0.1
23	Apparel and other textile prod.	9.6	12.1	-3.1	16.5	16.5	-0.1
24	Lumber and wood products	9.5	9.2	-0.7	10.8	10.6	-0.0
25	Furniture and fixtures	8.0	9.1	-2.2	9.6	11.4	-2.1
26	Paper and allied products	3.9	3.6	-0.4	5.3	5.4	-0.3
27	Printing and publishing	5.8	7.4	-2.4	8.5	9.0	-0.7
28	Chemicals and allied products	5.6	5.2	-0.4	6.8	6.4	0.2
30	Rubber and misc. plastics prod.	6.8	7.2	-1.5	7.1	6.5	0.6
31	Leather and leather products	8.5	7.3	0.6	8.0	10.5	-2.9
32	Stone, clay and glass products	5.0	6.1	-1.2	6.6	7.2	-0.7
33	Primary metal industries	4.3	5.0	-0.8	5.9	6.3	-0.5
34	Fabricated metal products	4.1	5.4	-1.9	6.1	6.7	-0.9
35	Industrial machinery	5.3	5.8	-0.9	7.0	6.9	-0.1
36	Electric & electronic equipment	7.0	7.3	-0.8	9.0	8.6	0.2
37	Transportation equipment	8.8	7.8	1.7	8.7	9.4	-1.0

| All sectors | 5.8 | 6.7 | -1.5 | 8.5 | 8.7 | -0.4 |

a The figures for the 13 states are calculated by subtracting from statewide totals the totals for the 64 enterprise zones in our sample. Note that although we cannot calculate move-in or move-out rates by state (because moves include all moves from one ZIP code to another, not just from one state to another), we can calculate net change by state, because moves between ZIP codes within a state will cancel out.

Table 6.6 The Comparative Advantage for Enterprise Zones

SIC	Sector name	% of total net decline in establishments over six-year period		Pct. pt. difference: states − zones	Capital per worker[a] ($)	Average annual wage ($)
		In the 64 zones	In remainder of 13 states			
Zones do relatively better than states						
25	Furniture and fixtures	4.6	16.8	12.2	41,893	19,391
37	Transportation equipment	−2.9	7.6	10.5	61,850	37,898
34	Fabricated metal products	19.9	25.6	5.8	116,686	26,188
32	Stone, clay and glass products	3.0	8.2	5.2	99,311	26,656
31	Leather and leather products	−0.3	4.5	4.8	31,308	15,584
27	Printing and publishing	29.0	33.6	4.6	33,495	24,122
	Total[b]	53.3	96.4	43.1		
	Weighted average[c]				66,071	25,458
Zones do about the same						
33	Primary metal industries	1.8	2.9	1.0	181,192	33,199
26	Paper and allied products	0.7	1.5	0.8	169,425	31,597
24	Lumber and wood products	1.7	0.8	−0.9	27,007	19,939
	Total[b]	4.2	5.1	0.9		
	Weighted average[c]				83,137	24,662

Zones do relatively worse than states

28	Chemicals and allied products	1.3	-1.6	-3.0	153,610	34,944
36	Electric & electronic equipment	2.4	-2.3	-4.7	177,904	24,392
38	Instruments and related prod.	5.6	0.6	-5.0	150,489	28,397
23	Apparel and other textile prod.	8.9	2.6	-6.3	34,238	13,905
35	Industrial machinery	11.8	5.4	-6.4	101,698	28,814
20	Food and kindred products	8.0	0.9	-7.1	68,930	22,643
30	Rubber and misc. plastics prod.	4.6	-7.1	-11.7	173,115	22,593
	Total[b]	42.5	-1.5	-44.0		
	Weighted average[c]				109,916	24,901
	Total for all 16 sectors	100.0	100.0	0.00		

[a] Property, plant, and equipment per worker.
[b] Totals for percent of net decline.
[c] The weight for a sector is that sector's share of total establishments in mid 1989 in the corresponding group of sectors, for the 13 states.

cent of the shrinkage in the zones; these are the sectors in which the zones appear to have an overall comparative advantage. At the bottom of the table are seven sectors that accounted for 43 percent of the shrinkage in the zones, but only 1.5 percent in the states (on average they grew elsewhere in the 13 states); these are the sectors in which zones appear to have a relative disadvantage.

Are there systematic differences between the sectors in which the zones did relatively better than the states and the sectors in which they did relatively worse? To explore this question, we looked at two industry characteristics: capital intensity and wages. Table 6.6 shows the level of capital intensity for each sector, as measured by the value of property, plant, and equipment per worker, and the average annual wage of production workers; for each group of sectors we then calculated a weighted average (see table footnote). These figures are national averages, of course, and thus are merely suggestive of the actual capital intensity or wage rates for the particular firms found in our 64 zones and 13 states.

On the basis of these average figures, there is no appreciable difference in the typical wages in the sectors in which the zones do relatively well versus the sectors in which the zones do relatively poorly. The zones appear to have a comparative advantage in one of the highest wage sectors, transportation equipment, which actually grew in number of establishments within the zones during the period 1989–1995. On the other hand, zones also did relatively well in two of the lowest wage sectors, furniture and leather products. If one focuses instead on capital intensity, however, distinct differences appear. The sectors in which the zones fare best in net terms have distinctly lower capital per worker than the sectors in which zones do the poorest. Of the six sectors with the greatest average investment in capital per worker ($150,000 or more), the zones performed poorer than the states in four of the six, and about the same as the states in the other two.

Although enterprise zones are sectorally diverse and have experienced rapid turnover in many sectors, they are still clearly focused on "old economy" industries. This is not surprising given the overall purpose of enterprise zones and the nature of the targeted labor pool. Nevertheless, it raises concerns about the long-term industrial viability of zones.

EFFECTS OF THE NATIONAL ECONOMIC EXPANSION

Thus far we have presented data for the entire time period, 1989–1995. During the first of the two-year periods, 1989–1991, the economy was sliding into recession, while the second period, 1991–1993, saw the beginnings of recovery, which then continued throughout the rest of the decade. Figure 6.1 displays the rates of growth and decline, and the percentage of establishments expanding and contracting, for each of the three periods. (See Appendix Table F.5 for the actual numbers, by employment-size class.) In terms of births and deaths, the three periods are very similar. However, the middle period, when the economy was moving out of a recession, showed much higher numbers moving both into and out of zones than the period before or after, and this was true for all establishment sizes.

The most striking trend evident in Figure 6.1 is that the percent of establishments that remained in the zone and expanded increased with each two-year period, while the percent that remained but reduced employment declined. Expansion rates exceeded contraction rates by a wide margin in the most recent period, and this was especially true for the two smaller-size classes (see Appendix Table F.5). It is quite possible that in the 1993–1995 period there was net employment growth in existing establishments in these zones sufficient to offset, or more than offset, the job losses due to exits exceeding entries. If these most recent trends continued through the economic expansion of the latter 1990s, the overall job base in these zones could have been restored to the level that obtained in 1989, prior to the recession. This is purely speculative, of course, but the data suggest that such a result is plausible.

CONCLUSIONS

Enterprise zones do not appear to be the stagnant backwaters of the economy, as often assumed. They contain a surprising amount of diversity, in terms of manufacturing sectors with a presence in the zones, and a surprising amount of movement of establishments into and out of

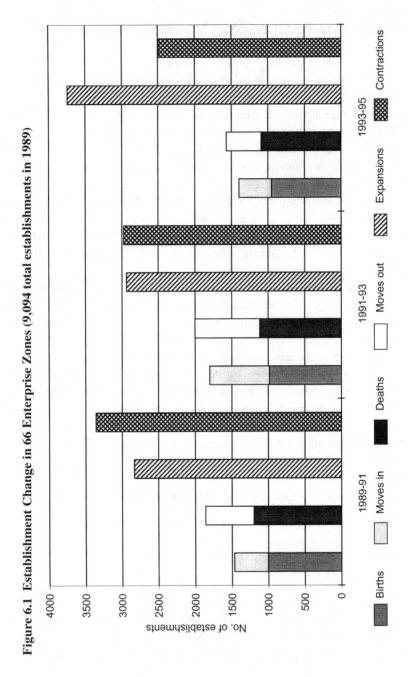

Figure 6.1 Establishment Change in 66 Enterprise Zones (9,094 total establishments in 1989)

the zones. The average zone among the 64 we studied started out with about 111 manufacturing establishments distributed across 6 or 7 sectors in 1989, and in the ensuing six years experienced an influx of about 11 manufacturing establishments each year through births or migrations from elsewhere. But the average zone also lost about 12.4 establishments each year, and thus was left with a net decline in manufacturing establishments, though at a rate of only about 1.2 percent per year. The gross rates of growth are significant for the estimation of fiscal effects, for it is the influx of new establishments, not the net change, that drives incentive expenditure, at least to the extent that new establishments require investments in facilities and equipment.

The economic performance of enterprise zones must be placed against the backdrop of the larger economy, of course. When compared with the remaining portions of the 13 states of which our 64 sample zones are a part, the zones did indeed perform more poorly than those states, as one would expect. The six-year period 1989–1995 saw relative stability in the manufacturing sector in the 13 states we examined, with small rates of establishment growth in some sectors offset by small rates of decline in other sectors. Manufacturing establishment numbers declined more rapidly within the zones than within the states in almost all sectors, the notable exception being transportation equipment.

We assessed the zones' comparative advantage or disadvantage for types of manufacturing. We compared sectors in which zones did relatively better than the states (six sectors that accounted for 96 percent of the state decline, but only 53 percent of the zone decline), and sectors in which zones did relatively worse (accounting for 43 percent of zone decline, but actually increasing for the states). There was no clear difference between the two groups of firms in terms of national average wages paid in those sectors. But zones appeared to have a pronounced disadvantage in attracting and retaining the more capital-intensive sectors of manufacturing. This is at least consistent with the nature of incentives in zones: they are more likely to favor labor than are other nontargeted incentives. Still, we would be surprised if incentives had much to do with the apparent zone comparative advantage in more labor-intensive sectors. Slack labor markets are a more plausible explanation, given the very meager value of labor incentives in terms of their wage equivalent (see Chapter 3) and given the very limited ability of labor incentives to reduce wage costs at the margin (see Chapter 4). It is also clear that manufacturing in enterprise zones remains concentrated in "old economy" sectors.

When trends were examined over time, there was a pronounced improvement in the manufacturing sector as the economy pulled out of the recession of the early 1990s. In particular, the number of firms expanding employment greatly exceeded the number contracting employment in the third period, 1993–1995, when the expansion was really getting underway. The likelihood is that this continued in the latter 1990s.

What the essentially descriptive analysis of this chapter leaves out is the "causal" connection between enterprise zones and growth. While we know that enterprise zones saw considerable establishment turnover during the first half of the 1990s, and that enterprise zones performed more poorly than their containing states during that period, we still do not know whether the incentives offered in zones have had any impact on economic growth in those zones. It is to this issue that we now turn.

Notes

1. We looked at 16 of the 20 two-digit industries, omitting those in which significant geographic mobility was clearly lacking, such as petroleum refining. See Appendix A (especially Table A.1) for a description of the sectors.
2. It should be noted that the employment-size class of firms is based on the number of employees in March of the first year of the period, with the exception of births (establishments that did not exist in the first year). Thus a death or exit of a plant in the largest-size class means that, for example, an establishment that had over 100 employees in March 1989 and then died or moved out of the zone in 1990 or 1991 will be recorded as the loss of a large firm in our database. We do not know how many employees it had when it actually closed or moved, and it may well have shrunk between March 1989 and the date of closing to the point that it was a small firm when it finally closed. Nonetheless, we show it as the loss of a large firm, which appropriately reflects the significance of the job loss for that period of time; showing it as the loss of a small firm would not do so.
3. Move-in and move-out rates at the state level are not shown because the SSEL data are at the ZIP code level, so that a plant that moves from one ZIP to another within the same state is nonetheless recorded as a move in and as a move out for that state. Thus the state move-in rates overstate the actual extent of moving into the state, and the state move-out rates overstate the extent of plants moving out of the state. The data do not identify the origin ZIP code for a move in or the destination ZIP

code for a move out, so it is not possible to determine the extent of within-state moves. We assume that this problem is minimal at the zone level, since the typical zone will involve a very small number of ZIP codes.

4. We cannot use the data showing moves in or moves out at the state level because (as noted in the prior footnote) the data do not allow us to distinguish a move from one ZIP to another within the state from a move into the state. However, we can combine the two figures to arrive at net moves in or out, since moves within the state will cancel out and we will have an accurate net outflow or inflow. Thus the net-change figures for the states and the zones are comparable.

7
Enterprise Zones, Incentives, and Local Economic Growth

In the previous chapter we looked at broad growth trends in enterprise zones. In this chapter we try to answer a more specific question: Can enterprise zones reasonably be expected to generate local economic growth? Our intention then is to draw some broader conclusions about the overall effectiveness of enterprise zone policy. The first part of this chapter discusses some of the broader issues relating to the modeling of taxes and growth and reviews the results of previous econometric studies of the effects of taxes in general, and enterprise zones in particular, on growth. In the second section, we review some of the technical issues involved in building an econometric model; this is followed by a description of how we dealt with the major methodological issues in constructing our own series of statistical models of taxes and growth. In the final section, we provide our econometric results, based on two separate analyses. The first relies on our sample of 65 enterprise zones in 13 states. The second is a more spatially focused analysis of 104 enterprise zone and non-enterprise zone communities in Ohio.

Before proceeding any further it is worth reiterating two points. First, from the national perspective, it is unclear whether incentives, including enterprise zone incentives, actually result in—or *cause*—entirely new growth, rather than merely shifting investment spatially. In this chapter, growth means growth in the particular localities in our study; we do not prejudge the wider question of the effect of incentives on net growth for the nation as a whole. Second, to the extent that they are not capitalized in land prices, enterprise zone incentives reduce the costs associated with a new business investment and thus increase the income derived from that investment. As we argued in Chapter 2 (see note 22), it is most unlikely that incentives are fully capitalized. Later, in Chapter 3, we provided estimates of the income advantage afforded by an enterprise zone location and the savings from enterprise zone incentives compared to another important location cost—wages. We found that enterprise zone incentives were fairly small when translated into wage equivalents—so small, in fact, that even quite limited local variation in wage rates could easily wipe out the business income advantages conferred by incentives. Thus our non-econometric evidence suggests that it is likely that zone incentives influence business location and investment decisions only in exceptional circumstances.

When we began writing this book, we had expected to find confirmation, at the enterprise zone level, of what has become the current consensus in the taxes and growth literature—that taxes and tax incentives have positive, but modest, effects on local growth. Our results do not confirm this position. Indeed, both our national and Ohio models show that enterprise zone incentives have no appreciable impact on local establishment growth. Given one of the important (non-econometric) findings of Chapter 3 (that the local benefits of incentives could be easily wiped out by local differentials in labor costs), and given the recent econometric literature on enterprise zones (more than half of which suggests that enterprise zone incentives have little impact on local growth), our results should not be surprising. Nevertheless, we feel it incumbent on us to say that since the extant literature on enterprise zone incentives and growth is still small, it would be foolish to claim that the models we present in this chapter are the final word on the relationship between enterprise zone incentives and local economic activity. They are not.

MODELS OF TAXES AND GROWTH—
BACKGROUND ISSUES

At heart, the relationship between enterprise zones and economic growth is merely a part of a much broader, well-studied problem: the relationship between state and local taxes—including tax incentives—and economic growth. We will begin our discussion of modeling by looking at how researchers have approached the broader issue and only then move on to the particular case of enterprise zones.

Econometric Models and Alternative Approaches

While politicians and a few policy analysts have been happy to view the relationship between taxes and growth quite simplistically—

seeing whether low-tax states have high levels of growth—most academics looking at this issue have employed various econometric modeling methods. The reason the econometric approach dominates academic work on the connection between state and local taxes and growth is probably partly institutional—applied economists dominate the field—and partly substantive. Given that so many factors could cause local economic growth, attempting to identify the impact of any single factor raises the old counterfactual issue: "Was growth a function of this particular factor x or some other less visible factor y?" In principle, the statistical techniques on which econometric models are based allow the researcher to hold constant other important factors and thus to be able to focus on particular important policy factors, one at a time.

Consider this example. Some high business tax states—for instance, California—have, at times, experienced long periods of growth. Correlating growth and taxes in such states would lead to the conclusion that high taxes cause high growth and, presumably, low business taxes cause low growth. This conclusion is almost certainly wrong because it fails to account for the other factors causing growth, including high population growth, defense spending, high levels of entrepreneurialism in some fast-growing industries, and so on. In order to see the "true" relationship between state and local business taxes and California's economic growth, we have to be able to control for these other factors. Indeed, the central difficulty encountered by econometric researchers in the area of taxes and growth is how best empirically to account for—or model—these other factors.

In order to better understand the usefulness of econometric models in the study of taxes and growth, it would be helpful to consider the problems associated with alternative non-econometric approaches to this issue. Four broad categories of alterative approaches can be identified: 1) surveys of business opinion on taxes; 2) case studies of the impact of particular taxes and incentives on growth; 3) general equilibrium models; and 4) hypothetical firm models.[1] Business surveys have a number of well-documented problems: response rates tend to be very low; those not directly involved in new investment or relocation decisions may be the ones to fill out the survey instrument, significantly distorting results; respondents have an incentive to lie about the importance of taxes (and incentives) in their decision-making process since business executives have a material interest in lower taxes. Moreover, it is difficult to know what the ranking of different factors—which most surveys require of respondents—may actually mean in practice. The problems here are both behavioral—how well such things are remembered—and theoretical—to what common denominator are, say, environmental rules, tax regimes, community support for business, and so on, to be reduced? The net result of these problems is that it is extremely difficult to use the survey method to resolve what we have called the "counterfactual problem"—measuring factors one at a time, each time holding all other factors constant.

The ultimate problem with the case-study method is much the same. Work in this tradition—and a large amount of work on enterprise zones has been in this tradition[2]—takes a region to which some tax and incentive policy measure has been applied and then compares growth levels before and after the application. The obvious problem is that if, say, Los Angeles were doing poorly in 1990 and well in 1999, and there had been some lessening of the business tax burden in the intervening years, jumping to the conclusion that the tax change caused renewed growth would be premature, possibly entirely false. As we indicated earlier, other factors may have caused that growth. Indeed, in the case of California, it is clear that other factors were the important ones.

In better examples of the case-study method, some attempt is made to control for the counterfactual problem. For instance, the basic case-study technique may be combined with a survey attempting to determine how many firms actually responded to a change in tax regime (see, for instance, Rubin 1991). Or shift-share techniques are used to try to eliminate, or hold constant, growth caused by other factors and thus identify "unusual," "unexpected," local growth (see, for instance, Rubin and Wilder 1989). However, the shift-share method is, for this purpose anyway, crude. The so-called differential-shift (or regional-shift) term—the term that measures the level of "unusual" growth—then accounts for all other local factors, only one of which is the change in taxes.[3] Thus the term contains too much to be used as a control for all other causal factors.[4]

While there appears to be agreement that the relationship between state and local taxes and growth would best be examined in the broader framework of some general (and spatial) equilibrium model, since this would allow a much more comprehensive coverage of the forces interacting with the local economy, the practical and empirical difficulties associated with doing this have discouraged much use of the method (Morgan, Mutti, and Partridge 1989; Isard et al. 1998). Certainly, no applications of this technique to American enterprise zones exist, though we expect this situation to change over the next few years.

The final non-econometric approach to studying the relation between taxes and growth—one that we and a few others have adopted—is to attack the problem from an entirely different angle: to measure what a particular tax or incentive does for a particular firm's income. For instance, one could measure the extent to which an investment tax credit raises an investment's internal rate of return as we do in Chapter 3. The counterfactual problem can then be resolved two different ways. First, tax costs can be compared to precise estimates of other important, spatially variant factor costs borne by the firm. We have tried to do this in some previous work as well as in Chapter 3 of this book: compare tax costs to labor costs.[5] Although this method has much to recommend it, a number of problems exist. While there is no theoretical reason why other nonlabor costs could not be compared to tax costs, in practice they have not been. Indeed, the practical difficulties here are large, so large we are not sure that this is an entirely viable strategy. Moreover, this method suffers from a problem latent in the other methods, but most clearly visible here. Taxes are paid in return for state and local government goods and services. There is no control for the worth of these goods and services to individual firms. One could imagine creating a model that contained such a control, but again the practical difficulties are enormous.

It is hard to know how important the public service problem is. There is some evidence that firms massively overpay state and local taxes compared to the benefits they receive from government (Oakland and Testa 1996). If this is indeed true then there is less damage to be done by merely focusing on the tax end. It is also likely that in making new investment and location decisions, business—after assembling a set of locations that meets its most important locational needs—responds more to the current state and local tax regime than to expectations of state- and city-produced goods and services.[6]

Probably the best way of dealing with the counterfactual problem is to put the tax results of a hypothetical firm model into the right-hand side of an econometric model of taxes and growth. The additional factors that need controlling may then be represented by other right-hand side variables: labor costs (productivity-adjusted), access to markets, the quality of government goods and services, and so on. A few researchers have adopted just such a strategy (Steinnes 1984; L. Papke 1987; Tannenwald and Kendrick 1995; Tannenwald 1996), as indeed we do later in this chapter.

The Contradictory Findings of Econometric Studies

Early surveys of the literature suggested that, at best, state and local taxes have only a minor influence on business location decisions (Due 1961; Oakland 1978). Various reasons continue to be given for this seemingly counterintuitive proposition, but the most persuasive are:

- State and local taxes account for such a small share of spatially variable business costs that their influence is swamped by other larger costs, such as labor and transportation.
- Federal taxes massively reduce the actual variability of state and local taxes.
- State and local tax differences reflect differences in the quality and quantity of state and local government services.

More recent reviews of the literature tend to be increasingly positive on the impacts of state and local taxes on location decisions and growth. Newman and Sullivan's (1988) influential review, which paid special attention to issues of model specification, concludes: "The most recent studies, employing more detailed data sets and more refined econometric techniques, have generated results which cast some doubt on the received conclusion that tax effects are generally negligible" (Newman and Sullivan 1988, p. 232). Then in 1991, Bartik published a most comprehensive review of the post-1979 literature and concluded that there was growing consensus that state and local taxes have a small but significant influence on location decisions. Moreover, Bartik was prepared to say what that consensus was. Averaging the results of a very large number of studies:

> The long-run elasticity of business activity with respect to state and local taxes appears to lie in the range of –0.1 to –0.6 for inter-metropolitan or interstate business location decisions, and –1.0 to –3.0 for intrametropolitan business location decisions. That is, if a small suburban jurisdiction within a metropolitan area raises its

taxes 10 percent, it can expect in the long run a reduction in its business activity from 10 to 30 percent. If an entire metropolitan area or state raises its taxes by 10 percent, the estimated long-run effect would be a reduction of business activity between 1 percent and 6 percent. (Bartik 1991, p. 43)

The reasons for the development of a research consensus on a link between taxes and growth have got to do with technical improvements in the literature—a point Newman and Sullivan (1988) also made—and with the increasing homogenization of other spatially variable factor costs across the U.S. Wasylenko's (1997) more recent review for the Boston Federal Reserve generally supports Bartik's claims although Wasylenko cautions that the results appear to be dependent on the data sets used, time periods covered and the variables included in the estimating equations. In a review of the literature on the effect of non-tax incentives on growth, also for the Boston Federal Reserve, we argue that while the research uniformly shows a statistically and substantively significant link between non-tax incentives and growth, these results may be entirely spurious given that they are all dependent on fairly dubious data sets (Fisher and Peters 1997a).

Other respected researchers in the field remain unconvinced by the "consensus position" and the matter remains anything but settled (McGuire 1992, 1997; Netzer 1997). Crucial issues are the variability of elasticity estimates, findings with regard to specific tax incentives appearing to contradict those for general taxes, and skepticism that the tax models capture the way firms make investment and location decisions (see also Ady 1997). Certainly, the best and most numerous studies are at the interstate and intermetropolitan level, but even here the elasticities (the actual measure of the effect of taxes on growth) are not large. On the other hand, the intrametropolitan studies are very few in number, and the results are all over the landscape. Frankly we are skeptical that a 33 percent business tax cut would induce a 100 percent increase in business activity, which Bartik claims is a credible upper limit on the effect.

The econometric literature that focuses on taxes and incentives in enterprise zones, as opposed to the effects of taxes generally, is small. As with the survey method, some of the early statistical work focused on issues of correct zone management where the relationship between enterprise zones and growth is only implicit. Elling and Sheldon

(1991), for instance, developed models looking at enterprise zone success—the number of firms qualifying for zone benefits by investing in the zone—in four states: Illinois, Indiana, Kentucky, and Ohio. They found enterprise zones to have been largely ineffective, and argue that "business cost-reduction tools"—in other words, tax incentives—were of little consequences to zone success because "they are so widely available and, hence, do little to differentiate a zone from any other location in the eyes of relocating firms" (Elling and Sheldon 1991, p. 151).[7] The most successful zones they found were where what they call a "pure" zone strategy—tax incentives—had been complemented by more traditional economic development support (technical assistance, location and site analysis, and so on). Insofar as they reflect on the relationship between enterprise zones and growth, Elling and Sheldon's conclusions are open to question. Their measures of taxes and incentives (as well as regulatory relief) are by current standards poor indeed, and their models—leaving out, as they do, almost all traditional location factors—suggest mis-specification for our purposes.

Erickson and Friedman (1990a) were the first to address the enterprise zone-growth issue directly.[8] They looked at two measures of zone success: first, jobs created or saved by firms investing in the zones after designation; and second, the number of firms investing in the zone after designation. Exogenous variables included 1) a number of policy variables meant to define how zones were administered, 2) a crude incentive variable—the number of verified incentives offered by the state, 3) a set of welfare variables reflecting zone designation and incentive criteria, but usefully also measuring the economic distress of zone residents, and 4) various control variables (population and area of the zone, and employment change in the surrounding MSA or county). In both the establishments and the jobs equations, the incentive variable was statistically significant and very positive. These conclusions are clearly at odds with Elling and Sheldon's and suggest that incentives offered in enterprise zones do generate local growth. Unfortunately, it would be unwise to put too much store by these results. Besides the problems associated with the way the incentive variable was measured, the jobs and establishments figures come from the reports of zone managers. There is every reason to believe that such a data set is highly unreliable.

As we indicated in Chapter 2, Leslie Papke (1994) has done some of the most convincing and sophisticated work in this area. She analyzed the Indiana enterprise zone program. Her research is notable for the geographical spatial scale of the data, the care taken in model building, and the incentive and "growth" variables analyzed—changes in the levels of machinery and equipment and inventories investment, and unemployment claims. The first two variables were defined at the Indiana taxing-district level and unemployment by claims made to local unemployment claims offices. Although there are serious questions about the reliability of her three outcomes data sets, her work represents one the best attempts to separate out the enterprise zone from its surrounding communities. Papke then estimates a number of different specifications of her model (all of which include jurisdictional fixed effects).

Papke's most consistent findings are that zone designation leads to 1) a decline in machinery and equipment, 2) an increase in inventories, and 3) a decrease in unemployment claims of about 19 percent in the year after designation. Papke (1994, pp. 43–44) notes that since the most valuable Indiana incentive applies to the stock of inventory (which is otherwise subject to high Indiana property-tax rates), the first two findings may represent a shift "in the composition of assets from depreciable property toward inventories." The third finding suggests very substantial employment effects. Related work by Papke (1993) on the census blocks composing the Indiana zones appears to validate her econometric results—for instance, unemployment fell more in zones than non-zones—although the "zone effects estimated with the census data [were] weaker than those estimated econometrically" (L. Papke 1993, p. 60).

However, more recent studies, done with as much care as Papke's, do not support her conclusions. Boarnet and Bogart (1996), using methods similar to Papke's, found no evidence that the New Jersey enterprise zone program resulted in increased economic activity. Admittedly, Boarnet and Bogart caution that the Indiana and New Jersey programs are very different and the differences in findings could reflect this fact. However, Greenbaum (1998), in a very well-designed study, examined the impact of state enterprise zones on both business and housing market outcomes in six major states. The analysis was undertaken at the ZIP-code level, in part using the same SSEL data source (though not the same data) that we used in the previous chapter and use again in this one. He found that while enterprise zones may create new business activity, these gains tend to be offset by shrinking business establishments in zones. The result is that overall zones have little impact on business outcomes. He finds also that zones have no impact on overall employment growth (but some impact on employment growth among new establishments).

Most recently, Bondonio and Engberg (2000) found that, as predictors of growth, neither the monetary value of enterprise zone incentives offered nor the particular features of enterprise zone programs mattered very much. This is confirmed by Greenbaum and Engberg (2000), who found that enterprise zones have little positive impact on housing market, income, or employment outcomes. Thus the majority of the recent literature comes down on the side of enterprise zones having little or no impact on growth.

The variation in the conclusions among these studies may have many causes. The differences may reflect divergence in effectiveness across states. As likely is that the variation reflects the difficulties of measurement, the discussion of which will occupy much of this chapter. There are no perfect data sets, and there is continuing debate on appropriate methodology. Nevertheless, the important point here is that the variation in conclusions suggests policy caution.

BUILDING ECONOMETRIC MODELS OF TAXES AND GROWTH

It should be clear by now that econometric studies of taxes and growth are controversial and that the results of these studies are not in agreement. Leaving aside the broader issue of the appropriateness of the methodology, there are a number of complex technical issues which each econometric study of this question must successfully address. It is to these technical issues that we now turn.

Broader Methodological Issues

As supporters of the survey technique like to point out, business location decisions are complex (Calzonetti and Walker 1991). For instance, it is now well understood that a firm's location decision will actually encompass a sequential set of decisions at increasingly refined geographical scales. A firm may, for instance, first focus on a region of the country with particularly good access to markets, energy costs and so on; then may choose a subregion on the basis of a set of other variables, such as labor costs, unionization, and possibly state taxation; then narrow the location decision down to the metropolitan level (possibly focusing on highway access), then the city level (possibly looking at local taxes among other things), and then within a set of cities, various actual sites.[9] This poses two major problems for typical econometric models. 1) There are a vast number of potential costs that firms may respond to; how a particular firm responds to a particular cost is likely to depend on that firm's particular factor composition. 2) The sequential decision-making process may mean, for instance, that a state with very low taxes is excluded from the selection process because it did not make the first "regional" cut. Some researchers do not believe it is currently possible to capture these complexities in econometric equations.

Likewise, while most econometric models try to explain aggregate economic activity in an area—such as net changes in employment, state product, and so on—the estimating equations tend to focus on only one aspect of aggregate local growth—the location of new branch plants.[10] But aggregate local growth is made up of a number of business decisions apart from the location of new branch plants—plant expansions, contractions, closings, and restructuring and small business start-up decisions. Each of these components of aggregate economic change will have its own, partially unique, set of determinants.

Finally there is the concern that many of the key factors influencing either aggregate local growth or the location of new branch plants may not be amenable to empirical measurement. Public services, wages, taxes, and state and local regulation of business are typical examples. Although the federal government publishes a number of different wage data series, the econometric problem is that, in the best of worlds, wages would need to be adjusted for productivity and possibly the cost of supplying certain mandated benefits, such as unemployment insurance.[11] With regard to public services, we need to measure outputs: the quality and quantity of the services produced. Unfortunately, there are few uncontroversial output measures, and public service inputs—the costs of providing services—are a poor guide to outputs. Even if they were a better guide, the quantity and quality of public goods and services are functions not only of current spending but also of historical spending (roads and bridges being a good example of this). With regard to taxes, one needs to be able to measure the real tax burden on firms, and there is solid evidence that tax burdens do not correlate with state business income tax rates or even with so-called effective tax rates (J. Papke 1995; Fisher and Peters 1998). Finally, state and local regulation of economic activity is an area only recently receiving the attention it deserves, and issues such as local land-use and zoning controls are almost entirely absent from the econometric literature.

As the discussion in Chapter 3 indicates, we believe there are ways of resolving the measurement of business taxes. These do require massive effort, but the result is a much more sensitive—though not perfect—measurement of business taxes. We believe the other difficult factors are also amenable to comprehensive measurement, although much of the work, particularly in the area of state and local regulation, still needs to be done.[12] We do not undertake that work in this book.

Technical Issues of Model Structure

There is broad agreement on the major technical questions that models of taxes and growth must address. But providing convincing answers to these issues within an empirical modeling setting is anything but a simple task. Besides resolving the issues raised above, models of state and local taxes and growth must also be able to control for so-called fixed effects, the endogeneity of some explanatory variables, and the durability of both capital and agglomeration economies. Simply put, in state and local taxes/growth models, fixed-effect controls are designed to account statistically for the unobservable characteristics of regions or states or cities, characteristics that may affect growth but that are not captured by the other variables in the equation(s). Typically, this requires creating regional (or state or city) dummy variables. Failure to do this will result in omitted variable bias—essentially, the impact of the omitted variables will show up in the estimated parameters of the included explanatory variables.

The relationship between the dependent variable (some measure of growth) and the explanatory variables is often causally complex. For instance, all else being equal, lower wages in an area would tend to increase the growth in that area. But higher growth would tend to increase the demand for labor and thus wages would increase, and so on. Other explanatory variables found in taxes/growth models, particularly policy variables, often cause the same problem. In particular, low taxes may induce growth, but growth in the industrial tax base may in turn permit reductions in the property-tax rate. The problem—endogeneity—is that the explanatory variables are having causal effects on the dependent variable, *and* vice versa. It can be shown that failure to deal with this problem will result in both biased and inconsistent parameter estimates. In the case of the effect of taxes on growth, there will be a tendency to exaggerate the negative impact on growth. One possible solution to this problem is to find instrumental variables that replace the offending endogenous variables in the estimating equations.

Also, an area's economic climate today will tend to be correlated with its climate yesterday, or a year ago, or two years ago. The reason for this is that both capital and agglomeration economies are durable. Thus a good part of the explanation of why city x is growing during period t is its growth in period $t-1$. Typically, some lagged measure of economic growth is used to control for this problem.

Special Modeling Problems Posed by Enterprise Zones

Over and above the technical issues just described, constructing a rigorous model of taxes and growth at the level of the enterprise zone poses serious empirical problems. Enterprise zones are usually subcounty, subcity regions. They tend not to be coterminous with tracts or sets of tracts (although they are almost always coterminous with sets of blocks). Most economic data are published at the county level, and even at this level, the requirements of privacy mean that in many smaller- and medium-sized counties, much data cannot be made public. Some economic data are indeed published at the ZIP-code level (*County Business Patterns*, for instance), but here the issues of privacy are that much worse, with much less useful data resulting. Moreover, from research and policy points of view, enterprise zones exist both in cities and in contradistinction to those cities. In the best of worlds the researcher would want to be able to compare the economic performance of the enterprise zone with the city in which it exists. But many of the factors that are commonly used to explain business location decisions are impossible or difficult to measure at the subcounty or subplace level. The fixed-effects estimation method can be very useful here since any characteristic of an enterprise zone that is constant over the period of the analysis—local infrastructure, labor, distance to markets, and so on—is controlled for by the individual enterprise zone effects. Unfortunately, where the fixed-effect controls used are regional, as they are in the analyses presented later in this chapter (for the national analysis, they are state specific), this is not possible.

Labor market data pose both theoretical and empirical difficulties. Labor markets—and thus the productivity and cost of labor—are usually seen as being defined by Metropolitan Statistical Area (MSA) boundaries. Indeed, MSAs are constructed, in part, out of commuting flow data. If labor markets are, in fact, defined by MSA boundaries, then labor (supply) differences between city and the enterprise zone markets may be illusory. But there is evidence—admittedly limited—from both the spatial mismatch and the gender and employment literatures which suggests that for some workers, functional labor markets are defined very narrowly and are certainly much smaller than MSAs. For instance, in a series of studies based on Worcester, Massachusetts, labor markets, Hanson and Pratt (1990, 1991, 1995) found that some blue-collar employees traveled very limited distances to their work sites; job-search behavior was consistent with this distance. Part of the reason for this appears to be that sometimes information about work opportunities does not flow freely; rather, it is disseminated by informal and often restricted social networks.

Early work in the spatial mismatch paradigm suggested that close access to buoyant job markets has important positive impacts on job-search behavior, labor-force participation, and employment rates and wages (Clark and Whiteman 1983).[13] If this is true then it is possible that taxes/growth models should be able to distinguish enterprise zone labor markets from city labor markets.[14] And if the latter is true, then further practical problems arise. There is little useful labor market information published at the subcounty and subplace level; furthermore, what information there is poses the sort of geographical issues we discuss in Appendix E (for instance, although there are ZIP-code region labor force data,[15] ZIP-code regions are not coterminous with enterprise zones).

Other right-hand-side factors bring further problems. Given the original intent of enterprise zones, one would expect them to be in older, inner-city areas. One would expect such areas to be more likely to have older, more decrepit infrastructure, older factories, and so on

(Dabney 1991). Thus enterprise zones should tend to be at some disadvantage compared to newer suburban industrial areas. If one is to measure the effect that particular enterprise zone tax credits have on local growth, then one must be able to control for the quality and quantity of enterprise zone infrastructure, or more generally, the quality and quantity of enterprise zone public services. The problem is that even outside of enterprise zones, there is no entirely acceptable way of measuring the quality and quantity of local or even regional infrastructure. Indeed, there were a number of research projects during the 1990s devoted entirely to this issue.[16] In subplace regions, such as enterprise zones, where records are seldom kept, the situation is that much worse.

Another important factor is access to markets. In many standard taxes/growth models this is reduced to differences in transportation costs incurred at various sites. Again, if the issue is the difference between the enterprise zone and the city, then the question is to what extent the transportation costs in the enterprise zone are higher than in the rest of the city. In an ideal world one would measure the average transportation cost to each major (or possibly every) market, using a geographic information system that would have the entire U.S. road network programmed into it. The true cost differential between transporting a good from site A in city x to its various markets and transporting the good from enterprise zone site B in city x could then be calculated. But this has never been done in the context of econometric models of growth and taxes. Our market information is too poor and the computerized network models too underdeveloped.

Given these problems, it is common to approach the transportation-cost issue in a considerably cruder manner. For instance, how far from a highway on-ramp is the enterprise zone compared to non-enterprise zone industrial sites in the city? In early versions of the research we undertook for this book, in fact, we used precisely such a measure. The problem is that even a cursory look at the road networks of most cities indicates that in medium-sized and larger cities access to the single closest on-ramp massively distorts real-world transportation choices. It also results in some serious anomalies. One Ohio enterprise zone we include in our intraregional model had fairly good access to a four-lane highway on-ramp, but this highway peters out before connecting to any other four-lane highway. So the question cannot be: Does the enterprise zone have better access to an on-ramp? Rather, it should be: Does the enterprise zone provide better or worse access to the wider transportation infrastructure available? The latter question is not easily answered. One further point here. For factories that transport their goods far or transport their goods in the snowy North where there is considerable variability in road speeds and thus transportation time, a mean five- or ten-minute disadvantage getting onto the highway system may have a marginal or non-existent impact on final business location choices.

Similar sorts of problems obtain for the other factors that are sometimes included in tax and growth models. The upshot is that while there are difficult statistical issues that need to be dealt with, there are also a range of more mundane empirical issues that hamper our ability to build such models.

THE STRUCTURE OF OUR MODEL

The SSEL Data and Constraints on Spatial and Temporal Comparisons

The SSEL data that are used to create the dependent variables in our econometric models of growth, while having a number of important advantages over other data sets, impose a certain structure on our models. The data are at the ZIP-code-region level—they are not for individual firms. Thus, we are unable to model the location decisions of individual firms with the result that our analysis takes a fairly traditional regional cross-section form. The data are organized into three periods: 1989–1991, 1991–1993, and 1993–1995. At the time we requested special census runs from the Bureau of the Census, 1989 was the first year for which linked, longitudinal SSEL data were available, while 1995 was the last year that would be available in time for completion of this research project. Therefore, historical models, with areas that were not enterprise zones becoming enterprise zones during one of the three periods, were impossible to construct for the national sample (although this was possible for our Ohio sample).

Our national model compares 65 enterprise zones in 13 states *to each other*, not to the cities in which they exist. Each data point is an enterprise zone. The model is intended to answer the question: Do zones with greater tax advantages experience more rapid growth in manufacturing establishments than zones with relatively disadvantageous tax and incentive regimes? Such a model does not allow us to say whether designation of a zone generates growth apart from the incentives offered in the zone. We look at the effect of enterprise zone incentives on growth, but not at the effect of enterprise zone designation (or the effects of other local development activities that may go on within zones).

Two methodological questions arise. First, regression analysis requires that the sample universe be "real." Do enterprise zones represent such a universe, or are they so varied across states that they should not be classed as a single policy tool? If we were considering all U.S. state-level enterprise zones, this problem would indeed pose serious obstacles to our research. We have chosen states, however, with programs that accord as a whole with the traditional zone approach, especially the focus on geographic targeting (we exclude states in which zones are little more than delivery mechanisms for standard state economic development policy). For instance, we have not included Louisiana with its thousands of zones since these clearly represent an entirely different sort of policy beast. We have included Ohio—which has a large number of nontargeted zones—but for our national model we include only those Ohio enterprise zones that qualify under economic distress criteria and thus are the recipients of special targeted incentives. Moreover, the whole point of the TAIM^{ez} model is to reduce various sorts of incentives to a common denominator, one that is both theoretically sound and methodologically feasible: the impact of incentives on business income. Thus we believe we do have a coherent universe for our regressions.

Second, since we do not have control groups in our national models (areas that are not zones or were not zones for some of the time during the analysis period that we compare our sample to), are we not just doing a traditional cross-sectional tax model, but with even less variation in the tax variable than traditional tax models? Essentially, there are four related criticisms here:

- Our models are not really enterprise zone models, but merely traditional cross-sectional tax models of the sort commonly found in the taxes/growth literature.

- There is likely to be less variation in effective tax rates among enterprise zones than among states or cities.
- Our models lack a spatial control group—areas that we compare our enterprise zones to.
- Our models lack an historical control group—we do not compare zone performance *after* designation to performance *prior to* designation.

With regard to the first two criticisms, while it is true that our national models do not measure zone effects per se—but the *effects* of variation in zone incentive levels—this is still an interesting and important issue. This is so because the broad tax effects on growth that have been found throughout the United States do not necessarily apply to enterprise zones. The major reason for this is that the "locational negatives" of zones may effectively neutralize zone incentives. Zone incentives may very well have effects different from those predicted by broader tax models. Moreover, contrary to the claims of Eisinger (1988) and others, incentives do not work to mitigate spatial variation in basic tax structure across states and cities, but rather to exaggerate the variation (Fisher and Peters 1998).

With regard to the criticism that we lack a spatial control group, there is reason to be skeptical about econometric attempts to compare zones to non-zones. In the states we analyze, enterprise zones have been selected for a range of specific policy reasons. They are not random policy experiments. Thus a case could be made that no true comparison regions exist. If this is correct then direct comparison of zones and non-zones may result in selection bias. Moreover, generating controls would have been a massive task. In all but a few cases, zones are shaped perversely; given the shape of ZIP-code regions, coherent zone/non-zone regions are close to impossible to construct.[17] Note, however, that in our Ohio models we do have both zone and non-zone *communities* in our sample. In this case the comparison is appropriate since the Ohio models are not restricted (and could not be restricted) to targeted zones.

With regard to lack of historical controls and the failure to look at the differences in enterprise zone areas prior to and after designation, two further points need be made. Generating historical controls (say, pre- and post-designation) was impossible for the national sample, given the SSEL data we used. This data set has other attributes that make it particularly useful in evaluating the performance of zones (for instance, completeness even when sectorally disaggregated). Furthermore, over anything but the shortest term, we doubt that firms respond merely to zone designation. Rather, they respond to the benefits that designation brings, that is, zone incentives. Thus, focusing on incentives is at least as methodologically appropriate as comparing zones to non-zones.

An important concern, however, is that it is possible that enterprise zones may be more than the incentives offered and that firms do react to "mere" designation. Some studies of enterprise zone effects have found that designation is more important than the incentives offered (U.S. Department of Housing and Urban Development (HUD) 1986). In a survey of the recent literature, Wilder and Rubin (1996, p. 481) wrote:

> Virtually every study has found that employment and investment activity increased in *most* zones after program implementation. However, there was seldom a simple or direct relationship between the new economic activity and the development incentives. Some studies found that many qualified zone firms had not taken advantage of incentives, yet had engaged in new or expanded activity. This outcome . . . reflects a more indirect effect of enterprise zones: that is, that the business community takes the mere existence of the zone as a signal that the city and state have made a commitment to the zone area. That perceived commitment has a positive influence on decisions about investment and location.

If this is true, then enterprise zone designation acts as a marketing device (Wolkoff 1992) and plays a symbolic role serving as an indicator of the local business climate and commitment by the public sector (Wilder and Rubin 1996, p. 482). Designation indicates to business that incentives will be offered, that land-use issues will be dealt with more promptly, and so on. The evidence on this issue is anything but settled. Certainly, many of the studies covered in Wilder and Rubin (1996) did not fully separate designation from incentives—however, many of those that did found that incentives were substantively important, even if only at the margin of location and investment decisions.[18] And most location theory suggests that insofar as firms react to state and local fiscal regimes, it is differences in actual tax costs that are important. All in all, we felt concerns over the designation/incentives issue need to be addressed directly. Thus we constructed a set of models for 104 Ohio cities able to distinguish between zones and non-zones, and including areas which became zones during one of our three time periods. In these models, zone designation enters into the equation separately from the financial benefits of zones (taxes and tax incentives). Of the 104 cities in our Ohio sample (drawn from cities over 15,000 population), 50 had one or more zones in 1990, 57 in 1992, and 65 in 1994. That is, 15 cities established zones between 1990 and 1994. There were 51 zones in the 50 cities in 1990, 60 zones in 1992, and 68 zones in 1994.

Again, the Ohio analyses are conducted at the ZIP-code level and growth data are from the SSEL. The analysis is restricted to Ohio because that is one of the few states in the nation that collects and publishes comprehensive local tax data. Also, Ohio has well over 200 zones, making this sort of analysis feasible. Note, however, that zones are not being compared to the cities in which they exist—rather, Ohio zone cities are being compared to non-zone cities. More often than not, in Ohio cities with enterprise zones nearly all land zoned for industry is contained by the zone. Many of the cities in the Ohio sample, in fact, consist of a single ZIP-code region. For the sake of comparability we try to keep our Ohio model as close as possible to our main model. The Ohio models draw on a sample that covers cities without zones, cities with targeted zones, and cities with nontargeted zones.

The Question of Panel Data

For both our national and Ohio equations we have cross-sections ($N = 65$ different locations for the national model, $N = 104$ for the Ohio model) and panels or time periods ($t = 3$). In order to improve the efficiency of the parameter estimates, it is common practice to pool cross-sections with time periods, giving nearly 189 cases for our national sample, for instance.[19] Pooling raises questions of model structure, however. If one can be certain the regression parameters will remain constant across cross-sections and panels, then a simple pooling of cases is appropriate—this is sometimes referred to as the "constant coefficients" model (Sayrs 1989). Unfortunately, in state and local taxes/ growth models, there is seldom good reason to assume such constancy.

One alternative is the addition of spatial and temporal fixed effects. Earlier in this chapter, as part of a more general discussion of the structure of tax/growth models, we indicated the usefulness of geographical fixed effects in accounting for unobserved state or local characteristics that may affect growth. Pooled models with spatial or temporal fixed effects are sometimes called covariance models[20] and have the advantage of permitting equation intercepts to vary by space and time.[21] Covariance models have been widely utilized in the taxes/growth literature. Provided the standard assumptions about the disturbance term are met, ordinary least squares estimates of parameters will be unbiased and consistent but not efficient (except when t is large).

Unfortunately, covariance models also have their problems. The addition of large numbers of dummy variables will decrease a model's degrees of freedom and, thus, its statistical power. One consequence of this is that researchers often specify models that include only cross-sectional fixed effects, ignoring temporal fixed effects (Isard et al. 1998, p. 189; Pindyck and Rubinfeld 1998, p. 253). For much the same reason, in the taxes/growth literature (and indeed in the following analysis), regional rather than cross-sectional fixed effects are sometimes used. Another problem is that the space and time dummy variables are substantively meaningless.

A third alternative is a "random effects" model, or some variation on this. In this approach, the error term of a cross-sectional panel model (ε_{it}) is broken into three components: cross-sectional error (u_i); time error (v_t); and a combined error component (w_{it}). Unlike the covariance model, where the time and cross-section dummies represent essentially our lack of knowledge about the impact of time and geography, in the random effects model our lack of knowledge—the error specific to time and cross-section—is described directly in the (first two) components of the disturbance term. This gives rise to the central advantage the random effects model has over the covariance model—it uses up fewer degrees of freedom and thus is statistically more powerful. However, the method requires that the error term components not be correlated with the explanatory variables in the model. If that assumption is not met, parameter estimates may be inconsistent. Generalized least squares procedures are often used for parameter estimation, although, if one is prepared to assume normal distribution of the error components, the maximum likelihood method may be preferred. It should also be noted that there are variations on the covariance and random effects models (see Hsiao 1986); moreover, there are a number of alternative ways of dealing with pooled data sets, including structural equation models (Sayrs 1989).

Although there are statistical tests comparing the power of models using these three methods, the appropriateness of the model used will also depend on the data at hand and the explanatory needs of the analysis. For our main national model we present estimates based on the covariance or fixed effects model although we also ran various constant coefficients and random effects (using maximum likelihood estimators) models. We focus on our fixed effect results since we doubt that the constant parameter assumption of the constant coefficient model can be met,[22] and we doubt that the error components of the random effects model are indeed uncorrelated with the explanatory variables. Also, the limited number of time periods suggests that without time intercepts the random effects model is inappropriate. Later in this chapter we mention certain multi-equation models used to analyze issues of potential variable simultaneity. Here the use of the random effects model is considerably more difficult to implement and does not provide preferred solutions over the simpler but more robust OLS models (Hsiao 1986; Sayrs 1989). Overall then, we believe the fixed effects models to be our strongest.

RESULTS

Our national base model was run for all 65 enterprise zones (in 13 states) in our national data set for three time periods. The model was run for all of manufacturing with the dependent variable the rate of growth of *new* establishments in the enterprise zone—technically, the new births and moves in expressed as a percent of the number of establishments at the beginning of the period.[23] We report parameters from the ordinary least squares fixed effects estimates. Not reported here are the time and state[24] intercepts of the fixed effects models. The Ohio models generally mirror the national models.

Independent variables in our models fall into four groups: 1) proxies for major spatially variant costs—wages, market access, electricity, public services, and agglomeration; 2) taxes and incentives and enterprise zone designation; 3) measures of the demographic characteristics of enterprise zones—race, poverty, unemployment, and skills; and 4) appropriate controls, including a measure of earlier growth. The main variables used in both the national and Ohio models are summarized in Table 7.1; note that not all variables are used in all equations. In the Ohio models variables irrelevant at the intraregional level (for instance, transportation costs to national markets) have been removed, and various other controls necessary for the structure of the model have been changed.

In the national models, each record is an enterprise zone, where an enterprise zone is defined as a set of ZIP codes. Where possible and appropriate, ZIP-code level data from the *Census of Population, County Business Patterns,* and the SSEL databases were aggregated to construct enterprise zone level characteristics. The aggregation was performed in a Geographic Information System on the standard enterprise zone boundary definition file, as described in Appendix E. Some data were available only at a broader geographic scale than the ZIP or enterprise zone—in these cases no aggregation was necessary.

With the exception of unemployment rate, all the demographic characteristics of enterprise zones are measured at the ZIP-code level—the percentage African American, the percentage in poverty, and the percentage of the population with degrees. This is appropriate since the demographic variables are meant to describe the peculiar neighborhood characteristics of enterprise zones. On the other hand, the major cost variables are measured at a number of different spatial scales, the precise scale depending on the quality of the data available and on the nature of the cost. Wages rates are set in broader metropolitan labor markets, not at the neighborhood level. Moreover, reliable wage data require going to the county or MSA scale. Public service expenditures are set at the city level, although the neighborhoods that comprise an enterprise zone may have previously suffered from city service neglect. Unfortunately, more spatially disaggregated service data are not available. Electric rates for industrial users are generally the same throughout the service territory of a given electric utility; in most cases, the cities in our sample fell entirely within one service area, so that electric rates for zones could be determined unambiguously.

Table 7.1 Variables Used in Models

AGGLOMERATION	MSA or county population from Census of Population, 1990.
DISTRESS	Distress categorization for some Ohio zones.
EDUCATION	Proportion of adult population with college degree, by ZIP, weighted average for zone, Census of Population, 1990.
ELECTRIC	Average cost of electric power for industrial users, by city, 1990, 1992, 1994.
GROWTH	Births and moves in for time period t, divided by total establishments at beginning of the time period t, by ZIP, weighted average of enterprise zones, SSEL.
INFRASTRUCTURE	Proportion of housing built before 1939, by ZIP, weighted average for enterprise zone, Census of Population, 1990.
MARKET ACCESS	Proportion within 500 miles, calculated by county, calculated from city centroid, divided by 1,000,000.
POVERTY	Proportion of individuals in poverty, by ZIP, weighted average for zone, Census of Population, 1990.
PREVIOUS GROWTH	Proportion change in manufacturing employment in the MSA for preceeding three years (1986–1989 for the 1989–1991 period, for example).
RACE	Proportion African American, by ZIP, weighted average for zone, 1990.
SERVICES	Per capita city expenditure on highways, police and fire protection, 1991–1992.
TAXNET	Calculated tax rate, net of incentives, by firm in sector or weighted average of sectors for manufacturing, calculated by TAIM^{ez} for 1990, 1992, and 1994.
UNEMPLOYMENT	Average annual unemployment rate in surrounding county for the beginning-of-period year 1989, 1991, or 1993.
WAGE	County average hourly wage for all manufacturing; 1987 used for periods 1 and 2; 1992 used for period 3. Where no county wage data are available MSA wage is substituted.

Our proxy for market access is given by the population within a day's drive (500 miles) of the enterprise zone. By definition, agglomeration economies[25]—essentially, the productivity advantages that accrue to larger places—occur at the broader MSA or county level. Our proxy for the quality of enterprise zone infrastructure—the percent of housing built before 1939—is measured at the ZIP-code level. This is appropriate since there is evidence that the poor quality of neighborhood infrastructure is a significant location deterrent to new investment in enterprise zones. Finally, our measurement of both establishment births and moves in and effective tax rates is at the enterprise zone level.

In Table 7.2 we provide descriptive statistics for the main variables in the national base model. For the average zone in our national sample, 23 percent of the population is African American, 19 percent are in poverty, and 20 percent of adults have a college degree. The county or MSA unemployment rate was around 6.5 percent and the wage rate $11.56. The ZIPs that comprised the enterprise zones were old—close to a third of the housing units were built before 1939. The average zone was within a day's drive of around 72 million Americans and was in a metropolitan area of over 1 million people. The effective tax rate after

Table 7.2 Descriptive Statistics of Variables in National Base Model

Variables	Mean	Std. dev.
AGGLOMERATION (millions)	1.44	2.05
EDUCATION	0.20	0.05
ELECTRIC	5.52	1.81
GROWTH	0.19	0.08
INFRASTRUCTURE	0.30	0.16
MARKET ACCESS	72.08	28.18
POVERTY	0.19	0.08
PREVIOUS GROWTH	−0.02	0.08
RACE	0.23	0.23
SERVICES	301.37	94.10
TAXNET	0.06	0.02
UNEMPLOYMENT	6.56	2.64
WAGE	11.56	2.42

all incentives was around 6 percent and the growth rate of establish-ment births and moves in was around 19 percent per two-year period. However, the metropolitan areas in which the enterprise zones existed had seen a net decline in manufacturing employment over the three years preceding our measurement year.

Table 7.3 summarizes the results for the main national models while Table 7.4 provides elasticity estimates derived from these results. GROWTH (the growth rate of establishment births and moves in) was de-pendent. We find no evidence that more generous enterprise zone in-centives or lower net tax rates result in increased growth. Indeed, the intercept for TAXNET (the net state-local tax rate, after incentives) consis-tently has the wrong sign—if the taxes/growth literature is to be be-lieved, higher taxes should result in lower growth, not higher growth. The t value on the TAXNET parameter estimate is not statistically signifi-cant. Moreover, the estimate is substantively unimportant. A 1 percent

Table 7.3 Results from National Base and Sectoral Models[a]

	National base model		National sectoral model	
Variable	Estimate	t	Estimate	t
GROWTH, dependent				
AGGLOMERATION	0.005	1.19	0.004	0.80
EDUCATION	0.344	2.92	0.342	3.09
ELECTRIC	−0.001	0.14	0.008	1.49
INFRASTRUCTURE	−0.232	0.48	−0.159	2.98
MARKET ACCESS	0.000	0.05	−0.008	1.32
POVERTY	0.129	1.28	0.060	0.62
PREVIOUS GROWTH	0.079	1.00	0.202	2.79
RACE	−0.088	2.57	−0.038	1.00
SERVICES	0.000	0.04	0.000	1.40
TAXNET	0.277	0.76	0.213	0.82
UNEMPLOYMENT	0.006	2.37	0.000	0.00
WAGE	−0.002	0.65	−0.002	0.67
n		193		605
Adj. R^2		0.44		0.27

[a] Fixed-effect intercepts are not reported

**Table 7.4 National Base and Sectoral Models,
Elasticity Estimates**

Variable	National base model	National sectoral model
AGGLOMERATION	0.03	0.03
EDUCATION	0.35	0.37
ELECTRIC	−0.02	0.22
INFRASTRUCTURE	−0.37	−0.27
MARKET ACCESS	0.01	−0.31
POVERTY	0.13	0.06
PREVIOUS GROWTH	−0.01	−0.02
RACE	−0.10	−0.05
SERVICES	0.05	−0.13
TAXNET	0.09	0.07
UNEMPLOYMENT	0.20	0.00
WAGE	−0.11	−0.12

increase in taxes is likely to result in only a 9/100 percent increase in growth. Thus, a full doubling of taxes increases growth by only 9 percent. The mean two-year growth rate in our sample zones was 19 percent so a 100 percent increase in taxes would increase the growth rate (in births and moves in) from 19 percent to just under 21 percent. In other words, in the typical zone with around 100 existing establishments, a full doubling of taxes would result in an additional two new births or moves in. A more realistic 10 percent tax change would result in no visible net change in growth in establishments. Moreover, even a dramatic 20 percent tax change would still be too small to alter the expected number of new business births or move-ins.

We varied the tax variable in a number of ways. In some models, a TAIM^{ez}-derived measure of the size of tax incentives was used to replace TAXNET; in others, two tax variables were entered into the equation separately: 1) a TAIM^{ez} measure of basic taxes before incentives, and 2) the value of incentives expressed as a tax rate reduction. These changes did not alter our results: there was no indication that the size of enterprise zone incentives alone, basic taxes alone, or incentives and basic taxes in combination are statistically or substantively important to the rate of births and moves in.

In Chapter 4 (and elsewhere) we argued that taxes have important sectoral effects. All else being equal, firms that use a greater proportion of equipment in their production processes will have more to gain from property-tax abatements, firms that use more labor will have more to gain from jobs credits, and so on. It is thus quite possible that state and local enterprise zone incentives will not work evenly among industrial sectors. The national—and later, Ohio—sectoral models allow us to analyze this issue. The models include the necessary controls for industrial sector (we do not present parameter estimates for sectoral controls). Unfortunately, at this disaggregated level, there are sectors for which there were no establishments in a particular zone at the beginning of a period; therefore calculation of the dependent variable, GROWTH, would result in an attempted division by zero. We modified our growth variable accordingly: for the calculation of the modified GROWTH, the denominator was total establishments at the *end* of the time period. Sectors in some enterprise zones ("zone sectors") had zero ending establishments; such records were necessarily excluded from our models.

Focusing on sectors raised a number of other concerns. Many zone sectors saw no birth or move-in activity with the consequence that the GROWTH distribution was heavily skewed toward "0." Moreover, there were a number of zone sectors with high GROWTH values merely because they started out with very few establishments in that sector. A zone sector that began with only one business, saw one birth from t to $t+1$, and thus ended up with two businesses, would have a growth rate of 100 percent. But a firm that started with 10 zone sector businesses would have to have added 10 businesses to achieve the same 100 percent growth rate. Since we had decided not to use a "counts" model because enterprise zones differ so greatly in size, our solution was to limit the analysis to zone sectors that had more than 10 businesses at the beginning of each time period and that had seen some growth activity.

The national sectoral estimates from the fixed effects models are given in Table 7.3. As before, TAXNET has the wrong sign and is far from being statistically significant. The elasticity estimate from the national sectoral model is surprisingly similar to that of the national base model—0.07 compared to 0.09 (see Table 7.4). As with the national base model, replacing TAXNET with our various alternative measures of taxes and incentives had no important impact on the resulting estimates.

Most of the non-tax variables behaved in consistent ways for the base and sectoral models. For instance, higher wages (WAGE), a higher percentage of African Americans (RACE), and older infrastructure (INFRASTRUCTURE) have a consistently negative effect on growth in all models. The estimate of the agglomeration variable (AGGLOMERATION) is uniformly tiny and insignificant. The percentage of residents with degrees (EDUCATION) is consistently, positively, and significantly associated with growth.

Two other points need be made about the sectoral model. We noticed that the sectoral model worked much better for some sectors than others, so we decided to combine sectors with similar tax rates, collapsing the 16 sectors into 7, thereby reducing the problems with small numbers of establishments in particular zones.[26] The TAXNET estimate remained positive, very small, and statistically insignificant. We were concerned about the impact of our "beginning size threshold" of 10 on the results.[27] Increasing the threshold to 15 or decreasing it to 5 had almost no effect on the TAXNET coefficient (though increasing it to 15 greatly improved the R^2 of the model). Removing the threshold entirely increased the estimate. But the substantive effect on estimates of likely growth was tiny.

Our conclusion is that enterprise zone incentives have no discernible positive effect on new economic activity. In fact, a very small negative effect is discernible in all our models. This is not entirely surprising, given the results of the econometric literature on enterprise zones and growth (where around half of the studies show very little or no impact), given the size of actual incentives (Chapter 3), and given the locational difficulties many zones must overcome (in Chapter 6 we concluded that zones were performing more poorly than their containing states). Moreover, these econometric results support the conclusions we reached in Chapter 3—based on our hypothetical-firm analysis—about the likely effects of zones incentives on firm behavior. There we concluded that most of the time enterprise zone incentives were probably too small to matter.

A number of other methodological issues remain:

- Are the models any good at analyzing the components of new establishment growth and of overall establishment growth? Many traditional taxes/growth models use net establishment growth or employment growth as the dependent variable. These numbers are used because they are more easily available. As we illustrated in the previous chapter, though, a small net establishment change figure is often the result of large gross changes in opposite directions; and it is gross growth that receives the incentives. Moreover, location models tend to be appropriate to only some of the components of overall establishment or employment change. The main reason here is that location models focus on relocations and starts—thus the independent variables in these equations are more appropriate as predictors of births and moves in, than as predictors of expansions, contractions, deaths, or moves out.

Finally, like location models, much of the economic-development literature has been concerned with the issue of relocations, euphemistically called the "war between the states." An advantage of our data set is that the individual components of growth are explicit.

We also ran models with alternative dependent variables: overall growth in establishments, rate of expansions, rate of contractions, rate of constants, rate of deaths, and rate of moves out. With the exception of the expansions equations—where the sign on TAXNET was correct (negative) and the parameter was statistically significant though still small—all equations performed much worse than the base models. This should caution against the use of overall establishment or employment change as a proxy for relocations into an area in tax/growth models.

- To what extent are the results of the base models dependent on the ZIP-code definitions of enterprise zone boundaries? We discuss our algorithms for translating enterprise zone boundaries into ZIP-code regions in Appendix E. As we indicate there, the result is a "liberal" selection of ZIP-code regions. Consequently, in some of the selected ZIPs, only a small portion of the sampled ZIP-code regions were actually in enterprise zones. We tried making our decision rules more rigorous (20 percent, 50 percent, and 70 percent of the ZIP region had to be in an enterprise zone). One consequence of this was that the number of ZIPs in our model declined drastically, as did the total number of enterprise zones (some zones are smaller than a single ZIP). Unsurprisingly, our models performed poorly. There was no case where the TAXNET parameter was negative, statistically significant, and substantively important.

- Do the base models suffer from simultaneity bias? As we indicated earlier in this chapter, in models like ours variables such as wages, unemployment, and incentives may be endogenous. Greater growth will increase demand for labor and thus increase wages, reduce unemployment, and possibly reduce the desire to provide incentives. We have attempted to avoid all simultaneity bias by measuring all explanatory variables at the beginning of each growth period. For the 1989–1991 and 1991–1993 panels, wages were measured for 1987, for the 1993–1995 panel, 1993. Unemployment was measured for the first year of each panel, and taxes and incentives for the middle year of the panel (although set legislatively in the first year). Thus, simultaneity should not be an important problem.

It could be argued that the time frames we use are fairly arbitrary, however, and that "causally" some broader growth time frame may be determining some historically broader setting of tax incentives. In theory this could explain the sign of the TAXNET estimate. For instance, it is conceivable that higher levels of longer-term growth will result in a smaller public appetite for economic-development expenditures. Under this scenario it would be a history of strong growth that is causing the relatively high level of taxation and low level of incentives, and poor growth low taxation and high incentives. Given the way we constructed the tax and incentive variables (using the TAIM^{ez} model), we do not believe this to be the case.[28] Nevertheless, to test simultaneity we developed two-stage least squares (2SLS) models with one or all of TAXNET, INCENTIVE, and WAGE endogenous. Although the TAXNET parameter declined in size, its performance in the 2SLS equations was consistent with the analysis above.[29]

Most of the location-theory literature suggests that taxes and incentives will have a much greater effect at the intraregional level rather than the interregional level. The reason for this is that many locational costs are less spatially variable within regions than among regions, thus accentuating the impact of those costs, such as taxes, which do show considerable intraregional variation. Empirical estimates of growth elasticities with regard to taxes are much greater intraregionally than interregionally, but there are fewer intraregional studies and thus this conclusion is not well established (Wasylenko 1997; Bartik 1991).

We developed one intraregional data set—for Ohio. In the national models, only targeted Ohio zones were included; however, for the intra-Ohio models we were forced to include both targeted and nontargeted zones. To account for this difficulty, the Ohio models also include a DISTRESS variable—this is the state designation for targeted enterprise zones in troubled areas. Ohio provides firms locating in these distressed zones a larger incentive package than is available in nondistressed zones. As we indicated in the discussion of the sample, the Ohio data set also includes non-zone areas.

Table 7.5 provides results for two of our Ohio models. As indicated above, the Ohio models are very similar to the national models. In both these Ohio models, the denominator for GROWTH was the number of firms at the beginning of the period. For the sectoral model we selected industrial sectors with more than 10 enterprises in the zone at the beginning of the period. Since our Ohio models are also designed to focus on the issue of designation, in some models (not reported here) TAXNET was replaced by a dummy (DESIGNATION) indicating whether the zone was designated during one of the three time periods. This was meant to capture whether zone designation per se was important for growth. Unfortunately, the correlation between DESGINATION and TAXNET was very high and thus it was deemed inadvisable to include both variables in any single model. As with the national models, we also investigated whether replacing TAXNET with measures of basic taxes and incentives would alter the results.

Our Ohio results mirror our national results surprisingly closely. TAXNET, the measure of the size of taxes net of incentives, remains positive in both the Ohio base and Ohio sectoral models. In neither are the results statistically significant, and in both the estimates are substantively tiny. Indeed, the Ohio TAXNET parameter estimates were very similar to the national estimates. Replacing TAXNET with DESIGNATION results in a negative estimate on that variable (also insignificant and substantively small). That is, zone designation results in very slightly lower growth. This is consistent with the estimate for TAXNET. In other words,

Table 7.5 Results From Ohio Base and Sectoral Models[a]

Variable	Ohio base models		Ohio sectoral model	
	Estimate	*t*	Estimate	*t*
GROWTH, dependent				
AGGLOMERATION	0.000	0.26	0.000	0.00
DISTRESS	0.009	0.47	0.032	0.01
EDUCATION	0.240	3.42	0.164	0.07
ELECTRIC	−0.002	−0.40	−0.001	0.00
INFRASTRUCTURE	−0.314	−4.52	−0.107	0.05
POVERTY	0.300	1.97	0.073	0.10
PREVIOUS GROWTH	−0.168	−1.53	−0.132	0.10
RACE	−0.031	−0.51	−0.035	0.04
TAXNET	0.242	0.64	0.241	0.26
UNEMPLOYMENT	−0.006	−0.98	0.002	0.01
WAGE	0.000	0.03	−0.003	0.00
n		300		710
Adj. R^2		0.24		0.10

[a] Fixed-effect intercepts are not reported.

these two variables suggest that neither enterprise zone designation nor enterprise zone incentives increase local growth.

The value on the DISTRESS parameter is very small indeed and not statistically significant. Given Dabney's (1991) argument about the difficulty enterprise zones have in making up for their inherent locational negatives, one would expect that once TAXNET has been controlled for, DISTRESS would have a negative sign. It does not. At least in Ohio, the targeting of zone incentives appears not to make much appreciable difference to growth.

As with the national models, replacing TAXNET with separate measures of basic taxes and incentives had no impact on the results. The statistically significant variables in both the Ohio models were similar to those in the national models. Older infrastructure resulted in less growth, and a greater percentage of the population with degrees resulted in more growth. The sectoral model performed poorly—nevertheless, all variables (including TAXNET and DISTRESS) but two had the same sign as they did in the Ohio base model. Variations on the measurement and taxes and incentives did not alter the results in any important ways. The upshot is that there is no evidence from Ohio that enterprise zone incentives result in greater growth.

We also ran a constant coefficient version of our national base model, and random effects versions of the national base and sectoral models. For reasons we discussed earlier in this chapter, we do not believe the assumption of these alternative models can be sustained. Nevertheless, if the results of these alternatives were radically different from those of the fixed-effects estimates, there might be some cause for concern. In the national base models, the signs on all variables remain the same for the fixed-effects, constant-coefficients, and random-effects estimating techniques. Naturally, parameter estimates and their t-scores did vary for the models. For the national sectoral models, all variables but two kept the same sign, but these two variables (MARKET ACCESS and SERVICES) have very small and statistically insignificant parameters in both models. Otherwise, the fixed-effects and random-effects estimates produced very similar results.

CONCLUSIONS AND FURTHER DISCUSSION

The consensus position in the taxes/growth literature over the past two decades is that taxes have a small but nevertheless significant negative impact on economic growth. Work on discretionary incentives, such as grants and loans, has generally reached conclusions similar to the taxes/growth results—more incentives lead to greater growth. However, the research on enterprise zones, with few exceptions, has not found much evidence that zones or zone incentives result in more growth. Our simulations presented in this chapter accord with most of the recent enterprise zone literature. We found that enterprise zones are not effective engines of economic expansion.

Why would the findings for general state and local taxes and for discretionary incentives not also be true for enterprise zones? After all, from an economic-development point of view, enterprise zones are merely a set of targeted tax (and discretionary) incentives. Various sorts of answers can be given to this question, none of them definitive.

First, many of the zones are in older, distressed, inner-city neighborhoods. As Dabney (1991) has argued, such places suffer from a number of important locational deterrents—high levels of crime, poor infrastructure, poorly skilled workers, and so on—and it is unlikely that tax incentives alone will make up for these negatives.

Second, enterprise zone incentives are mostly just too small to affect firm behavior. As we showed in Chapter 3, the income benefits provided by zone incentives can be wiped out by fairly small local differentials in wages. Of course, in some places enterprise zone incentives are so generous that it is likely they are successful in generating growth. We cannot prove it but we are strongly inclined to believe that the Michigan Renaissance Zone's munificence ensures that it can't help but be effective, though at great cost in state and local tax revenue. A few other states have very generous enterprise zone regimes. Consequently, the income difference for a firm between the most-generous and least-generous sites can be substantial. But for the most part the tax advantages of enterprise zone status are not huge and the differences in tax generosity among different enterprise zones (or between enterprise zones and non-zone areas) are usually quite small. While enterprise zones probably do work in the extreme cases, it is entirely unsurprising that they do not have much effect on growth overall.

The argument of the last paragraph should not, however, be taken to imply that states would be wise to increase massively the generosity of their enterprise zone programs. As the results in Chapter 5 show, such a strategy could be fiscally deleterious. As long as the elasticity of economic activity with respect to taxes is less than one, incentives will generate fiscal losses, and the larger the incentives the larger the total losses per zone. Moreover, if all states upped their incentive ante, the relative competitiveness of any one state's incentives would necessarily decline.

Third, there is reason to be skeptical of the consensus position that general (that is, non-enterprise zone) taxes and incentives do have an important impact on growth. A significant minority of researchers in the field do not believe the matter has been settled. Much of the work on which the consensus is based is itself flawed and reproducibility of results remains an issue.

As we have said, our results generally conform to those in most of the econometric literature on enterprise zones. But are our results reliable? By the standards of the literature, our analysis is comprehensive. We do not limit our analysis to programs in a few "model" states. The study is undertaken at two geographical levels. Where appropriate, it is disaggregated sectorally. The dependent variables used are in line with those recommended as best practice—we do not merely look at overall growth but measure the specific components of that growth (births, moves-in, deaths, expansions, and so forth) that are the theoretical focus of most models. Likewise the database we use is complete (no records were removed to maintain privacy) and the data are, by the standards common to the literature, highly disaggregated spatially. As far as we are aware, we are among the first to use this database in a taxes/growth analysis. Moreover, we use what is probably the best and most comprehensive measurement of the impact of enterprise zone incentives on firm income available today (the estimates from the TAIM^{ez} model). And we have used a variety of statistical procedures—many not reported in this book—all with fairly consistent results. We have investigated likely sources of empirical and specification error in our model. The most worrying of these is clearly the impact of the algorithms used to translate each enterprise zone into a series of ZIP-code regions. Nevertheless, the results have remained broadly consistent.

Our conclusions do not *prove* that a substantively strong positive relationship between enterprise zone incentives and growth does not exist; much more research will be necessary to establish that incontrovertibly. Furthermore, our modeling effort is open to a number of important technical and empirical criticisms—and our answers to these criticisms are unlikely to convince all in the field. But our conclusions certainly provide no support for the idea that enterprise zones generate new growth in targeted areas. What we don't know is whether or not enterprise zone incentives that were targeted appropriately, were managed correctly, and were quite large could be effective.

The next chapter focuses on a related question: Do enterprise zones improve the access to employment opportunities of targeted populations? It is conceivable that although enterprise zones don't create new employment growth, they are nevertheless worthwhile because they encourage business to use the sorts of labor cohorts (the unemployed, those loosely attached to the labor force, those out of the labor force, and so on) that would otherwise be avoided.

Notes

1. None of this work should be confused with the multitude of academic and policy studies that has tried to investigate the cost-effectiveness of individual taxes and incentives. These latter studies, while often relying on estimates of the effect of taxes and incentives on growth, do not address the relationship between taxes and growth directly.

2. See, for instance, Part Two of Green's (1991) edited volume on enterprise zones.

3. In other words, the differential-shift term aggregates all growth or decline that cannot be explained by the performance of the national economy and by the sectoral mix in the local economy.

4. The case-study method can be dramatically improved through the use of experimental or quasi-experimental research designs. Unfortunately, these are extremely difficult to develop in an economic development policy setting, though Isserman (1999) presents a discussion and implementation of some of these techniques.

5. For comparisons of tax costs to labor costs see Fisher and Peters (1997a) and Fisher and Peters (1998, Chapter 5). Hunt (1985) and Hunt and O'Leary (1989) have used this method to measure other non-tax costs experienced by business. See also Tannenwald, O'Leary, and Huang (1999).

6. Debate still continues as to whether business even responds to state and local taxation. For instance, see Wasylenko (1997) and the discussion that followed this paper: Bartik (1997), Duncan (1997), McGuire (1997) and Ady (1997). For earlier, and very good, discussions of the technicalities of this debate, see Bartik (1991) and Newman and Sullivan (1988). Underlying this research are a set of serious theoretical questions about the relationship between business taxes and goods and services firms receive for paying those taxes and about the way firms choose among sites. For a summary of this debate see Kenyon (1997). For more theoretical accounts of the competition between jurisdictions, see Shannon (1991), Oates and Schwab (1991) and Netzer (1991).

7. See also Sheldon and Elling (1989).

8. See also Erickson and Friedman (1991).

9. See Blair and Premus (1987), Chapman and Walker (1990), and Ady (1997). In this case, we are actually focusing on a new branch plant location decision which is obviously only part of what determines the aggregate level of business activity in an area.

10. Part of the reason for this is that since its inception location theory has tended to emphasize the more tractable problem of new plant locations. Certainly, there are many exceptions to this claim. See, for instance, Bartik (1989) regarding small business start-ups.

11. See Tannenwald, O'Leary, and Huang (1999) for an important attempt to do this for unemployment insurance.

12. In this regard see the recent reviews of the literature on public services and

growth (Fisher 1997) and regulation and growth (Tannenwald 1997). Also see Tannenwald, O'Leary, and Huang (1999) on the application of the hypothetical-firm method to other costs and Wasylenko's (1997) brief but very useful discussion of the dependent and explanatory variables used in the econometric models of taxes and growth.

13. These points are confirmed by more recent studies, for instance Holzer and Ihlanfeldt (1996) and Mayer (1996), although there is still considerable debate here. We take up this issue again in Chapter 8. Some of the most interesting literature in this area has focused on gender, spatial mismatch, and employment. For a recent review, see MacDonald (1999).

14. In fact, in the next chapter we show that enterprise zones do draw on wider metropolitan level labor markets, so that distinguishing between the two is probably inappropriate. Nevertheless, this remains an important theoretical issue.

15. Supply data are from the ZIP-code publications of the *Census of Population and Housing*, demand data from the ZIP-code publications of *County Business Patterns* and the *Census of Manufacturers*.

16. For a broad discussion of the state of the literature on the impact of public services and infrastructure on growth, see Fisher (1997). There is also a very useful, short discussion on Bartik (1991) on the difficulties involved in measuring the impact of infrastructure on economic development.

17. The perversity of enterprise zone boundaries presents a huge problem in creating spatial controls. One could not simply compare enterprise zones to cities; enterprise zones would have to be compared to other *similar geographical units*. This would require that all enterprise zones in the system be digitized (a very time-consuming task) in order to ensure the non-zone regions are truly non-zone and provide appropriate comparisons. It would also require defining what a *similar geographical unit* is.

There are also problems adopting various simplifications to overcome these problems: either using the area just outside the sample zones, or using other similar areas—say, blighted old industrial areas—in the sample cities. Unfortunately, areas just outside the sample ZIPs are often rural with little or no manufacturing and thus are inappropriate comparison regions. Moreover, it is nearly always impossible to find appropriate alternative ZIPs within (or even partly within) a city's boundaries. The reason is simply that except for the very biggest cities in our sample, there are just too few ZIPs per city (we found this to be true even of cities as big as St. Louis).

What are *similar geographical units*? Appropriate comparison ZIPs would have to have a similar industrial structure and similar demography. Typically, factor analysis would be used to generate industrial/demographic profiles of enterprise zone ZIPs, and then the resulting factors could be used in the selection of comparison ZIPs. Early in this project we attempted to do just this, focusing on bigger cities (at this stage in the project we were contemplating using a matched-pair methodology). But even in big cities, there were too few enterprise zone ZIPs to generate adequate factors. Use of simple industrial/demographic profile indices rather than factors did not improve the situation. The indices tended to reflect the policy concerns (and indeed designation criteria) of the state enterprise zone legislation. Thus, similar ZIPs also tended to be actual designated enterprise zones.

18. Of the regression studies covered, see Erickson, Friedman, and McCluskey (1989) and Sheldon and Elling (1989).

19. "Nearly" because one enterprise zone in our example came into being only during the third period and another three only during the second period.

20. They are also referred to as "least squares dummy variable" (LSDV) or "fixed effects" models.

21. A comprehensive treatment of analysis with cross-sectional panel data is provided by Hsiao (1986). Other useful guides are provided by Greene (1997) and Sayrs (1989). For a more general treatment, see Pindyck and Rubinfeld (1998).

22. Certainly the large error sum of squares change suggests opting for the fixed effects model over the constant coefficients model.

23. For reasons we mentioned in the last chapter, the distinction between birth and moves in is somewhat arbitrary.

24. In the model reported, we use regional (state) fixed effects.

25. We assume that the effects of localization economies (the effect of the mass of activity within a particular sector or closely allied group of sectors) will be caught by our measure of urbanization economies (the effect of the overall size of the local economy).

26. The seven combined sectors were as follows: 1) SIC 27, 2) SIC 20 and SIC 26, 3) SIC 24 and SIC 23, 4) SIC 25 and SIC 32, 5) SIC 28 and SIC 34, 6) SIC 30 and SIC 37, and 7) SIC 35 and SIC 36 and SIC 38. Sectors were grouped by effective tax rate because other measures of similarity between sectors would average out divergence in tax effects.

27. For modeling purposes, the requirement that there be some growth activity was retained.

28. The reason for this is that TAIM^{ez} measures the tax burden on the firm, not legislative decisions about rates, incentives, apportionment, and so on (the tax structure). The size of the model could be taken as indirect proof of the numerically complicated relationship between the tax burden and the tax structure.

29. We also built preliminary structural equation models that looked not only at the impact of enterprise zones on growth, but also on the causes of incentive generosity. While the results of these models have not been good, they have not led us to alter our conclusions on the impact of enterprise zone incentives on growth.

8
Enterprise Zones and Access to Employment

Thus far we have described the incentives available to firms locating in enterprise zones, what these incentives are worth to relocating firms, the effect of these incentives on the investment behavior of firms—in particular, the likelihood that labor will be substituted for capital, the cost of those incentives, and, finally, the impact of enterprise zone incentives on growth. Essentially, for much of this book we have focused on whether enterprise zones are likely to get businesses to modify their investment behavior in ways which might produce particular, potentially socially useful, outcomes. However, even if an enterprise zone has been successful with regard to these outcomes, the enterprise zone strategy may still not have been successful overall. As we argued in Chapter 2, for enterprise zones to fulfill their original promise, they must also provide the economically disadvantaged with improved access to these new jobs. In other words, creating jobs may not be enough; besides, there are other, probably more efficient, economic-development tools aimed at job creation. Enterprise zones must be able to create appropriate job opportunities for those who currently have difficulty in the labor market.

In Chapter 2 we argued that the traditional understanding was that providing access to jobs for targeted populations required the creation of enterprise zones close to those populations. However, by the late 1990s it was clear that most states believed that this was not enough; the favored enterprise zone strategy was by then enlarged to include enhancing access through incentive instruments that give targeted groups some special employment advantage, usually by offering more generous incentives for hiring disadvantaged persons or zone residents. Other strategies exist—for instance, leaving enterprise zones to focus simply on employment creation while improving the access of disadvantaged groups through changes in transportation policy or housing policy or through improved job-placement services.[1] The latter approach moves the access question out from enterprise zone design into other areas of policy and thus is beyond the scope of this research.

Nevertheless, the belief that enterprise zones need not address access issues directly raises important questions about the relevance of much enterprise zone policy; we come back to this issue in the conclusions to this chapter and again in the final chapter.

WHY ACCESS MATTERS

When the enterprise zone idea was first developed, the issue of job access was understood to mean that employment should be provided locally—close to or within the areas of economic decline. Enterprise zones should create jobs in (or, more correctly, relocate jobs to) the right sort of places, usually depressed inner-city areas. Underlying this idea was the belief—usually justified by reference to the spatial mismatch hypothesis—that inner-city unemployment was due, in part, to two related processes and one broad transportation constraint:

- For most of the twentieth century, but particularly after World War II, business relocated out of inner-cities and into the suburbs, effectively reducing the accessibility of work to inner-city residents.
- Discrimination in housing markets limits the ability of minorities to move to growing suburban locations.
- Reverse commuting from residences in inner-city locations to suburban work sites is difficult for government or the public sector to organize, is less efficient than commuting downtown, and is thus expensive. Moreover, given the extra time involved in reverse commuting (using public transit), reverse commuting usually involves some welfare loss for users.[2]

However, there is reason to be skeptical that spatial access alone—or even in major part—explains higher levels of inner-city unemployment and lower levels of labor-force participation. Some important early work suggested that racial discrimination in labor markets is a much more potent reason for inner-city unemployment than the dislocation of low-income residences and low-skilled jobs (Ellwood 1986),[3] although this situation is complicated by the strong possibility that the location decisions of firms are driven, in part, by the racial preferences of executives and customers (Mieszkowski and Mills 1993). Some recent empirical examinations of the impact of proximity to jobs provide little or no support for the "strict form"[4] of the spatial mismatch hypothesis (Cutler and Glaeser 1995; Taylor and Ong 1995; O'Regan and Quigley 1996; Zhang and Bingham 2000).[5] However, the situation is anything but settled and conclusions depend on the precise form of the spatial mismatch hypothesis being evaluated. For instance, Holzer and Ihlanfeldt (1996, p. 79) showed that "employers' proximity to black residences and to public transit both increase the likelihood that they will hire black employees" and saw this as consistent with spatial mismatch. But they also argued that improving the access of inner-city minorities to suburban work sites would not necessarily improve employment and earnings if other barriers to employment continue to exist. Two of the other barriers widely cited in the literature are the so-called skills-mismatch—inner-city residents may not have the skills appropriate to the needs of employers—and discrimination in labor markets. Along similar lines, Immergluck (1998) found that job proximity has a significant but modest effect on neighborhood employment rates, but he also found that educational attainment and race—essentially the skills mismatch and labor market discrimination—have much greater effects.

Consequently, it now looks as though interpreting job access in terms of the enterprise zone location is unnecessarily limiting. Merely reducing the distance between targeted groups of people and jobs may have a comparatively small impact on either unemployment rates or labor-force participation rates if the major determinants of these rates lie elsewhere. Moreover, labor markets are bigger, indeed usually much bigger, than enterprise zones, although it is true that low-income and low-skilled workers tend to have geographically smaller labor markets (Theodore and Carlson 1996; Hanson and Pratt 1995). Thus, there should be no surprise in finding many of the residents of enterprise zones working outside of the zones, and residents of non-zone neighborhoods, including homeowners in far-off middle-class suburbs, commuting into the zones for employment. But if the spatial location of jobs is less important, then some other way must be found to give targeted populations special access to the jobs created in the enterprise zones. Various possibilities exist, although the most common method is to tie enterprise zone business incentives to the employment of targeted individuals. In the next section we explore how this is done in the states we studied.

TARGETING IN ENTERPRISE ZONE
JOBS CREDIT PROGRAMS

Eleven of the 13 states we have analyzed have jobs credit programs for firms locating in an enterprise zone, and all 11 target those credits in one way or another, either to zone residents or to population groups that are in some way economically disadvantaged. Table 8.1 shows the nature of the targeting for each state over the period 1994 through 1998 (unless otherwise noted, the targeting criteria remained the same over this period). Indiana is the only state that restricts credits to new hires who are residents of the enterprise zone, though two states (Virginia and Wisconsin) provide larger credits for zone residents than for other new hires. Four states (Illinois, Kentucky, Ohio, and Wisconsin) restrict credits to employees who fall into one or more categories of economic disadvantage, such as welfare recipients, the unemployed, or those eligible for JTPA (Job Training Partnership Act) services. New York provides credits for all new hires, but allows larger credits for those who are economically disadvantaged. Four states (California, Connecticut, Florida, and Missouri) provide credits for new hires who are either zone residents or fall into one or more categories of economic disadvantage.[6] Missouri has a second credit program that requires that at least 30 percent of new hires be either zone residents or economically disadvantaged, but if this threshold is exceeded, the firm receives credits for all new hires.

Overall, 7 of the 11 states with targeted jobs credits reward firms that hire zone residents; 10 of the 11 reward firms that hire persons suffering some kind of economic disadvantage. The reward may be in the form of eligibility for any credits at all or in the form of larger credits (usually two or three times as large) for those who meet the targeting criteria. Thus, targeting of jobs credits appears to overcome to a degree one argument against enterprise zones as a strategy for improving the welfare of low-income zone residents, the argument that the labor market is much larger than the zone so that the creation of jobs in enterprise zones will not do much to increase the employment prospects of zone residents. Even the targeting at the economically disadvantaged entails *de facto* targeting of zone residents to the extent that economic disadvantage is concentrated in the enterprise zone.

There are some major caveats to this conclusion, however. The first is that capital (and other) incentives tend to dominate labor incentives, as shown in Chapter 4. Firms are presumably attracted by the total incentive package, but if the jobs credit component is only a small part of the package, the jobs credit may be viewed as irrelevant. The second is that the targeting of jobs credits is effective only if firms are able and willing to use them. The Ohio jobs credit, for example, is fairly generous as such credits go ($3,000 per job), but fewer than 10 percent of firms locating in enterprise zones take advantage of the credits (Ohio Enterprise Zone Annual Report). One reason may be the onerous task of certifying eligibility under one of five criteria, employee by employee. The other reason may be that at least 25 percent of new hires must meet the eligibility criteria for the firm to receive any credits at all; this threshold may be too difficult for most firms to attain readily and they may judge that the credits are not worth the cost of restricting their hiring criteria. In Connecticut, at least 50 percent of new employees must be either zone residents or federal Joint Training Partnership Act (JTPA) eligible for the firm to receive any credits. This is a very high threshold.[7]

Third, jobs credit targeting increases job offers to zone residents only to the extent that it changes firm behavior. The firm is rewarded for hiring members of targeted groups even if those persons would have been hired anyway. Take an average jobs credit of $2,000 per job, and an average manufacturing wage of about $25,000 annually or $12.00 per hour (the median among our 16 representative firms). Let's assume the credit is fully utilized in the first two years; then it effectively reduces wage costs for the first two years by 4 percent, which is equivalent to a cut in the hourly wage rate of about 48 cents. The question is: How many targeted individuals become attractive hires at a wage of $11.50 for the first two years (which could be viewed as a sort of training wage) who would not have been hired at the standard wage of $12.00? To make a difference in hiring decisions, the 50-cent wage differential must be enough to overcome employers' assessments of productivity differences. If zone employers are indifferent between

Table 8.1 Demographic Targeting in Enterprise Zone Jobs Credit Programs in 13 States, 1994–1998

State	Program	Targeting
Calif.	Hiring credit	Credit only for new hires who are 1) eligible for JTPA or GAIN; 2) residents of a high-density unemployment area or Targeted Economic Area; 3) economically disadvantaged persons; 4) disabled; 5) ex-offenders; 6) Native Americans; 7) eligible for SSI, AFDC, GA or food stamps; or 8) displaced workers.
Conn.	Job grants	Credit only for eligible new hires: those who are 1) residents of the enterprise zone or 2) JTPA eligible. At least 50% of new plant employees, or 150 employees, must be eligible for firm to receive any credits.
Fla.	Jobs tax credit	In 1994: Credit only for new hires who are 1) residents of the enterprise zone, 2) AFDC recipients, or 3) JTPA participants. After 1994: All new hires are eligible but larger credits are awarded to those earning under $1,500 per month, and the largest credits are awarded to 1) employees earning under $1,500 if at least 20% of all employees are zone residents, and 2) participants in a welfare-to-work program.
Ill.	1299D Jobs tax credit	Credit only for new hires who are dislocated workers or economically disadvantaged individuals. Firm must hire at least 5 eligible employees.
Ind.	Employee credit	Credit only for new hires who are residents of the enterprise zone.
Ky.	Employee credit	Credit only for new hires who are AFDC recipients or persons unemployed for 90 days or more.
Mo.	New & expanded business facility credits in an EZ	Qualified employees: 1) zone residents, 2) those unemployed at least 3 months, and 3) recipients of public assistance. At least 30% of new hires must be qualified employees for the firm to be eligible for any credits; if this threshold is met, all new hires get a basic credit, and additional credits are awarded for qualified employees.

Mo.	Training credit	Credit only for new hires who are zone residents or the difficult to employ. Targeted employees: all those who are paid at least 135% of the federal minimum wage and 1) are eligible under JTPA or the Work Opportunity Credit program, 2) are recipients of public assistance, or 3) have income below the poverty level. All new hires get basic credit; double credit for targeted employees.
N.Y.	Wage tax credit	
Ohio	Employee training credit	Credit only for new hires who are qualified employees: Resident of county for one year; or resident of county six months and 1) JTPA eligible; 2) unemployed; 3) recipient of AFDC, general assistance, or disability assistance; or 4) handicapped. At least 25% of new hires must be qualified employees for the firm to be eligible for any credits.
Pa.	None	
Tex.	None	
Va.	Job grants (1995 or later)	All new hires are eligible. Larger credits awarded for zone residents. At least 40% of new hires must either be zone residents or have family income (prior to employment) below 80% of the area median income.
Wis.	Jobs credit	Credits only for eligible employees: 1) referrals by a voc rehab program, 2) economically disadvantaged Vietnam-era veterans, 3) economically disadvantaged youths age 18–23, 4) SSI recipients, 5) GA recipients, 6) youths in a coop education program from economically disadvantaged families, 7) economically disadvantaged ex-convicts, 8) AFDC work incentive employees, 9) persons unemployed as a result of a business closing or mass layoff, and 10) dislocated workers. Economically disadvantaged means having income below 70% of the Bureau of Labor Statistics lower living standard. Additional credit for zone residents.

NOTE: EZ = Enterprise Zone or the equivalent; JTPA = federal Job Training Partnership Act; GAIN is a California employment program for welfare recipients; SSI = Supplemental Security Income; GA = general assistance; AFDC = Aid to Families with Dependent Children (replaced by TANF).

hiring members of the targeted group and hiring others, then of course a small wage differential could have a large effect. On the other hand, it is easy to imagine that there are real or perceived productivity differences that would be valued at far more than 50 cents to most zone employers.

Finally, the jobs credits apply only when employment is expanded as a result of building a new plant. As targeted employees leave, there is no incentive to replace them with new employees who are members of targeted groups. Thus, any short-run gain in jobs for zone residents produced by targeting probably disappears in the long run. It also may be that excessive targeting causes firms to discount the value of the jobs credits when making expansion or location decisions because of the increased uncertainty with regard to the extent to which the firm will benefit. The imposition of thresholds no doubt exacerbates this problem; one can imagine that firms considering a Connecticut zone discount the job grants entirely.

ENTERPRISE ZONES AND COMMUTING BEHAVIOR

Do enterprise zones improve *spatial* access to employment opportunities? As far as we are aware, this question has received close to no empirical attention in the enterprise zone literature. The accessibility of employment opportunities to economically disadvantaged persons, however, is a very well researched problem. Moreover, in the recent past the problem has been analyzed in increasingly sophisticated ways, using origin-destination data sets allowing the residences of employees to be digitally connected to their places of work. For instance, O'Regan and Quigley (1996) used the *Census Transportation Planning Package* (CTPP) data for Newark, New Jersey, to measure the impact of job accessibility on, among other things, youth idleness. They found little impact. In our research, accessibility was measured using the standard gravity/entropy models from the commuting literature[8]—essentially, the impact of distance between residences and places of work (controlling for appropriate occupations) was quantified and treated as a constraint on mobility. Sen et al.'s (1999) work on the matching of welfare clients to job openings in the Chicago area does much the same. Since current geographic information system (GIS) technology allows dynamic connection between journey-to-work origins (homes) and destinations (work sites) using real transportation networks (roads, cars, and buses), it is likely that matching models will become considerably more refined over the next few years, with a significant improvement in our understanding of how people perceive and react to accessibility of employment.

The problem with enterprise zones is that the standard models used to measure accessibility are not entirely appropriate, and advances in GIS models of commuting are unlikely to change this situation. In O'Regan and Quigley's (1996) and Sen et al.'s (1999) research, there are distinct jobs and job seekers. The problem is finding out whether the distance between the two poses a hindrance to the job seekers' finding and taking the available jobs. Likewise, in recent research looking at potential work opportunities for welfare recipients in Boston, the distances between the welfare recipients and the jobs available to them are measurable (Lacombe 1998). In principle then, if one were studying job access for some targeted group, one would simply want to know if reduced distance increased the probability of getting a job. In the case of enterprise zones, if there were a significant distance effect (say for zone residents), then providing jobs within the zone should increase employment. To investigate this, one needs to define: 1) the employment opportunities provided by the enterprise zone; and 2) the population at which they are targeted.

With regard to the first issue, it is clear that only the new, induced jobs—the jobs that would not be there *but for* the existence of the enterprise zone incentives—should be counted. Noninduced jobs would exist in the zone anyway and therefore do not provide any new accessibility advantage. Unfortunately, further difficulties arise here. It is unclear what should count as induced employment. As we argued in the previous chapter, most econometric studies of enterprise zones find little or no inducement. Leaving aside this issue and presuming that zone incentives do indeed lead to new growth, at least some of the growth in the zone will likely derive from transfers from elsewhere in the city that contain the zone. If the city is a better approximation of the local labor market than the enterprise zone itself, transfers of jobs into a zone from the non-zone parts of the containing city will not increase the total number of job opportunities available to targeted job seekers. But if

spatial proximity is important for the employment of targeted job seekers (in other words, if the geographical size of the labor market for the
targeted job seekers is very small), then to the extent that firms are
moving into a zone from elsewhere in the containing city, they may indeed provide new job opportunities. From an accessibility perspective,
in the first instance, intracity moves into enterprise zones should not
count as induced jobs; in the second instance, they should.

In Chapter 2 we gave estimates from the taxes/growth literature on
the elasticity of employment growth with respect to taxes. In the previous chapter we gave our own, specifically enterprise zone, estimates of
investment elasticity with respect to tax incentives available in enterprise zones. Our estimates, which are in line with most of the recent
econometric research on enterprise zones, indicate that enterprise zone
incentives have at best a tiny positive impact on induced investment in
zones and, thus, presumably on induced employment in zones. Note
that our national estimates use the liberal second definition of induced
investment (intracity moves are counted in) and thus may *overstate* the
actual impact since at least some of the growth in an enterprise zone
will derive from transfers from elsewhere in the containing cities.
Thus, it is likely that the number of truly induced jobs in an enterprise
zone is very small indeed.

Finally, who are the job seekers to be targeted? Are they all those
who live in the enterprise zone? Surely this definition is too geographically conservative (residents of poor neighborhoods surrounding the
enterprise zone are excluded) while being too demographically liberal
(wealthy enterprise zone residents are included). Are all those "targeted populations" as defined by the state statutes and local ordinances enabling the existence of the enterprise zone? If a metropolitan area describes the true geography of a labor market, then the research question
is whether the enterprise zone reduces the commuting distance of targeted individuals in the MSA. We could then go on to define targeted
individuals in various ways (say, for instance, those with an annual income of less than $12,000). However, if poorer, less-skilled people ex-
perience much smaller geographical labor markets (and in Chapter 2
we argued that the claim that they did underpinned early arguments for
enterprise zones), then the targeted population must either reside in, or
at least be close to, the enterprise zone. Complicating matters, a few
zones have very few residents.

Given these difficulties, we decided not to build full commuting models for each enterprise zone but merely to answer a series of fairly simple, but nevertheless important, questions:

- What proportion of jobs available in enterprise zones are taken by enterprise zone residents (and correspondingly, what proportion of enterprise zone jobs are taken by nonresidents)?
- What proportion of employed enterprise zone residents actually work in the zone (and correspondingly, what proportion of working enterprise zone residents travel out of the zone to find employment)?

The answer to the first question indicates the extent to which enterprise zone jobs have been "infiltrated" by others in the metropolitan labor market. In other words, it gives some idea of how truly targeted a zone is. The answer to the second question indicates whether enterprise zones are part of a truly *local* labor market. Needless to say, it is possible that an enterprise zone will attract few of its own residents but may nevertheless capture labor from poor neighborhoods surrounding the enterprise zone. In this case, the level of non-enterprise zone "infiltration" would appear large and the enterprise zone would appear to be unsuccessful. In reality, however, the opposite would be true. Therefore, it is important to know where the infiltration comes from; if it is mainly from distant—and presumably wealthier—suburbs, then the enterprise zone is failing to provide greater local accessibility to jobs; if it is from close-by—and presumably poorer—communities, then the enterprise zone may be succeeding.

In preliminary studies for this chapter, we developed maps for each of a small sample of enterprise zones, showing both the flow of employees into the zone from every commuting subregion (Traffic Analysis Zone, or TAZ) of the metropolitan area (these are sometimes called "desire line" maps) and the average earnings of residents in each of these subregions. In a fairly consistent pattern, these maps showed that enterprise zones attract employees from far and wide and that many of the commuters into enterprise zones reside in wealthy suburban areas. Because these maps are too complex to present in this book, we provide two summary measures here for each zone: the average distance to work of all workers in the metropolitan area,[9] and the distance to work of those employed in enterprise zones. If enterprise zones were indeed attracting local workers, one would expect the commute distance of enterprise zone workers to be *considerably* shorter than that of all workers in the wider metropolitan region.[10]

Before presenting our results we need to make a few comments on the data and our analysis of it. The answers we provide for these two sets of questions are far from being as comprehensive or rigorous as we would like: partly this is a result of the data set itself and partly it is a result of the small number of enterprise zones in our commuting subsample. The analysis in this chapter relies on the CTPP, a reorganization of the decennial *Census of Population and Housing* data, allowing households (commuting origins) to be connected, via commuting matrices, with places-of-work (commuting destinations).[11] For our purposes, the main deficiency in the CTPP is that, although we can get complete summary demographic data on residents of a particular TAZ, or employees working in a particular TAZ, we cannot get occupation or income data cross-classified by TAZ of residence and TAZ of employment. That is, we don't know much about zone residents who work in the zone and how they differ from zone residents who work outside the zone, and how these groups differ from non-zone residents who work in the zone. The results presented in this section are therefore far from being conclusive. Better evidence will require future model building based on individual data records of commuters into and out of enterprise zones, data sets that do not now exist.

Commuting Into and Out of Enterprise Zones

In most of the enterprise zones in our commuting subsample, a fairly small proportion of residents actually worked in the zone—averaged over the 14 zones, just under 10 percent (see Table 8.2). In other words, about 90 percent of zone residents commuted elsewhere in the metropolitan region for employment. Naturally, these numbers varied among zones. The Beloit zone managed to employ over 30 percent of its residents while the South Bend zone kept only 2.6 percent. The reasons for this have to do with the relative sizes of zones, the proportion of the city's industrial land that is covered by the zone, the extent of a match between the skills of zone residents and the skills demanded by zone employers, the targeting of zone jobs at zone residents, and, finally, the algorithms we used to translate enterprise zone boundaries into

TAZ regions (see Appendix E). The fact that 90 percent of zone residents on average work outside the zone certainly does not support the argument that zone residents find work only within a very constrained geographic area. Of course, it may still be the case that there is a sizeable subset of zone residents who are currently jobless and who are more spatially constrained than those who are employed.

Averaged over the 14 zones, zone residents took about one-fifth of the jobs offered in the zone. Again this percentage varied considerably. In Springfield, Missouri, close to 35 percent of jobs were taken by residents, but in South Bend, Indiana only 11.7 percent were. Overall, the vast majority (four-fifths) of jobs were taken by commuters into the enterprise zones. Moreover, these commuters came from far and wide.

In Table 8.2, distance is measured using the following equation:

$$(1) \quad MCD = \frac{\sum D_{ij} C_{ij}}{C},$$

where MCD is the weighted mean commute distance, D is the zone centroid to zone centroid distance between each TAZ pair, i being the origin or residence zone and j being the work zone, and C_{ij} the number of commuters living in i and working in j. C without the subscripts is the total number of commuters in the system. This calculation makes use of the most geographically precise commuting data in the CTPP, the origin-destination matrices.

In exactly half of the zones in the subsample, those who worked in enterprise zones actually had *longer* commutes than those who worked elsewhere in the region. Another three zones had employees with weighted average commuting distances within a tenth of a mile of the average for the region. Unsurprisingly, Beloit—the zone able to provide the highest percentage of its residents with zone jobs—had the biggest difference between average distance to work of zone and non-zone workers. Zones are not attracting workers from a highly localized labor market.

Since workers experience the friction of distance in terms of time, not the miles traveled (even less the miles between zone centroids), it is possible that our results misrepresent the true accessibility of zone jobs. To test this we built a standard time-to-work regression for each zone in our sample (see Appendix H for a detailed description of this model

Table 8.2 Employment in Enterprise Zones by Residence and Distance to Work of Zone Employees

City	Zone residents employed in zone (%)	Zone jobs taken by zone residents (%)	Distance to work, all workers in transportation region (miles, weighted average)[a]	Distance to work, enterprise zone employees (miles, weighted average)[a]
Beloit, Wis.	30.4	26.2	4.8	2.3
Canton, Ohio	11.7	29.9	5.0	5.4
Evanville, Ind.	5.6	15.5	4.9	4.5
Fort Wayne, Ind.	3.0	13.2	4.9	4.8
Green Bay, Wis.	5.5	13.4	4.0	3.1
Jacksonville, Fla.	10.1	31.5	8.4	8.6
Lexington, Ky.	14.8	30.1	4.2	4.2
Milwaukee, Wis.	6.3	15.1	6.6	6.9
Muncie, Ind.	7.8	19.6	3.4	3.5
Pittsburg, Pa.	4.4	19.7	6.9	7.5
Porterville, Calif.	6.6	21.9	7.3	6.4
South Bend, Ind.	2.6	11.7	4.8	5.0
Springfield, Mo.	15.5	34.2	5.8	5.9
Syracuse, N.Y.	10.2	27.5	6.4	6.3

[a] Mean miles to work (MCD) is calculated by the distance from zone centroid to zone centroid for each zone pair and weighted by actual commuters between each zone pair.

and further results for an earlier sample of zones). In these regressions commute time was the dependent variable, and the income (or occupation) of workers, the mode of transportation to work, and whether the work site was an enterprise zone or not were all independent. Since zone residents tend to be poorer than the rest of the metropolitan population, and will therefore be more likely to use *slower* public transit, a control for transportation mode is crucial; since the literature suggests that better-paid and more-skilled workers are prepared to commute longer distances, a control for income (or occupation) is also necessary. We found further evidence for our earlier conclusion: even when taking into account the time effects of transportation mode and income, in almost all cases zone workers had a *longer* commute time than non-zone workers.[12]

In summary, the vast majority of zone residents actually worked outside of the zone and the vast majority of zone jobs were taken by non-zone residents. Where did those commuting into zones live? In most instances, the homes of zone workers were nearly as dispersed across the metropolitan area as the homes of those who worked outside of the zone. It does not appear that jobs created within zones offer much in the way of a local accessibility advantage to residents of zones.

Why are enterprise zones attracting workers from afar and employing so few of their residents? At this stage we have only speculative answers to this question. It is likely that the truth of the claim that labor markets for lower-skilled workers are quite spatially limited has been massively exaggerated. For example, the recent commuting literature suggests that minorities—who are often overrepresented among lesser-skilled workers—often travel *further* to work than non-minorities (MacDonald 1999). Over and above arguments about the size of labor markets, it is probably the case that, controlling for industry, the range of skills demanded in enterprise zones is little different from the range of skills demanded in the rest of the metropolitan area. It would be very surprising indeed if the residents of enterprise zones—who tend to be poorer and less educated than the rest of the population—were able to supply the full range of labor skills demanded by firms located in the enterprise zones. Moreover, the zones we have looked at tend to focus on manufacturing, whereas many of the jobs requiring lesser skills are in other sectors, particularly services.

We should not be surprised to find that many of the residents of enterprise zones commute to lower-skill jobs more abundantly available in other parts of the city.

CONCLUSIONS

Do enterprise zones enhance the accessibility of work for disadvantaged workers and job seekers? Enterprise zone programs attempt to do this in two ways: by placing zones in areas where disadvantaged workers are concentrated, in the hopes that spatial proximity by itself will increase employment of such persons, and by tying job incentives (for zone firms or for all firms) to the employment of disadvantaged workers. Almost all state enterprise zone legislation calls for the tying of some portion of available jobs credits to "disadvantaged" workers and job seekers. But as we saw in Chapter 4, jobs credits on average make up a relatively small proportion of incentives offered in enterprise zones. Thus the actual percentage of potential credits tied to or targeted at disadvantaged persons is very small indeed. Moreover, there is some evidence that firms may avoid using incentives which require the employment of disadvantaged persons. If this is so, it should come as no surprise that the targeting apparent in state zone legislation is much less obvious when looking at the employees working in enterprise zones. We doubt that the tying of jobs credits to the employment of disadvantaged persons has increased the accessibility of employment for those persons very much.

In this study we have focused on states that enforce some level of spatial targeting through the criteria for establishing zones; in other words, we have focused on states that presume job proximity is important. There are other states that allow zones in areas that are not depressed but give bigger incentives if the zone is *near* targeted populations. There are also states in which enterprise zones are little more than delivery mechanisms for standard state incentives without any particular geographical focus. Even where there is proximity between zones and disadvantaged persons, however, it is still unclear if the disadvantaged gain any special accessibility to employment opportunities.

First, incentives create very few additional jobs in zones. Second, enterprise zones function in the context of much broader regional labor markets; many, or even most, of the jobs will go to persons residing outside the zone. Finally, it is unclear whether the spatial mismatch hypothesis explains much of inner-city unemployment and labor-force participation.

Many individuals commute into and out of the enterprise zone for employment. Of those commuting in, many appear to come from wealthier neighborhoods and suburbs. In the cases we examined, enterprise zones were as likely as not to have more long-distance commuters than non-zone areas of the city-region. Thus, it is hard to see that spatial proximity of jobs has provided much in the way of increased accessibility. Again we need to emphasize that the analysis presented in this chapter is quite preliminary. Our results are based on a very small sample of enterprise zones and the data we use are not rich enough to define comprehensively the accessibility provided by enterprise zones.

As we mentioned in the introduction to this chapter, there are other ways of providing accessibility. It is possible that declining inner-city locations are poor places for business to develop. Some have argued that in comparison to greenfield suburban sites, these places are racked by poor infrastructure, high crime, and so on (Dabney 1991). If this is true, it may be better to abandon efforts to increase the spatial proximity of jobs and targeted persons and to resolve the issue of accessibility to employment in a more comprehensive way. Better job placement services would be a start; these would better disseminate information about suburban job opportunities to inner-city residents. Better transit-based reverse commuting would be another help, allowing inner-city residents to get to suburban jobs. Residential programs that move people out of the inner-city and place them in suburban locations may be another useful, if highly controversial, option. Helping overcome racial stereotyping (and geographical stereotyping) would almost certainly help. We have looked at none of these strategies in this book, but it is clear to us that the accessibility of employment to economically disadvantaged people has not been resolved by enterprise zones and that other policy approaches need to be tried. In the conclusion we return to these issues.

Notes

1. Hughes and Sternberg (1992) argued for the provision of "job mobility" through transportation and job-placement services. For instance, public transit that enabled reverse commuting would improve the accessibility of suburban jobs, appropriate placement programs would allow inner-city residents, spatially removed from buoyant job markets, to "hear" about suburban job openings. Others are skeptical of the ability of either public transit or placement approaches to overcome employment barriers and have argued instead for "residential mobility" programs, such as the Gautreaux housing experiment in Chicago (Rosenbaum et al. 1991; Kain 1992). Rosenbaum (1996) argued forcefully that residential mobility programs have a much greater chance of reducing a wider range of labor market barriers to minority employment than traditional approaches. For instance, potential employers may take a suburban address as a positive indicator of future work performance, compared to an inner-city address.

2. For the original statement of the spatial mismatch hypothesis, see Kain (1968). Also see the papers developing the hypothesis, in particular, Gordon, Kumar, and Richardson (1989), Jencks and Mayer (1990), Blackley (1990), Holzer (1991), Holzer and Vroman (1992), Ihlanfeldt (1994), and Holzer and Ihlanfeldt (1996). Also see Kain's (1992) restatement. For work on the constraint, see Peterson and Vroman (1992) and Ihlanfeldt and Sjoquist (1998).

3. Audit studies provide the most compelling evidence of hiring discrimination against blacks. See Fix and Struyk's (1994) review.

4. Glaeser (1996) distinguished between the loose form of the spatial mismatch hypothesis (segregation by race and income affects employment outcomes) and the strict form (location matters because of transportation distance to work). We doubt that any of the evidence here contradicts the loose form.

5. Also see Cooke (1997), who found that proximity to intrametropolitan job opportunities has no effect on African-American labor-force participation, but it does have a positive effect on labor-force participation among white married mothers, for instance. Part of the difficulty with the spatial mismatch hypothesis is that there appears to be significant gender differentiation within individual race categories. See McLafferty and Preston (1996) for a statement of this issue.

6. California targets residents of a high-density unemployment area or Targeted Economic Area, rather than the enterprise zone per se.

7. In fact, we assumed in our TAIM^{ez} simulations that no firms qualified for the jobs credit in Connecticut.

8. Gravity or entropy models are widely used as a way of understanding spatial accessibility. See Appendix G for a discussion of these models in this context.

9. Note that for convenience we use "transportation region" and "metropolitan area" interchangeably. For the purposes of this section the distinction between these two regions is unimportant. Nevertheless, transportation regions as defined by the Bureau of Transportation Statistics and Metropolitan Statistical Areas (MSAs) are not identical entities.

10. Enterprise zones tend to be in or near central cities. Here TAZ regions—the local unit of geographical analysis in this section—tend to be smaller; thus zone-to-zone (commute) distances are shorter. Consequently, one would expect that, on average, those working in enterprise zone TAZs would have shorter commuting distances than other workers. Thus, if enterprise zones do provide some special accessibility advantage, commuting distances for those working in enterprise zones should be even shorter.

11. The CTPP does three unique things: 1) it uses Traffic Analysis Zones (TAZs), which are small commuting regions, as the basic unit of geography; 2) It includes a reorganization of Census data so that the characteristics of persons and households by their place-of-work is obtained; and 3) It includes commuting flow matrices of beginnings (origins) and ends (destinations) for the journey-to-work. The data are used mainly by traffic planners and engineers for forecasting traffic flows, but they may also be used to analyze a range of other policy-oriented commuting issues. See, for instance, O'Regan and Quigley 1996.

12. Unfortunately, the data used in these regressions are from Part II—the place of work data—of the CTPP. The reason for this is that the CTPP does not provide information on the occupation or income of those residing in a particular zone and working in a particular zone. See Appendix H for more information on the regressions.

9
Conclusions and Policy Recommendations

Enterprise zones remain the principal, if not the only, form of urban policy at the state level in the majority of U.S. states; in fact, their use expanded in the late 1990s. Is this a trend to be applauded or decried? We begin this chapter by reviewing the principal findings of our research on enterprise zones. We then revisit the policy issues raised in the first two chapters and reexamine them in light of our research. Are enterprise zone incentives in fact a useful policy instrument for raising the incomes of the poor, enhancing city economic development, or redeveloping depressed neighborhoods? We conclude the chapter with recommendations for improving state enterprise zone programs.

A REVIEW OF THE RESEARCH FINDINGS

What are the Most Common Enterprise Zone Incentives and How Much are They Worth?

The typical package of incentives available to firms locating in an enterprise zone consists of an investment credit and a jobs credit under the state corporate income tax, and local property-tax abatements. Among 20 of the most industrialized states, the average incentive package increased in value from $4,061 per job in 1990 to $5,338 per job in 1998, where value is measured by the increase in the present value of the 20-year cash flow attributable to investment in a new plant. Looking at just the 13 states that had substantial enterprise zone programs in place by 1990, the average package among our 75 sampled cities was worth $5,048 per job in 1994. Among the 75 cities, half had at least one sector for which the total incentive package exceeded $10,000 per job, and 14 cities would have granted at least one sector more than $20,000 per job. Incentives of this magnitude are equivalent to a gross undiscounted value in the range of $20,000 to $60,000 per job, which is not trivial in comparison to the reported packages offered to some firms in the past 10 years.

Another way of getting at the question of incentive size and importance is to consider the size of the wage premium that a given incentive package would just offset. If we look at the average across the 13 states for each of the sectors, we find that the incentive packages were equivalent to a 1.6 percent to 7.1 percent cut in wages. A relatively small wage premium would be sufficient, in many locations, to wipe out the advantages created by the incentive packages there. Thus one would not expect incentives to have large effects on location decisions when they appear small relative to wages—the major factor cost for manufacturing firms.

How Do Enterprise Zone Incentives Compare to More Widely Available State and Local Incentives?

The total incentive package values reported above included both incentives available only within enterprise zones and incentives available anywhere in the state. On average among the 20 states, the enterprise zone incentives per se accounted for 63 percent of the total package in 1990, but only 52 percent by 1998. Looking just at the 75-city sample, the enterprise zone share fell from 65 percent in 1990 to 56 percent in 1994 (though in 3 of the 13 states, zone incentives represented 100 percent of the package). General incentives have been increasing more rapidly than enterprise zone incentives. Still, for the typical manufacturing firm, the incentive package more than doubles if the firm chooses an enterprise zone location over a non-zone location in the same state.

While on average states are attempting to confer a substantial competitive advantage on enterprise zones through more generous incentives, there were two contradictory trends in the 1990s among the 20 states: 1) some states embarked on new enterprise zone programs, or increased the competitive advantage of existing zones or other targeted areas;[1] 2) other states weakened the advantage of geographically targeted areas by reducing targeted incentives or, more commonly, by expanding nontargeted incentives. Perhaps more importantly, the trend in many states with long-standing enterprise zone programs (or the equivalent) was to increase the maximum number of such zones allowed.

This further weakened the targeting effect of zone programs, as a larger and larger portion of the state fell under the "targeted" program.

Are Larger Incentives Compensating for Higher Taxes?

Competition among states and localities for manufacturing investment has led to reductions in basic state taxes as well as increases in state and local incentives. The importance of these tax and incentive changes can best be measured by their effect on the overall state-local tax rate on new investment. The overall trend in the 1990s has been overwhelmingly to reduce basic taxes on corporations. Among the 20 states, the median basic tax rate was reduced from 8.5 percent in 1990 to 7.9 percent in 1998. Larger reductions in the median effective tax rate occurred when general incentives were included (from 7.6 percent to 6.7 percent) and when targeted incentives were added (from 6.3 percent to 5.2 percent).

Has there been any convergence among these 20 states in terms of their tax rates on new investment? The short answer is "No." In 1990, incentives were not, by and large, offsetting unusually high basic tax rates but were in fact reducing tax rates that were already below average. By 1998, the variability in basic tax rates among states had actually increased, but incentives no longer added to (or subtracted from) this variability. Thus, tax rate and incentive competition continued through the 1990s with no indication that this was producing convergence; the process resembled a game of leapfrog, with no state apparently content to be merely average. The most striking evidence of this is the prevalence, by 1998, of *negative* tax rates on new investment: not only did the construction of a new plant, and the generation of sales and income from it, fail to generate additional tax liability to the state in which the plant was located, but the plant actually reduced the firm's *existing* tax liability to that state in many instances because new plant credits exceeded the entire new plant tax.

Do Enterprise Zone Incentives Appear to Favor Particular Industrial Sectors?

Some states have relatively high corporate income tax rates, while others are noted for high local property-tax rates; income tax credits may favor labor or capital, and the property-tax base may tax only real property or most forms of personal property as well. This variation in state-local tax systems, combined with variation among manufacturing firms in terms of profitability, capital intensity, and asset composition, produces wide variation in effective tax rates on a given industry across our 75 city sample, and wide variation within cities in terms of effective rates imposed on one sector versus another. All but 4 of the 16 sectors end up as the most-competitive sector (in terms of effective tax rate) for at least one of the cities, while all but 4 end up as some city's least-competitive sector. Within a given city, it is quite common for the most heavily taxed sector to be facing a state-local tax rate two (or even three) times the rate on the least-taxed sector.

All this amounts to implicit industrial policies, with states and cities providing favored tax treatment to a few industrial sectors. Our major concern here is that it is very likely that little or no thought has gone into the industrial policy consequences of most states' and cities' tax systems. Industrial policy has developed almost by default, as a by-product of decisions taken about other state and local policy issues.

Do Enterprise Zone Incentives Favor Labor over Capital?

One would assume that job creation is the predominant objective of enterprise zone programs, given the concern with higher rates of poverty and unemployment in zone areas. State tax policy, on the other hand, generally may simply be aimed at "economic development," where investment is the primary objective (with more jobs assumed to follow, of course). This is borne out to a limited extent by the pattern of state tax incentives in the 13 states that are the focus of this study: jobs credits are a little more likely to be provided in enterprise zones than to be provided generally throughout the state.

It is more instructive to look at incentives that actually lower the price of labor at the margin versus incentives that lower the price of capital at the margin, since some incentives that appear to do so, do not in many instances, functioning instead as lump-sum grants to the firm. Looked at in this way, we found that 4 of the 13 states provide, at the state level, a set of incentives to zone firms that clearly lowers the price of labor without an offsetting capital-matching "grant." Four other states have a clear capital bias. In the other five states, state credits provide no clear reduction in labor or capital prices at the margin. When local incentives—property-tax abatements, primarily—are brought into the picture, however, the capital bias becomes quite strong.

The possible effects of incentives on a firm's choice of technology, and the relative use of capital and labor in the production process, depend not on the dollar amount of incentives but on changes in the prices of capital and labor. We estimated these price changes for each of the 16 manufacturing sectors and each of our 75 enterprise zone cities. The effects of labor incentives on the price of labor are quite small. In only two states does the average price reduction exceed 1.0 percent, and the maximum price reduction among the 16 sectors never exceeds 3.0 percent in any state. Capital incentives, on the other hand, have substantial price effects in several of the states. The average price reduction among sectors exceeds 5.0 percent in 8 of the 13 states, and in 6 states the maximum exceeds 20 percent for at least 1 sector. Our results show that overall there is a clear bias of incentive systems in favor of capital in all but 2 of the 13 states.

Given the significant substitutability between capital and labor in manufacturing reported in empirical studies, it is likely that this capital bias in incentives will cause firms to adopt at least somewhat more capital intensive methods of production. This substitution of capital for labor could occur in any firm benefiting from the subsidies, including those whose location decisions were unaffected. If this substitution effect is large enough, it is possible that the net effect of zone incentives is to lower employment rather than to increase it.

Do Enterprise Zone Incentives Produce a State or Local Fiscal Surplus?

The case for providing tax incentives for investment in enterprise zones would be stronger if it could be shown that states or localities experience a net gain in revenues as a result of the incentive program, at least in the long run. The increased revenues could be used to upgrade infrastructure or education systems or to provide job training, thus augmenting the development effects of the direct job creation. If fiscal losses occur, on the other hand, the opposite is true: incentives weaken the ability of government to provide the public services that businesses depend on, directly and indirectly.

Our research indicates that the direct revenue effects of enterprise zone incentives are very likely to be negative, and rather strongly so. In the average enterprise zone city, among our sample of 75, each job that is actually induced by the zone incentives would generate about $7,200 in net additional revenue to state government (in present value terms over 20 years) and another $11,000 in local revenue. On the other hand, the state would lose about $4,600 for every new job that was not attributable to incentives (because some growth would have occurred anyway), and localities would lose about $3,200 for each noninduced job. The key to determining fiscal break-even is identifying the percentage of new jobs that were in fact created only because of the incentives—the induced jobs as a percentage of all new jobs. In the average city, as long as this percentage was more than 30 percent, state and local government combined would come out ahead. The problem is, research (ours and others) suggests that the percentage is likely to be much lower than 30 percent. If the elasticity of jobs with respect to taxes is about –0.3, the inducement percentage would be about 9 percent and the annual net state-local revenue loss would be about $7,130 per induced job in our average city. These losses would mount over time as gross job growth causes more incentive spending each year. The eventual effect of a typical set of zone incentives for the average-sized zone in our sample would be a total state-local revenue loss (for the zone as a whole) of about $1.5 million annually.

While it appears unlikely that enterprise zone incentives will produce fiscal gains for state government, or for a state's localities in the aggregate, it is possible that local incentives produce local gains. This is because there is reason to believe that incentives have a greater effect moving investment around within a metropolitan area than from one state or metro area to another. Shifts in location within a metropolitan area would produce no net gain for the state or for localities collectively, but the city that gains business could gain fiscally. This depends on how sensitive intrametropolitan location decisions—in particular, decisions to locate in a central city enterprise zone versus a suburban greenfield site—are to differences in local tax rates, about which we know very little.

The conventional wisdom favors granting firms temporary and declining tax credits or abatements. Eventually, the argument will go, these firms we have attracted will be paying the full freight in taxes, and it will be worth the temporary loss in revenue to get the permanent gain. This assumption ignores the fact that establishments do not live forever. By front-loading, one is increasing the odds that a given establishment will get most or all of the potential incentives but will pay full freight for only a few years, or none at all; by the time the incentives are phased out, many establishments will have died or moved on to start the incentive pattern over again in another community. Our research shows in fact that governments will lose more revenue the more they front-load their incentives. A permanent tax cut on new investment or jobs is more likely to produce positive revenues than a temporary cut with the same power to create jobs (in other words, with the same value to the firm over some decision-making time horizon). The most cost-effective incentive program, in terms of revenue loss or gain per new job, is a back-loaded one. The argument for back loading is strengthened by the fact that it rewards firms for staying in the community, instead of rewarding them just for arriving, and so may increase the average time over which new establishments, and the jobs they bring, benefit the community.

Did the Manufacturing Sector in the Enterprise Zones Shrink during the 1989–1995 Period?

When we examine the 13 states as a whole, we find that the six-year period 1989–1995 saw relative stability in the manufacturing sector, as measured by changes in the number of manufacturing establishments. Small rates of net growth in some sectors were offset by small rates of net decline in other sectors. On the other hand, enterprise zones within these states experienced relatively pervasive decline, though at a modest rate. This net decline in manufacturing establishments was produced not just by steady attrition, however. New plants were constantly emerging to replace older ones that disappeared, and in most sectors the gross changes in both directions were five to eight times as large as the net change. The average zone among the 64 we studied began the period with about 111 manufacturing establishments distributed across six or seven sectors. Each year, in the average zone, about 11 manufacturing establishments were born or moved into the zone, but about 12.4 establishments died or moved out. The net effect was a decline in establishments at an average rate of only about 1.2 percent per year. Of the 64 zones, 20 actually experienced a net gain in manufacturing establishments; on the other hand, 10 zones suffered net losses of 20 percent or more over the six-year period.

Establishments exiting the enterprise zones (through deaths or moves out) were, on average, just slightly larger than entering establishments. The percentage loss of manufacturing employment over the six-year period due to net loss in establishments was therefore likely to be a little more than the percentage loss of establishments. Zone employment is also greatly affected by the job expansions and contractions of existing firms that remain in the zone. Overall, of the establishments existing at the beginning of a given two-year period in these 64 zones, about one in three expanded employment within the two years, and about one in three reduced employment. (About one in five died or moved out.)

Larger establishments were much more likely to contract than smaller establishments, however, so it is likely that the net effect of expansions and contractions in these zones was further erosion in the job base, beyond the more than 9 percent attributable to net loss of establishments. When one examines expansions and contractions by time period one finds a striking trend, however: the percent of establishments that remained in the zone and expanded increased with each two-year period, while the percent that remained but reduced employment declined. Expansion rates exceeded contraction rates by a wide margin in the most recent period, 1993–1995, especially for the two smaller-size classes. It is quite possible that in the 1993–1995 period there was net employment growth in existing establishments in these zones sufficient to offset, or more than offset, the job losses due to exits exceeding entries. Whether this trend continued as the national economic expansion continued through the 1990s is open to speculation.

There is a surprising amount of sectoral diversity in the enterprise zones. In all but 4 of the zones, there were at least 5 of the 16 sectors significantly represented, and in 19 of the zones, there were 8 or more sectors. (A sector was considered to have a significant presence if it accounted for at least 5 percent of the total number of establishments in the zone.) In part, this reflects the fact that many zones are quite large, drawn to include a major portion—if not all—of the city's industrial land. The median number of sectors significantly represented among the births and moves in (those accounting for at least 5 percent of the total) was 7; all but 5 zones saw new establishments representing 5 or more different sectors.

We assessed the zones' comparative advantage or disadvantage for types of manufacturing. We compared sectors in which zones did relatively better than the states (six sectors that accounted for 96 percent of the state decline, but only 53 percent of the zone decline), and sectors in which zones did relatively worse (accounting for 43 percent of zone decline, although these sectors were actually increasing for the states). There was no clear difference between the two groups of firms in terms of national average wages paid in those sectors. (This analysis is based on national average wages by two-digit SIC code, however, not on actual wages for the particular establishments moving into and out of these zones or these states, so these results should be viewed with caution.) But zones appeared to have a pronounced disadvantage in attracting and retaining the more capital-intensive sectors of manufacturing. Moreover, zones are dominated by traditional—that is, non-technology—manufacturing sectors, particularly printing and publishing and fabricated metal products. Zones appeared to have a comparative disadvantage in electronic equipment, instruments, and chemicals. This may not bode too well for long-term zone growth.

Do Enterprise Zones Create Local Economic Growth?

If zone incentives are to be effective, then they must be sizeable enough to influence geographic investment decisions. Averaged across the 13 states for each of the sectors, we found that the incentive packages were equivalent to a 1.6 percent to 7.1 percent cut in wages. So in many locations a relatively small wage premium would be sufficient to wipe out the advantages created by the incentive packages there. With the exception of some extreme cases, therefore, one would not expect incentives to have large effects on location decisions. Our statistical models of enterprise zone incentives and growth bear out this deduction. At best the evidence shows that enterprise zones have little or no impact on the growth of establishments. It is almost certain then that they have as little impact on employment growth. Our conclusions here are in line with much, but not all, of the econometric work on enterprise zones and growth.

Why are enterprise zone incentives not affecting growth? Part of the explanation probably lies in the fact that many zones are in older, distressed, inner-city neighborhoods. Such places suffer from a number of important locational deterrents—high levels of crime, poor infrastructure, poorly skilled workers and so on—and it is unlikely that tax incentives alone, small as they usually are, will make up for these negatives. In other words, in growing places enterprise zones may do little more than reinforce growth trends, but in distressed places they are seldom likely to be large enough to make a huge difference. This suggests that enterprise zone incentives could be effective if they were targeted appropriately, were managed correctly, and were large.

In some places enterprise zone incentives are so large that it is probable that they are successful in generating growth. For instance, we are strongly inclined to believe that Michigan's Renaissance Zone program is so generous that it is effective. A few other states also have very generous enterprise zone regimes. Considering our entire sample, however, the incentive differences between the most generous and least generous sites were often substantial. But for the most part, the tax advantages of enterprise zone status are not huge and the differences in tax generosity among different enterprise zones are quite small. While enterprise zones probably do work in the extreme cases, it is entirely unsurprising that they do not have much effect on growth overall.

It is also important to recognize that the likely effectiveness of very generous incentives such as Michigan's comes at a high cost. As long as the elasticity of economic growth with respect to taxes is less than one, and there is reason to believe it is much less than one (for interstate location decisions), incentives generate net revenue losses, and the larger the incentives, the larger the losses (for a state and its localities in the aggregate). To understand how this works, recall that larger incentives will indeed mean that a larger share of the establishment growth in a locality is induced by those incentives; but the larger the incentives, the less the locality gains from each induced establishment, and the more it loses in revenues by granting incentives to firms that would have located there anyway.

Do Enterprise Zones Improve the Accessibility of Work for Targeted Workers?

Our answers to this question are decidedly preliminary. Nevertheless, two broad conclusions may be drawn. Tying the provision of business incentives to the requirement that recipient firms hire targeted workers appears not to have been a success. These requirements usually apply only to jobs credits, and jobs credits are typically only a small part of provided incentive packages. Moreover, it is possible that firms may avoid using incentives with strong "tying" provisions.

Improving access by locating zones in targeted areas also seems to be problematic. Enterprise zones attract workers from far and wide. In most of the enterprise zones we looked at, the majority of jobs were taken by commuters from outside. Indeed, commute time of those working in enterprise zones is often longer than the average for those working elsewhere in the containing regions. This suggests that spatial proximity between home and work does not necessarily improve the accessibility of jobs. Moreover, there is good reason to be skeptical that transportation costs—between home and work—are a major cause of higher levels of unemployment and lower levels of labor-force participation in inner-cities. Thus it is a mistake to believe that the location of enterprise zones in older inner-city neighborhoods will improve the employment opportunities available to inner-city residents.

ARE ENTERPRISE ZONES A USEFUL ECONOMIC-DEVELOPMENT TOOL?

Our work points to a basic confusion in the enterprise zone concept. Enterprise zones are seen as instruments for increasing business investment, creating jobs, and enhancing the tax base. But to what end? Is the objective merely to enlarge the economic base of the city— that is, are enterprise zones just another name for local economic development, or another way for "the urban growth coalition" to direct resources to capital investment? If so, one would permit enterprise zones to be drawn quite large and to incorporate the major industrial sections of the city, whether inhabited by lower-income persons or not; furthermore, one might allow enterprise zones outside of cities, in suburbs or rural areas. This in fact appears to be the implicit purpose in some state enterprise zone programs (most notably Ohio's), where the spatial targeting is limited to only some zones, individual zones sometimes include much of the city, and zones have proliferated.

Or is the objective to raise the incomes of the residents of depressed or inner-city neighborhoods? This certainly appears to be the goal of enterprise zones in those states in which zones are narrowly drawn, zones are limited in number, and zone eligibility is predicated on a showing of neighborhood distress. Here the idea is that proximity to work opportunities is essential to reducing the unemployment rates and boosting the labor-force participation rates of people who live in those neighborhoods, thus increasing their income. Buttressing this idea is the spatial-mismatch hypothesis—that the suburbanization of investment has reduced the work opportunities of inner-city minorities. If this is the objective, then one must confront the fact that there are many strategies for raising incomes, including programs to enhance access to suburban jobs, programs to improve access to suburban housing, and programs to increase the employability of residents, not to mention income transfers and social services. Where are the public's limited resources best spent—on a jobs-to-people strategy through zone incentives or on other approaches?

Finally, enterprise zones may be seen as part of a neighborhood redevelopment policy. In many cities the zone is just one more program layered on top of existing neighborhood-based programs operated by the city, by local churches, by community development corporations, or by other nonprofit organizations, often through alliances with the private sector. The zone tax incentives—which are often provided to a wide range of businesses, including retail and service establishments—are part of a broader, neighborhood-based approach to revitalizing depressed areas that might include such things as job training, social services, housing rehabilitation, infrastructure improvements, education reform, and commercial redevelopment. Our research is certainly not meant to be a criticism of such broad-based community development strategies. Rather, we ask the question: Are enterprise zone incentives that are aimed at basic economic sectors, such as manufacturing, a useful and important component of such a strategy? Again, the question should be: Where are the community's limited resources best spent— on incentives to attract manufacturing establishments or on other programs more directly and clearly affecting the quality of inner-city neighborhoods?

Let us focus our attention on enterprise zones as a distinctive strategy involving spatially targeted incentives aimed at creating jobs in depressed neighborhoods, rather than zones as just another name for general economic development. The relevant questions then become: Do zone incentives create jobs in such places, and if so, at what cost? Do these jobs raise the employment rates and income levels of low-income residents of the neighborhood? And most importantly, given the cost of creating a job in a zone that goes to a low-income zone resident, could these public funds be better spent in other ways? If we can answer these questions we will have addressed the neighborhood development issue as well: if zone incentives have any role to play here it is because higher income levels would support a larger local commercial sector and better-quality housing and schools.

The accessibility of economically disadvantaged populations to employment could be enhanced in a number of ways besides bringing jobs to the inner city.[2] Better job-placement services, for example, would let the residents of inner-city neighborhoods know about suburban job opportunities. Run properly, placement services could enhance access to such jobs by reducing the transaction costs and prejudices of suburban employers if such employers come to trust the agency as an effective initial screener of prospective inner-city employees. Such an agency should also provide the kinds of services commonly employed in effective welfare-to-work programs—an assessment of job readiness, classes in job readiness, and job-search assistance—and perhaps referral to other programs such as GED classes, English as a Second Language classes, or more extensive job training.

Likewise, transit options could be developed that reduce the costs associated with reverse commuting. In fact, there are placement services and temporary employment agencies that run their own minivans from inner-city neighborhoods out to suburban work sites. Federal support for reverse commuting initiatives has recently expanded and these programs have now been in place long enough in some larger cities that researchers have begun to provide some preliminary assessments of their effectiveness and limitations (Blumenberg 2000; Minton 1999).

Another option is to facilitate the movement of people from decayed neighborhoods to the suburbs. This has been tried a number of times in the United States, the most famous of these experiments being the Gautreaux program in Chicago. The evidence suggests that such programs can be effective, particularly if the impacts are measured over more than one generation. This strategy raises the incomes of those able to move closer to centers of employment and to places with better schools and better environments for children. It may worsen conditions, on the other hand, for those left behind as positive role models become more scarce and labor market networks thinner, and it is certainly not compatible with community-development goals.

Other possibilities exist. To the extent that the employment problem in the inner city is a mismatch of skills or work habits, rather than a spatial mismatch, job-training and work readiness programs, or programs to reduce high school drop-out rates, may be appropriate. The point is this: The alternative uses of funds are many, and the incentives offered in enterprise zones are not cheap. What if the revenues foregone through zone incentives were spent directly on other programs? Consider the following "thought experiment" involving alternative approaches to increasing the mobility of inner-city residents looking for work.

We begin by calculating a reasonable estimate of the direct state and local cost of creating one job for an enterprise zone resident. Let us take as a starting point the fiscal simulations reported on in Chapter 5. These simulations assumed a gross annual rate of job growth (births and moves in) of 10 percent, approximately equal to the observed rate in our zone sample over 1990–1995. Let us next assume that in the average zone 10 percent of the gross job growth is attributable to the tax incentives available in the zone; the other 90 percent would have occurred anyway. While 10 percent seems like a very low figure, it is actually quite optimistic, based on our estimates of the actual effects of zone incentives on growth and based on other studies of the elasticity of employment with respect to taxes.

If we take 10 percent inducement as a best case, for every 100 new jobs in the zone each year, the 10 induced jobs would generate a net state-local revenue gain of about $18,200 per job (the average among our 75 cities), or a total of about $182,000. The 90 noninduced jobs would entail a revenue loss of about $7,800 per job (the average incentive cost) or about $702,000 in total. The total net loss is $520,000, or about $52,000 per induced job. (These figures all represent the present value of gains or losses over 20 years.)

The next step is to estimate how many of the induced jobs are filled by enterprise zone residents. Based on the limited analyses presented in Chapter 8, it would be a reasonable guess to assume that on average about one in four jobs goes to a neighborhood resident; we will assume a best-case scenario of one in two. That means that state and local governments spent $520,000 on average to create just five jobs for zone residents, or about $104,000 per job. (And it only gets worse if we take into account that these five jobs may not represent a net gain in zone resident employment, since some of the jobs may be taken by zone residents leaving an existing zone job, which might then be filled by a non-zone resident.)

Our estimate of $104,000 per job is a present value cost over a 20-year period. At the 10 percent discount rate that we used, it is equivalent to an annual expenditure of about $12,200 over that period. (Keep in mind that this is the best case; a more probable set of assumptions would easily double or quadruple these figures.) So here is the thought experiment: What could we do with $104,000?

Suppose that each prospective inner-city worker was bought a new car. In 2000, the cheapest new cars on the market went for between $7,000 and $9,000—used vehicles for much less. Assume that insurance for the first three years for each car would average around $3,000 (estimating conservatively that it would take inner-city residents new to the work experience about three years to become attached to the labor market and thus able to afford their own transportation). Add to this a liberal administrative overhead of 25 percent (a full 10 percentage points more than JTPA allowed). Such an "access" policy would have a direct cost of between $12,500 and $15,000 per worker.[3]   There would be other indirect costs and benefits. More cars on the road would increase infrastructure costs for government and there would be some negative externalities for other road users. However, given that most of the new auto use would be reverse commuting, these extra costs might well be small. Moreover, given that the mobility of whole families, not merely prospective workers, would be improved, there would likely be welfare benefits beyond access to work for the one employee.

Clearly, a program such as the one described above would be difficult to implement (requiring, for instance, monitoring that cars were actually used to get to work), and would likely be challenged politically. For instance, there would likely be opposition to the unemployed being given free automobiles. Environmentalists would probably be opposed to the further government subsidies of automobile use. The policy experiment could be altered to take account of many of these challenges. Community minivan pools, for instance, could replace individual cars. No matter—the experiment shows that access to employment can be provided comparatively cheaply. If the function of enterprise zones is to provide access, then they are comparatively expensive tools.

Our thought experiment is not far from the recommendations of some working in the area of welfare and transportation policy. Waller and Hughes (1999) argue that both federal and state governments need to consider the provision of autos to families in poverty. At its broadest, their reasoning is that the United States is an auto-dominated society and it is unreasonable to expect poorer people to compete economically without access to cars. They are justifiably skeptical of the efficacy of reverse-commuting initiatives and of most transit-based responses to the problems associated with access to jobs by the poor. In response to the environmental and congestion objections to subsidizing automobile ownership for the poor, they write:

> While [clean air and congestion] are all worthy concerns, should we pursue them on the backs of poor people being compelled by time limits and work requirements? Lower income households undoubtedly drive older cars, which likely produce more air-polluting emissions. The answer is more assistance for better cars and maintenance, not excluding poor workers from the highways. More cars on these roads would undoubtedly add to congestion. The answer is congestion pricing and other ways to manage overall highway demand, not just managing poor workers' traffic. And if public transit is the magic bullet that would solve both air quality and highway congestion, then policymakers should increase its use by higher income workers rather than simply focus on maintaining a captive market share among poor workers who have no alternative. (Waller and Hughes 1999, p. 12)

In their survey of transportation support to welfare recipients, Waller and Hughes found widespread reliance on vouchers for public transit and mileage reimbursement for existing private automobiles. But they also found innovative funding solutions including paratransit alternatives such as van pools and new mechanisms that help clients acquire cars. For instance, Pennsylvania and Michigan provide grants to some families to buy cars; both states also provide for car repair. A few states help with getting drivers' licenses, and all states in their survey permit the use of Temporary Assistance for Needy Families Block Grant (TANF) funds for car repairs and for vehicle-operating expenses. About half the states excluded the value of at least one car from the eligibility determination of TANF-funded benefits. So our thought experiment is not too far from strategies already being used by states to encourage and support work among welfare recipients and others in need.

A possible argument against this line of thinking is that enterprise zones have at least two functions: encouraging employment and providing access. The thought experiment only deals with the latter of the two. Our answer here is that enterprise zone incentives do not appear to induce much employment. Enterprise zones would have to be radically more successful at inducing new investment than *anyone* has yet found for them to be judged a success. In those few cases where enterprise zone incentives are probably successful, they are extremely costly. Presumably, in such cases, state government could set a small portion of the direct subsidy package aside to provide direct support to improving accessibility.

Furthermore, our thought experiment thus far has spent only about $15,000 of our $104,000 in available funds. What could we do with the rest? Following some of the suggestions made by Hughes (1989) for a six-part mobility/income strategy for inner-city residents, a number of alternatives spring to mind: two years of community college education would cost a few thousand dollars per year; a $400 per month subsidy for day-care expenses would amount to $4,800 per year, enabling more single parents to work (and reducing welfare costs in the process). Some of the saved revenue could be invested in upgrading neighborhood schools and infrastructure, or operating a job-training and referral center, or on housing assistance. Some of the saved revenue could fund a state-earned income tax credit, which would supplement the wages of entry-level jobs. The point is this: it is not difficult to imagine a set of alternative programs that would enhance job access and improve incomes, immediately or in the long run, and that would cost less than the zone incentive strategy.

The possibilities for funding alternative kinds of strategies become clearer if we consider the total cost, in lost state and local revenues, for a typical enterprise zone. As we reported in Chapter 5, for an average zone in our sample of 75 cities, with a typical incentive package and average rates of firm births and deaths, the revenue losses from this incentive package would eventually rise to about $1.5 million per year for state and local governments combined. An annual expenditure of this magnitude clearly could fund alternative programs at a significant level.

IMPROVING ENTERPRISE ZONES

While we have doubts about the overall effectiveness of enterprise zone incentives, it appears that they will remain in place in the majority of states for the foreseeable future. One reason for their staying power is that their costs are hidden; like all tax expenditures, they can be portrayed as a tax-cut program rather than an expenditure program, and this greatly enhances their political viability. So it is important to consider how state enterprise zone programs could be improved. We take as given that existing zones (except in the few states with sunset provisions) will remain in place, and that tax incentives will remain a central policy tool. Within those parameters, a number of reforms are possible.

Let us assume for the moment that enterprise zone policy continues to be guided by the basic premise that zones should be depressed areas where additional jobs need to be created—in other words, it is a place-based investment strategy. It is important, then, to prevent the proliferation of zones, particularly into areas that are not really economically distressed since that weakens the relative tax advantages conferred on zones. States should also restructure the incentives offered in their zones. There are five problems with the kinds of tax incentives currently emphasized, generally a combination of state corporate income tax credits for jobs or investment and local property-tax abatements: 1) they tend to favor capital over labor; 2) they tend to favor certain sectors over others, but not in an explicit and purposeful way; 3) they do not aid in the retention of existing establishments but only in the attraction of new ones or investment in expansions; 4) they are front-loaded and, hence, are more costly than they need to be; and 5) they rob local governments of the ability to finance needed local services.

There is an alternative incentive strategy that addresses all five of these problems: exempting some percentage of zone income from state corporate income taxation. By exempting a share of taxable income, there is no bias in favor of any one factor of production, nor is there a bias in favor of one industry over another. The effective tax rate on income is reduced by the same percentage regardless of the economic sector. Since the income exemption applies to all firms with facilities and labor in an enterprise zone, it would create an incentive to remain in the zone as well as an incentive to locate or expand there. As such it would probably have a larger effect on total zone employment than investment incentives alone. Such an exemption is constant and permanent and therefore is not front-loaded; thus even though it would be more expensive in the short run (because existing firms would immediately qualify), since it is also more effective, in the long run it would probably achieve a given inducement effect at lower cost to state government than a credit or abatement. Finally, since it is entirely state financed, it would not drain tax resources from local governments.

Alternatively, one could reorient zone policy and think of enterprise zones as concentrations of the hard-to-employ; the goal of the policy, then, is to create incentives for firms, wherever they may be, to hire zone residents, instead of incentives for firms to locate in zones and then hire whoever they want. Of course, individuals identified as hard-to-employ can be found anywhere; a demographic-based zone strategy still makes sense to the extent that location itself is an important determinant of employability. This can occur for several reasons: the prejudices of employers against workers from certain areas, the culture of joblessness or lack of role models that some authors attribute to inner-city neighborhoods, the problem of transportation access, or the lack of connectedness to job markets. Zone residence could be a necessary and sufficient condition to qualify for the credits, or it could be a necessary condition combined with some other individual attributes that define the hard-to-employ, such as those unemployed for long periods of time, TANF recipients, or individuals who are JTPA eligible. A third possibility, of course, is to make either zone residence or employability a sufficient condition.

Under this alternative view, criteria for creation of zones would be based entirely on the demographics of the residents, particularly chronic joblessness and high poverty rates. The zones should be confined to such areas, again to avoid dilution of effectiveness, but should also be drawn to include all such areas within a given job market. (This is less of a concern with investment-based strategies, since jobs in one place can be filled by the hard-to-employ from neighboring areas, whereas here we are creating a spatial definition of who qualifies.) Logically, then, the incentives should be redesigned to consist entirely of state jobs credits. There should be no capital incentives, including local property-tax abatements.

The jobs credits need to be more generous than they typically have been if they are to make a significant dent in the costs of employing the hard-to-employ, and upper threshold limits should be eliminated, or at least raised, to create stronger incentives to hire more-skilled, higher-wage workers. Jobs credits are not sector neutral; they favor more labor intensive sectors, but that is entirely appropriate since they are designed to encourage hiring, not relocation per se. The incentives should not be front-loaded for two reasons: front-loaded incentives will be more costly in the long run, and it is important to create on-going incentives to retain the individuals hired. The credits should continue for as long as that individual remains on the job. The credits should also be available for replacement hires and should not be limited to hires associated with plant expansions. This would make it even more important for the incentives to continue, to avoid creating incentives for churning the labor force (getting rid of employees as soon as the credits are used up and hiring someone new to start the credit process over again.)

Regardless of whether zones are viewed as a place-based investment strategy or a people-based employment strategy, there is a need to integrate enterprise zones with transportation and social policy so that those most in need of jobs have better access to them. Encouraging reverse commuting either through changes to public transit or support for private van-pools would be useful. Better placement services, connecting inner-city residents to suburban job opportunities, would also be good. Finally, moving people out to suburban residences would probably be the most effective of all (though also most likely to face stiff political opposition). All this implies that for enterprise zones to become more effective, they must be part of a broader set of public policies aimed at encouraging people to work productively.

We believe the expectations of enterprise zone policy have been far too great. Enterprise zones, or for that matter any other simple economic-development policy, should not be expected to solve some of the most deep-rooted problems in American society: racial inequality, welfare dependency, inner-city crime and decay, the breakdown of big city education systems, and so on. At the very best, enterprise zones can only be expected to make a small dent in these vast problems. It seems to us that the problems enterprise zones were originally meant to tackle would be better addressed directly and massively. In this sense, enterprise zones are only stop-gaps until an effective social and economic policy response becomes politically palatable. Primarily for the same reasons, it should come as no surprise (although it did at first to us) that enterprise zones have not been successful.

Notes

1. It should be noted that Pennsylvania enacted the new Keystone Opportunity Zone Program, with very generous incentives, but that took effect in 1999, too late to be reflected in our 1998 effective tax rate comparisons.
2. Hughes (1989) describes a six-part mobility strategy to improve the mobility and thus income of inner-city residents: provide job training; create job information systems; restructure transportation systems; provide day-care facilities; increase the level of the earned income credit; and modify policing and correctional practices.
3. If it were assumed instead that it would take six years for workers to become attached to the labor force, then total direct costs would still be $16,250–$18,750. Assuming six years and very high administrative overhead (35 percent), direct costs would still only be $17,550–$20,250 per worker.

Appendix A

Details of the TAIM^{ez} Model

TAIM^{ez} (Tax and Incentive Model-Enterprise Zones) is what we call our new hypothetical-firm model for measuring effective tax rates on new investment and the value of incentives. It is a direct descendent of the original TAIM model that we used for much of our research in the mid 1990s, in particular the research for the Upjohn Institute that led to the book *Industrial Incentives* (Fisher and Peters 1998). The new TAIM^{ez} model is much larger, considerably more flexible, and capable of tax simulations we were not able to perform in the original model. It also contains our responses to issues raised by others about the original model (Netzer 1997; L. Papke 1997; Schwartz 1999). However, in basic structure and principle, the two models work in much the same way. The reader is referred to our earlier book, *Industrial Incentives*, for a more complete discussion of model structure and data sources.

There are very few hypothetical-firm models in the United States. Most have been built with specific purposes in mind and are therefore designed to undertake quite specific simulations. We have discussed at length in various academic papers how hypothetical-firm models should be evaluated.[1] Suffice it is to say here that the overall quality of a hypothetical model should be measured on how well certain pivotal tax questions are dealt with:

- Are federal and local taxes included?
- Are tax incentives included? If so, what range of tax incentives are included?
- Are sales taxes and sales tax exemptions and credits included?
- Does it model an existing firm's new investment so that marginal tax rates can be calculated, rather than the average tax burden on an established firm?
- Is the model multiyear, and if so how well does the model deal with the replacement of assets?
- How well are state apportionment formulae, including throwback rules, taken into account?
- How realistic is the model with regard to the distribution of firm payroll, plant, and sales?

The original TAIM model was designed to deal comprehensively with these seven questions. Since a number of methodological improvements were made to the hypothetical method to provide rigorous solutions to these questions, the new TAIM^{ez} provides a highly flexible environment for modeling state and local taxes and incentives.

HOW THE MODEL WORKS

The TAIM^{ez} model begins by simulating the firm's costs and revenues, and changes in its balance sheet, over a 20-year period, producing a stream of annual cash flows. The simulations are performed twice, the first with the firm operating in a "steady state" for 20 years with no new investment and constant sales and operating costs; the second, with the firm constructing a new plant in one of the states or cities in our study. The internal rate of return (IRR) or the increment to cash flow attributable to the operations of the new plant can be used as the measure of project returns; they capture the profitability of making an investment at a particular site. Differences in project returns among states and cities reflect differences in state and local tax structures and incentive packages.

TAIM^{ez}'s implementation of the hypothetical-firm method allows simulations to be performed with and without the various categories of incentives included in the analysis. For instance, a first run might include the basic tax structure and statewide tax incentives. A second run might add enterprise zone incentives (or a particular enterprise zone incentive). The difference between returns including enterprise zone incentives and without those incentives measures the value to the firm of the enterprise zone incentives. For example, one of the sectors we model is SIC 24, lumber and wood products. In one simulation of 1998 state and local taxes of a small firm in this sector (investing around $700,000 in plant and machinery and equipment, with 25 prospective employees), over the 20-year period of the simulation, the firm would see a return on that investment of around 16.4 percent (or an increment to cash flow of about $380,700) if it located in Ohio but outside an enterprise zone. However, the IRR would rise to 17.4 percent (or a $429,800 increment to cash flow) if it located in an Ohio enterprise zone and received State of Ohio enterprise zone incentives. In other words, the state enterprise zone program is worth about $49,100 more in income to this particular firm.[2]

Along the same lines, the difference between project returns with all incentives (including enterprise zone incentives) included and project returns with only the basic tax structure, measures the after-tax value of the entire incentive package. The difference between returns in Ohio and returns in another state measures the competitive (dis)advantage of Ohio. For instance, the same SIC 24 firm (mentioned above) locating a new plant in an Indiana enterprise zone would generate a 15.9 percent IRR and a $346,100 increment to cash flow. Thus, all else being equal,[3] for this particular firm and investment, the Ohio state enterprise zone program provides an $83,700 competitive advantage over the Indiana state program. One additional advantage of TAIM^{ez} is that individual elements of the tax code—a particular jobs or investment tax credit, for instance—can be evaluated, as can hypothetical changes in such programs.

The model generates a large amount of data besides project cash flow (income) and IRR. Since tax payments to all levels of government must be calculated as a part of the model, these numbers are themselves part of model output. For instance, a property-tax abatement or exemption offered by a community would likely raise the firm's income (its project returns). But in so doing, the exemption increases the taxes paid by the firm to other levels of government (state income tax, for instance) and jurisdictions of government (income taxes paid in other states, for example). Both tax and non-tax incentives thus have implicit intergovernmental revenue transfer consequences. TAIM^{ez} is able to keep track of these and is thus able to calculate the true net revenue costs to a state or local government unit using a particular incentive program. (The measurement of these net revenue costs should not be confused with fiscal impact studies—those in which the object is to measure the costs a project imposes on city- or state-provided services, as well as indirect revenue effects.)

TAIM^{ez}'s fiscal calculations allow us to compare the benefits that an incentive program provides to a firm with the net costs to government of that incentive, taking into account all, or an appropriate subset of, revenue transfers. Doing so allows incentive programs to be compared on the basis of each incentive's benefit-to-firm/cost-to-government ratio. The use of such a ratio has been widely recommended in the economic development literature (for instance, Rasmussen, Bendick, and Ledebur 1984), but has seldom been implemented. Other things being equal, one would want government to maximize usage of incentives that provide most benefit to the firm with least cost to government.

MANUFACTURING SECTORS MODELED

TAIM^{ez} incorporates financial and operating ratios for 16 hypothetical manufacturing firms, based on the characteristics of real firms in 16 manufacturing sectors. In general, we have chosen sectors at various stages in the employment growth cycle. The sectors also vary by labor and capital intensity, so that the full effects of labor and capital subsidies available in enterprise zones can be better understood. Each firm is assumed to construct a new plant, with assumed plant sizes based on employment and asset data for typical manufacturing establishments. Balance sheets, income statements, and statements of cash flows were developed for each firm based mostly on financial statements for actual manufacturing corporations in the commercial database Compustat. For each firm, we specified a new manufacturing facility (total plant and equipment and working capital needed, employment, sales, and so forth); the financial statements for the new plant mirror the characteristics of the parent firm.

Financial statements do not contain information on employment, wages or payroll, and these variables must be included in the firm profiles for the TAIM^{ez} model in order to simulate the effects of tax incentives tied to job creation. Such incentives are usually a dollar amount per new job or a percent of new plant wages. Firm financial statements also tell us nothing about the size of typical establishments (in terms of assets or employment). These problems were solved by relying on two additional sources of data. Annual new-plant payroll for each hypothetical firm was constructed using the average annual wage of production workers by two-digit SIC code from the Annual Survey of Manufactures and an assumed number of new-plant production workers. The new-plant employment figures, in turn, were based on data from two states (Nebraska and Ohio), by two-digit SIC code, that show new manufacturing plant assets and employment. The states collected these data from firms receiving state incentives. These data thus provide exactly what we need: establishment- (not firm-) level data for new manufacturing branch plants. From these data we constructed typical new plant employment sizes by two-digit SIC code. Since the state data also contained the total value of property, plant, and equipment (PP&E), we were able to construct a ratio of assets to employment that allowed us to scale the plant to the typical employment size. New plant PP&E then became the starting point for constructing the new plant financial statements: remaining statement items were constructed as ratios to PP&E, the ratios coming from the firm-level data in the Compustat database.

The most important operating ratios for the sectors that are the focus of this book are described in Table A.1. Capital intensity, as measured by the value of property, plant, and equipment per worker, ranges from $27,000 in the lumber and wood products sector to $181,000 in the primary metal industries. As a percent of total assets, inventories range from about 12 percent to nearly 37 percent, while machinery and equipment ranges from under 14 percent to almost 53 percent. The average annual wage of production workers is under

$14,000 in the apparel sector but reaches almost $38,000 in transportation equipment.

Note that we include no service sectors. This is an important omission, given that many enterprise zones seek to attract firms from a broad range of sectors, including wholesale trade, services, and even retail. Unfortunately, the modeling of sectors other than manufacturing is constrained by the lack of crucial pieces of data. The omission is less important than it might appear, however, given that previous research has shown that a large majority of the jobs that are claimed by enterprise zone administrators are in manufacturing (Erickson and Friedman 1990a).

THE FIRM'S FINANCIAL STATEMENTS

The heart of the TAIM^{ez} model consists of a set of pro-forma financial statements: an income statement, a balance sheet, and a statement of cash flows. The first year is the year prior to new-firm investment. If we are simulating the tax burden on a new plant to begin operation in 1994, for example, the firm's financial statements would begin with 1993, showing income and assets at the beginning of the year in the absence of the new plant. For present value calculations, 1993 is year 0, or the present. The pro-forma projections extend through year 20, or 2014.

In order to focus on the effects of incentives on returns from a new investment, we assume that each hypothetical firm would have been in a "steady state" but for the expansion. That is, each year the gross value of the depreciable assets in place on January 1, 1993 (to continue our example), is maintained by undertaking replacement investment equal to retirements. With straight-line depreciation, annual depreciation of these assets is constant, and therefore accumulated depreciation and the net value of these assets also remain constant. Replacement investment is financed by rolling over long-term debt, so that total long-term debt and interest expense for existing assets remain constant. The result is that the simulation of firm operations in the absence of new-plant investment produces a constant net income after taxes each year for the 20-year period; net income is also equal to cash flow.

Calculation of the steady-state or baseline set of financial statements was not as simple as one might think. This is because the model must calculate state income taxes in at least one state even in the baseline scenario (since we are simulating an existing firm, with assets somewhere) and these state taxes are deductible from income for federal tax purposes. Furthermore, some states

Table A.1 Characteristics of the Representative Firms

Characteristic	Food and kindred products 20[a]	Apparel and other textile products 23	Lumber and wood products 24	Furniture and fixtures 25	Paper and allied products 26	Printing and publishing 27	Chemicals and allied products 28	Rubber & plastics products 30
Firm								
Total assets ($ millions)	100.0	150.0	60.0	175.0	300.0	150.0	400.0	150.0
Total sales ($ millions)	139.9	227.2	162.6	300.6	354.7	207.7	418.8	218.4
New plant								
Total Assets ($ millions)	17.2	25.2	1.4	7.7	18.5	9.0	19.3	21.7
Property, plant & equipment, gross ($ millions)	10.3	7.7	0.7	4.2	12.7	5.0	11.5	13.0
Employees	150	225	25	100	75	150	75	75
Average annual wage ($)	22,643	13,905	19,939	19,391	31,597	24,122	34,944	22,593
Energy costs: % of operating costs	1.2	1.2	1.7	1.1	3.4	0.8	2.8	2.1
Asset composition: % of total assets								
Current assets	39.8	69.5	51.8	45.9	31.5	44.0	40.3	40.2
Inventories	18.0	36.9	21.7	17.9	11.6	12.0	13.7	15.1
Property, plant & equipment	60.2	30.5	48.2	54.1	68.5	56.0	59.7	59.8
Real property	24.2	13.1	23.5	21.7	15.6	14.8	19.8	14.0
Machinery & Equipment	36.1	17.4	24.7	32.4	52.9	41.2	40.0	45.8
Property, plant & equipment per worker ($)	68,930	34,238	27,007	41,893	169,425	33,495	153,610	173,115
Operating profit: % of sales	9.8	9.0	6.9	9.0	13.6	13.2	18.3	11.9
Rate of return (IRR) in a zero-tax state[b] (%)	10.8	13.8	18.2	12.8	13.8	17.4	20.4	17.7

Characteristic	Leather and leather products 31[a]	Stone, clay and glass products 32	Primary metal industries 33	Fabricated metal products 34	Industrial machinery 35	Electric & electronic equipment 36	Transportation equipment 37	Instruments & related products 38
Firm								
Total assets ($ millions)	50.0	200.0	250.0	60.0	50.0	40.0	100.0	100.0
Total sales ($ millions)	70.3	204.3	357.6	92.6	69.2	55.7	173.0	117.6
New plant								
Total Assets ($ millions)	13.9	11.4	45.6	17.1	27.6	42.4	35.2	37.1
Property, plant & equipment, gross ($ mill.)	3.1	7.4	27.2	8.8	10.2	17.8	18.6	15.0
Employees	100	75	150	75	100	100	300	100
Average annual wage	15,584	26,656	33,199	26,188	28,814	24,392	37,898	28,397
Energy costs: % of operating costs	1.0	4.7	4.5	1.5	0.8	0.8	0.6	0.8
Asset composition: % of total assets								
Current assets	77.5	34.9	40.4	48.9	63.2	58.0	47.3	59.5
Inventories	32.0	15.9	18.3	19.2	20.9	20.7	19.1	21.0
Property, plant & equipment	22.5	65.1	59.6	51.1	36.8	42.0	52.7	40.5
Real property	8.8	17.3	13.5	17.8	10.9	12.4	15.8	14.4
Machinery & Equipment	13.7	47.8	46.1	33.3	25.9	29.6	36.9	26.1
Property, plant & equipment per worker	31,308	99,311	181,192	116,686	101,698	177,904	61,850	150,489
Operating profit: % of sales	9.9	16.9	10.8	11.1	10.9	12.5	11.0	13.6
Rate of return (IRR) in a zero-tax state[b]	11.1	15.4	13.9	19.2	12.1	13.6	15.7	15.0

[a] Industry SIC code.
[b] Rate of return on investment in a new plant after federal taxes, if located in a state with no state or local taxes.

allow a deduction for other state income taxes or for federal income taxes. If the model were to allow contemporaneous deductions (so that in a reciprocal-deductibility state such as Iowa, 1992 Iowa taxes are deducted in calculating 1992 federal taxes and 1992 federal taxes are deducted in calculating 1992 Iowa taxes), there would be a circularity problem that would prevent the spreadsheets from calculating. To solve this, we created a separate set of proforma spreadsheets for computing the baseline cash flow; each year after the first year, state income taxes for the *previous* year are deducted in calculating federal income taxes in the current year, thus preventing circularity. Convergence is reached after a few years even in states such as Iowa with reciprocal deductibility; state and federal taxes remain the same each year (at least when rounded to the nearest dollar). The financial statements in the last year of the baseline run (at the point when convergence is assured) define the "steady state," and the baseline cash flow that is produced in the steady state becomes the model's counterfactual—the annual cash flow that would have been produced for the next 20 years in the absence of new-plant investment. The addition to cash flow each year attributable to the new-plant investment is simply the firm's total net cash flow with the new investment less the baseline cash flow.

The model begins by constructing a complete set of financial statements for one of the prototype firms. For 1994 tax simulations, the initial balance sheet is for January 1, 1993; the firm then builds a new establishment, with the new-plant assets going on the books at acquisition cost at the end of 1993. The new-plant assets generate income (and depreciation deductions) beginning January 1, 1994. Short-term assets and liabilities (inventories, accounts payable and receivable, and so forth) are increased proportionately as a result of the expansion. New PP&E is added in the same proportions to total assets as for the existing firm. Additional net working capital (current assets minus current liabilities) necessitated by the new plant, as well as the new-plant fixed assets, are financed by a combination of additional long-term debt, retained earnings, and the sale of common stock (if necessary), in such a way as to maintain the same ratio of debt to equity.

New-plant private debt-financing terms vary by asset class and loan size. The long-term rates (applied to financing land, plant, and infrastructure) are based on corporate A-rated bond rates; the short-term rates (3–4 years, for financing short-lived equipment and working capital) are based on Federal Reserve data on commercial and industrial fixed-rate bank loans, with interest rates declining substantially as loan size increases. Interpolation was used to derive rates for intermediate-term loans (for equipment lasting 7–12 years).

The new PP&E is depreciated for tax purposes according to the MACRS schedule that applies to buildings (straight line for 31.5 years prior to 1994, for

39 years in 1994 or later), infrastructure (15 years, 150 percent declining balance), and machinery and equipment (200 percent declining balance, over a period of 3, 5, or 7 years depending on the industry). The depreciable basis of each asset is its acquisition cost (from the database of firm financial characteristics) plus state and local sales taxes on machinery and equipment, where applicable. Depreciable assets are assumed to have zero salvage value and to be replaced at the end of the appropriate class life (20 years for infrastructure, 40 years for buildings, 5 to 15 years for machinery and equipment). Since we are using a 20-year time horizon, replacement schedules are modeled only for machinery and equipment. Assets are depreciated on the books according to the appropriate ADS straight-line schedule (20 years for infrastructure, 40 years for buildings, 5 to 15 years for machinery and equipment).

TAXES MODELED

Data on state taxes and tax incentives were obtained largely from Commerce Clearing House's *Multi State Corporate Income Tax Guide* and from copies of corporate income tax forms and instructions for each state. Data on local taxes were obtained from state reports, where available, or directly from each city. Local abatement schedules generally had to be obtained directly from the city.

Corporate Income Taxes

TAIM models only the major features of the corporate income and net worth taxes:

- rates,
- deductibility of income taxes paid to other states, the federal government, or one's own state,
- deductibility of property taxes,
- rules for apportionment of income,
- depreciation methods,
- the availability of general credits for other taxes paid, such as sales or property taxes,
- the treatment of nonbusiness income—how it is allocated and whether it is subject to apportionment,
- whether the property factor in the apportionment formula is measured by acquisition cost or book value,

- whether the sales factor includes nonbusiness receipts, and
- the availability of investment tax credits or jobs tax credits.

There seems to be agreement among the developers of hypothetical-firm models that there is little point in modeling the very minor differences in the measurement of the payroll factor or in modeling the differences in the treatment of subcategories of nonbusiness income: rents, royalties, interest on federal bonds, interest on state and local bonds, dividends from subsidiaries, capital gains, and so forth. We would argue that since the focus of our research is on the location of facilities for the generation of sales of products—business income—the treatment of such items is not relevant. There is a practical argument as well: data at this level of detail are not generally available, making the models excessively reliant on empirically unsupported conjectures about firm behavior. We make the simplifying assumption that the hypothetical firms have aggregate nonbusiness income as given by the statistical data sources, but it is entirely in the form of interest on corporate bonds, which is treated uniformly by the states. This approach allows us to model rules for the allocation or apportionment of nonbusiness income without getting into the details of what counts as nonbusiness income and what doesn't. We also ignore the treatment of foreign business income, foreign nonbusiness income, foreign tax credits, extraordinary items such as write-offs for plant closures, goodwill, recapture of federal investment tax credits, and adding back in federal job incentive credits (by creating firms that have no such income or asset category). We do not include firms with losses because of the logical and practical difficulties in doing so over a 20-year period; thus, net operating loss (NOL) provisions would never apply and are not modeled.

Sales Taxes

Most studies consider only the sales tax on purchases of fuel and electricity and of machinery and equipment. These are the two major categories of expenditure by manufacturers that are sometimes taxed and sometimes exempted by the states. The exemptions are most often targeted exclusively at manufacturing machinery, and at fuel and electricity used directly in the manufacturing process, which suggests that at least part of the motivation for the exemption is an economic-development one. Our model includes expenditures on machinery and equipment, furniture and fixtures, computers, and fuel and electricity; it does not include expenditures for office supplies, construction materials, or pollution-control equipment, so the results do not reflect the minor differences caused by state variation in taxing these latter items. Each state's sales tax is part of the model; to the extent that the state applies the sales tax fully to, or exempts, or applies a lower rate to, purchases of manufacturing machinery, computers, furniture and fixtures, transportation equipment, or other personal property, that will be reflected in a higher acquisition cost for those assets, and hence larger depreciation deductions and larger financing requirements. To the extent that the state taxes or exempts purchases of electricity or fuel, or exempts the portion used directly in the manufacturing process, the firm's operating costs will be more or less each year.

Property Taxes

All states allow localities to tax real property (or realty), which consists of land and buildings, and associated site improvements, such as access roads. States vary considerably in rules regarding the taxation of business personal property, which consists of inventories (of raw materials, goods in process, and finished products), manufacturing machinery and equipment, computers and other office machinery, furniture and fixtures, and transportation equipment.

The property-tax component of TAIM^{ez} begins with specification of state policy, which will generally determine whether local property taxes apply to business inventories and to personal property in general, whether categories of personal property such as manufacturing machinery and equipment are exempt, and whether different classes of property must be assessed at different ratios to market value. States also generally establish rules or guidelines for local assessors in determining the market value of personal property; typically, the state will publish schedules for depreciating machinery and equipment, which are usually by category (furniture and fixtures, transportation equipment) and industry (for manufacturing machinery and equipment), just as federal depreciation schedules are. The states that do not publish guidelines allow assessors to use whatever guidelines they think appropriate; for these states, we assume depreciation schedules representing the average of the other states. These state guidelines are used by the model to value personal property; real property is assumed to be valued at book value, using straight-line depreciation over the life of the building.

Property taxes are assumed to be paid in a given calendar year based on the value of property at the end of the previous calendar year. The calculation of property taxes begins with the valuation of taxable classes of property. Inventory and land values are constant from the year of new-plant construction onward, since we assume no inflation and neither asset depreciates. Three states tax inventories of raw materials, goods in process, and finished goods differently. We follow the Wisconsin tax study (1990) in assuming 40 percent of inventories are finished goods; we assume 25 percent are raw materials, 35 percent goods in process. The second step in the calculation of property taxes is the application of the assessment ratio (which may vary locally) to the value of each asset. Finally, the model multiplies the assessed value by the consolidated local property-tax rate—the sum of the rates for the city, the school district (if independent of the city), the county in which a majority of the city is located (where counties exist and levy taxes), and other special districts overlying the city. In the 20-state simulations of "average" locations in a state (rather than particular cities), a statewide effective property-tax rate is applied.

THE GEOGRAPHY OF THE FIRM AND THE DESTINATION OF SALES

Some studies using the hypothetical-firm approach to compare state business tax burdens treat each firm as if it were a single-plant firm, or at least a single-location firm. This may make sense for comparative tax studies, but it is not appropriate for the measurement of development incentives such as enterprise zones, which are provided for *new* investment. A firm with the financial characteristics and asset size of the average mature firm in the industry cannot be treated as if it were a brand new establishment. The sensible approach is to assume an ongoing profitable business that invests in a new branch plant.

Where the parent firm and the new plant are located matters because tax burdens can differ dramatically depending on where a firm's sales, property, and payroll are located. This is because the spatial pattern of the firm's investment determines what proportion of income is taxed in each state. In an analysis of five firms considering locations in 10 states, we found that for half of the states a multistate firm would experience more than a 10 percent better (or worse) rate of return than a single-state firm expanding in its home state (Fisher and Peters 1997b, Table 3).

Assumptions regarding the destination of the hypothetical firms' sales are critical because of the way in which states apportion business income for purposes of income taxation. Most states use a three-factor apportionment formula, where the three factors are payroll, property, and sales. The payroll factor, for example, is the ratio of the firm's payroll located within the state to the firm's payroll everywhere. The sales factor is the ratio of the firm's sales with a destination within the state to the firm's sales everywhere. A weighted average of the three factors produces the apportionment factor; when multiplied by the firm's taxable income derived from operations everywhere, the result is income taxable by the state in question. The weight applied to the sales factor varies from 33 percent in a number of states (equal weight given to the three factors) to 50 percent in many states (double-weighted sales) and 100 percent in a few states (single-factor apportionment).

The sales factor is complicated by throw-back rules. In several states, shipments from facilities in that state to states in which the firm has no tax nexus, or to the federal government, are thrown back to that state—in other words, counted as part of the numerator in the sales factor. Sales destined for states in which the firm is taxable (and in which those sales will be reflected in that state's apportionment formula) are never thrown back.

In constructing a hypothetical-firm simulation, assumptions must be made with respect to the proportion of firm sales destined for: 1) the state in which the new plant is located, 2) the state(s) in which the original firm is located, 3) other states in which the firm is taxable, and 4) other states in which the firm has no tax nexus. These assumptions significantly affect the results in terms of the apparent relative competitiveness of states. If a large share of sales is assumed to go to category (4), this assumption disadvantages a state such as Wisconsin, which requires throw-back of all such sales and which double-weights sales in the apportionment formula. On the other hand, assuming all sales are to states in which the firm is taxable increases the firm's tax liability to those states; this, in turn, puts a premium on the deductibility of other states' income taxes, allowed in only a few states, and eliminates throwback effects entirely.

The design of the model may constrain the sales assumptions that one can make. If the model permits each firm to be located and taxed in only one or two states, as most models do, one must assume that sales are quite unevenly distributed (with all or most sales going to just those one or two states) or one must assume that most sales are to the other 48 or 49 states and that the firm has no tax nexus (not even a sales office) in any of those states. Both these assumptions are unrealistic. Data from Wisconsin corporate income tax returns indicate that, among apportioning corporations, about 16 percent of total sales are thrown back, in the aggregate.

The creation of a median state, intended to represent all other states in which the firm has facilities, provides a solution to the sales allocation dilemma. We give this mythical state a population representing a large share of the total U.S. population, and then allocate sales among the particular actual state, the mythical median state, and the remaining (non-taxing) states in proportion to population. This has the effect of attributing only a small share of sales to non-taxing states (we assume 15 percent) without forcing the remainder to occur in the actual state; most of the remainder is destined instead for the median state, where the firm is taxed. This provides more accurate comparisons of throwback versus non-throwback states, as well as of states allowing deductions for other states' income taxes versus states that do not. It is also consistent with the national markets assumption; the actual state is allocated sales only in proportion to its share of national population.

MEASURING EFFECTS OVER TIME AND THE PROBLEM OF INFLATION

Almost all hypothetical-firm studies have assumed zero inflation; that is, the financial projections are in real terms. If all project revenues and costs inflated at the same rate, nominal cash flows discounted at the nominal discount rate would equal real flows discounted at the real rate, and the zero inflation assumption would be harmless. But depreciation deductions and interest expenses do not inflate; they are fixed at the time assets are purchased and financed. The higher inflation is, the more advantageous are accelerated forms of depreciation, since inflation erodes the real value of the deductions taken in later years. On the other hand, inflation reduces the real after-tax cost of debt.

The zero-inflation assumption could bias comparisons among states to the extent that depreciation rules or the timing of incentives differ. Almost all states allow federal MACRS depreciation, a notable exception being New Jersey, which requires a less accelerated form of depreciation. By ignoring inflation we ignore the lesser real value of New Jersey's depreciation rules compared to other states. Similarly, consider state A, which provides incentives up front in the form of grants, and state B, which provides incentives spread over 10 years (in the form of below-market rate loans). Inflation has no effect on the value of A's grants, but reduces the real value of B's annual interest cost reductions unless the interest subsidy is increased during periods of high inflation.

How substantial is the bias produced by assuming no inflation? Brooks, Tannenwald, Sale, and Puri (1986) tested the effects of a 5 percent inflation rate over the entire 60-year period of their analysis, which calculated after-tax rates of return on new investment at 16 sites in 11 states. Ten of the states allowed federal ACRS (accelerated) depreciation at that time; one (New York) required pre-ACRS depreciation, resulting in quite different allowances in the first few years. The analysis also provided a test of the significance of incentive-timing differences: investment tax credits were offered at various rates by 4 of the 11 states. (Unlike other tax features that apply uniformly from year to year, an ITC usually provides all its benefits in the year an asset is acquired.) Despite these differences among states, these researchers found that "the actual rankings of the sixteen sites are virtually identical to those calculated assuming zero inflation" (Brooks et al. 1986, p. 65).

Inflation could also affect comparisons of incentive packages available at different points in time. In this book, we compare the tax burdens and incentive packages based on 1990 tax law with those based on 1992, 1994, or 1998 tax law. In all comparisons, we use the same yardstick: representative firm financial ratios based on actual 1992 corporate financial statements and 1992 Census of Manufactures data. This yardstick fixes technology, prices, capacity utilization, and sales as they existed in 1992, which of course was a particular point in the business cycle. Our comparisons thus show how a manufacturing firm as it existed in 1992 would have fared if 1990, 1992, 1994, or 1998 tax law had been applied to its financial results. The tax and incentive differences that the model produces are therefore entirely due to tax law changes, and not to changes in technology, prices, or the point in the business cycle.

One must be careful, however, in interpreting differences in model results across years. If, for example, the incentive package per job in a particular state for a particular firm was worth $2,000 under 1990 law and $2,500 under 1998 law, that may or may not mean that incentives increased 25 percent in real terms between 1990 and 1998. Let us suppose that the incentive consisted entirely of an investment tax credit worth 8 percent of the value of new machinery in 1990, increased to 10 percent by 1998. This is clearly a real 25 percent increase in the value of the incentive. Incentives expressed as percentages are, in effect, automatically indexed to inflation (such as rises in the cost of the machinery). If we had built into the model inflation in industrial machinery prices, the nominal value of the incentive would have been more than $2,500 in 1998.

On the other hand, suppose that the incentive consisted entirely of a $2,000 per job credit in 1990, increased to $2,500 in 1998. Inflation will have eroded that value over the 8-year period. If wages had risen over that period, the firm would have received the statutory $2,500 in 1998 in nominal terms, but less than that in real (1990) dollars. The value of the credit as a percent of wages would have fallen. In practice, job credits are frequently expressed in this fashion, and the dollar amount is not adjusted for inflation in most states. There are also fixed dollar amounts in the form of thresholds and ceilings that affect incentive values. Thus, inflation can affect the real value of complex tax and incentive packages in complex ways that are not captured in our model, which assumes constant prices. In some states, the change in the real value of incentives over the period 1990 to 1998 will be less than the change shown by our model results.

DISCRETIONARY INCENTIVES

Probably the biggest hole in the current research is that we have tended to ignore discretionary agreements, including grant and loan programs, loan guarantees, and special discretionary deals.[4] Our earlier research paid considerable methodological attention to how the worth of discretionary incentives should be measured. While TAIM^{ez} is capable of simulating discretionary incentives, we have not gone out and collected information on what discretionary incentives were available in enterprise zones in 1990, 1992, 1994, 1996, and 1998. The task would have been much too large and, given the results of our earlier research on this matter (Fisher and Peters 1997b, 1998), it is unclear that the inclusion of such data would have had a substantive impact on our conclusions about enterprise zones.

Moreover, we believe that in the present study there are good methodological reasons for leaving out estimates of actual discretionary awards. Tax incentives are by far the largest incentive in enterprise zones. Even within individual enterprise zones offering discretionary incentives, variation in the size of the awards present important methodological difficulties for the sorts of econometric modeling we do later in this book. Furthermore, there is reason to believe that firms respond more to tax incentives than to discretionary incentives.

Appendix Notes

1. See Fisher and Peters (1997b, 1998).
2. The increments to cash flow are measured in present value terms; the annual increment to cash flow over 20 years is discounted at 10 percent.
3. What we mean by "all else being equal" is that TAIM^{ez} assumes that all non-tax costs (wage rates, for example) are equal in Ohio and Indiana. The only costs that vary are tax costs. We also assume that the factor composition of the investment at the two sites remains identical.

4. For instance, in Ohio it is not uncommon for a firm that has received a large property-tax abatement in an enterprise zone to donate money to the local school district in lieu of the tax payment. Such donations have tax consequences useful to the firm. Deals such as these are, more often than not, privately negotiated, and we found it impossible to gather good information on them.

Appendix B

Do High-Unemployment Places Have Lower Business Taxes? A Comparison of Results from TAIM and TAIM^{ez}

As we indicated in Chapter 2, Bartik (1991) has made a persuasive case for the plausibility of national economic benefits from state and local competition for jobs. Provided that tax cuts and incentive awards are more generous in areas with higher rates of unemployment, and therefore tend to redistribute employment toward such areas and away from areas of lower unemployment, there will be a net gain for the nation as a whole because 1) the benefits of a new job, measured as the wage the job offers minus the reservation wage of the person employed, are greater in high-unemployment areas because the reservation wage is inversely related to the local unemployment rate; 2) inflationary pressures may be reduced by increasing employment in labor surplus areas where cost-push effects will be minimal and reducing it in tight labor markets; 3) total employment may be increased because the overall level of labor subsidies nationally is increased; and 4) the distribution of income may become more equal, since the most pronounced effects will be felt by minorities with above-average rates of unemployment.

Whether competitive state and local economic-development policy enhances the welfare of the nation as a whole depends crucially on whether incentives do affect location and where such incentives are offered. The first issue has been researched extensively, and two recent and comprehensive reviews of that research have been published. Bartik's (1991 and 1994) reviews of the literature on the effects of taxes on investment, employment, or gross state product led him to conclude that the probable long-run interstate or interregional elasticity with respect to total state and local taxes is about –0.3. Wasylenko (1997) concludes that a reasonable estimate of this elasticity is about –0.2. In other words, a 10 percent across-the-board reduction in state and local taxes should produce about a 2 percent to 3 percent increase in business activity.

Earlier research has provided only limited, and somewhat contradictory, evidence on the second issue: what kind of places offer the lowest taxes or highest incentives. We have reported elsewhere (Fisher and Peters 1998) on whether the economic-development incentives offered by states and cities are significantly higher in high-unemployment places—in other words, whether there is evidence that the end result of competition for jobs *could* be a redistribution of jobs to regions that would benefit the most. The original study employed a hypothetical-firm model to analyze taxes and incentives in 24 states (that together accounted for about 85 percent of U.S. manufacturing employment) and a random sample of 112 cities in those states. This research concluded that state and local tax systems, considered in the absence of any investment or jobs incentives, were perverse in their effects, with higher-unemployment places tending to have higher taxes. The combined effects of statewide, citywide, and enterprise zone incentives were, however, sufficient (on average) to overcome the perversity of the state-local tax system. But the end result was a pattern of returns on investment that was essentially random: there was no discernible tendency for returns to be more attractive in high-unemployment or in low-unemployment places.

These results were consistent with the following two arguments (though they certainly cannot be taken as proof of either one). First, state and local tax reductions and development incentives are adopted for a variety of reasons; high unemployment perhaps is one, but slow growth and simple imitation of other states may be more important.[1] Furthermore, large deals struck with particular firms subsequently produce pressure to extend the same kinds of tax breaks to other firms in order to "level the playing field," regardless of the economic climate. The second argument is that even where economic distress (perhaps a recession) may have provided the original political impetus to cut business taxes or adopt incentives, these measures are likely to persist even if state economic performance improves.

As part of our current research project on enterprise zones, we have expanded the simulation model to incorporate state taxes and tax incentives for each year from 1990 through 1997, for 16 of the 24 states in the original study.[2] These 16 states include 88 of the 112 cities in the sample. To test the robustness of our results, we calculated the return on investment for each of 29 manufacturing sectors (the original model included only 8) for each of the 88 cities in 1990 and in 1997. The 16 states include all of the original 24 states that had active significant enterprise zone programs. Of the 88 cities, 34 had enterprise zones in 1990; 11 more established enterprise zones between 1991 and 1996.

The results of the simulations using the smaller sample of 88 cities with 1990 and 1997 taxes and incentives are shown in Table B.1. The basic result found in the earlier book was corroborated. The pattern of returns on investment in new plants considering only the basic state and local tax systems was negatively correlated with unemployment rates in 1990. Cities with higher unemployment had higher tax rates on investment. Incentives moderated this effect to a degree since they tended to be higher in high-unemployment cities. By

Table B.1 Correlation between City Unemployment Rate and Return on New Manufacturing Investment for 88 Cities in 16 States

Return on investment	1990[a]	1997[b]
Return		
After basic state and local taxes	−0.26	−0.14
After taxes and statewide incentives	−0.19	−0.08
With zone incentives	−0.14	−0.09
Value		
Total incentive package	0.16	0.05
Zone incentive package	0.07	−0.04

NOTE: Correlations shown are weighted averages of the correlations for each of 29 manufacturing sectors, where the weights are the sectors' shares of U.S. manufacturing employment in 1992.

[a] For 1990, return after 1990 taxes and incentives was corrrelated with the city unemployment rate in 1990.

[b] Return after 1997 taxes and incentives was correlated with 1996 unemployment rate.

1997, however, these effects were weaker. Basic tax systems were less perverse in their distributional pattern, and incentives exhibited no discernible spatial pattern.

This analysis was also performed at the state level, using a statewide average local tax system to represent a "typical" city for each state. While differences in local tax rates and tax abatements were substantial, it was largely changes in state policies between 1990 and 1997 that accounted for the changes in state-local tax rates on new investment over that period. Focusing on states allowed us to measure the size of the changes in state taxes and incentives. Table B.2 shows how the average state-local tax rate on investment was related to state average unemployment rates. For 1990, the pattern was very similar to the city results, as one would expect. The perverse distributional effects of basic state and local taxes were only partly offset by the slight tendency of non-zone incentives to be higher in higher-unemployment states. In 1997, however, the negative relation between basic taxes and unemployment had largely disappeared as had the positive relation between incentives and unemployment. Enterprise zone incentives, meanwhile, were *negatively*

Table B.2 Correlation between State Unemployment Rate and Return on New Manufacturing Investment at an Average Location in Each State

Return on investment	1990[a]	1997[b]
Return		
After basic state and local taxes	−0.22	−0.07
After taxes and statewide incentives	−0.14	0.08
With zone incentives	−0.19	−0.09
Value		
Total incentive package	0.09	−0.01
Zone incentive package	−0.01	−0.21

NOTE: Correlations shown are weighted averages of the correlations for each of 29 manufacturing sectors, where the weights are the sectors' shares of U.S. manufacturing employment in 1992.

[a] For 1990, return after 1990 taxes and incentives was correlated with state unemployment rate in 1990–1992.

[b] Return after 1997 taxes and incentives was correlated with 1996–1998 unemployment rate.

correlated with state unemployment, lower unemployment states offering larger zone incentives.

Differences between city and state results reflected the implicit weighting provided by the city sample. Since the cities were sampled without regard to state, the most populous states (California, Florida, and Texas) had a large proportion of the cities in the sample, so state policies in those populous states had a much larger effect on the city correlations. The negative relation between zone incentives and state unemployment in 1997 was largely due to the enactment of enterprise zone programs in Michigan and Iowa in 1996 and 1997, two states with lower-than-average unemployment. But since there were only six cities in these two states, these new zone programs had less effect on the city correlations. The state correlations also tended to overstate the effects of zones, since for the runs that included zone incentives the "average" site in each state was assumed to be in an enterprise zone, regardless of how widespread zones were in that state.

To get a sense of which states had made the most significant changes in tax and incentive policies between 1990 and 1997, we computed a weighted average rate of return on new investment for each state, where the return for each sector was weighted by that sector's share of manufacturing employment nationally. We then ranked the states by that average rate of return. Table B.3 shows the results; the eight states in the top half had below-average unemployment rates in the period 1996–1998 (and all but one also had rates at or below average in the recession years 1990–1992). The eight states in the bottom half had unemployment rates at or above the average in both 1990–1992 and 1996–1998.

There is no discernible relation between the state's average level of economic distress, as measured by unemployment rates, and that state's adoption of business tax cuts or development incentives between 1990 and 1997. In fact, the low-unemployment states improved their situation on average slightly more than the high-unemployment states. And while Michigan had the highest unemployment rate in the earlier period (8.5 percent) and subsequently enacted what stands as the most generous set of enterprise zone incentives among all the states, the Renaissance Zones (as they are called) were not enacted until 1996. At that point the unemployment rate had fallen to 4.9 percent; so although Michigan subsequently moved from 11th to 1st place overall, it would be difficult to argue causality in either direction, unemployment rates bringing about incentives or the Renaissance Zones being responsible for the decline in unemployment (they went into effect only in 1997).

Table B.3 States Ranked by Return on Investment after Taxes and Incentives, 1990–1997

State[a]	1990: IRR[b] after all incentives	Changes in IRR 1990–97		1997: IRR after all incentives	Unemployment rate 1990–92	Unemployment rate 1996–98
		Due to basic tax changes	Due to changes in incentive package			
With low unemployment						
Minn.	13	3	16	16	5.0	3.0
Iowa	4	1	15	4	4.5	3.1
Ind.	15	9	2	8	6.1	3.4
Wis.	7	11	11	10	5.0	3.4
Va.	6	16	4	7	5.5	3.8
Mich.	11	5	1	1	8.5	4.1
Ohio	3	6	5	3	6.4	4.2
Mo.	5	15	9	9	6.0	4.3
Average rank	8	8	8	7		
Average value	12.9	0.06	0.40	14.0	5.9	3.7
With high unemployment						
Ill.	2	12	13	6	6.5	4.7
Conn.	10	2	12	11	6.4	4.8
Fla.	9	7	14	12	7.1	4.8
Pa.	14	13	7	15	6.6	4.9
Ky.	8	14	3	5	6.7	5.0

Tex.	12	4	10	13	6.8	5.3
N.Y.	1	10	8	2	7.0	5.9
Calif.	16	8	6	14	7.4	6.4
Average rank	9	9	9	10		
Average value	12.9	0.04	0.18	13.7	6.8	5.2

NOTE: Highest rate of return or largest improvement in rate of return is ranked 1.

[a] States are listed in order by 1996–98 unemployment rate.

[b] Average rate of return (IRR) was calculated by weighting each of the 29 sectors by that sector's share of U.S. manufacturing employment in 1992.

Appendix Notes

1. State incentives of all kinds, and investment returns after all state taxes and incentives, were negatively correlated with state employment growth between 1980 and 1990; in other words, slower-growing states offered higher incentives and higher overall returns.
2. This sample, from our original research published in Fisher and Peters (1998) and elsewhere, is used nowhere else in this book. We use the original sample here to indicate the comparability of the original results and those reported in this book.

Appendix C

The Tax Elasticity of Employment
and Fiscal Break-Even

Bartik (1994) argued that the fiscal effects of tax cuts are bound to be negative, given the likely elasticities of economic activity with respect to differences in state and local taxes. Assuming the measure of activity is employment, this elasticity can be written:

$$(1) \quad E = \frac{dJ/J}{dT/T},$$

where T represents the state-local tax rate and J represents total employment. He then states that the net percentage change in state-local revenue resulting from a new job, denoted dR/R, is approximately equal to dT/T plus dJ/J. Tax revenues will increase by the percentage increase in jobs, and decrease by the percentage reduction in tax rate. Substituting terms, he arrives at the formula for the net change in revenue per new job:

$$(2) \quad \frac{dR}{dJ} = \frac{R}{J}(1 + 1/E).$$

For the R/J term, Bartik (1994, p. 860) substituted the national average state-local direct business tax revenue per job across all business sectors, which is about \$1,620. Assuming an elasticity of -0.3, the fiscal effect of a new job on average would then be $-\$3,780$.

Bartik also showed that fiscal break-even occurs when the elasticity is equal to -1.0. Break-even occurs when dR/dJ in Equation 2 is equal to zero. If we set $(R/J)(1 + 1/E)$ equal to zero and solve for E the result is -1.

One can also derive the conditions for fiscal breakeven in the context of changes in *marginal* state-local tax rates (taking into account investment or job-creation incentives) and changes in the *gross flow* of new jobs, rather than changes in average tax rates and the level of employment. We will use the following notation:

T = total or gross taxes paid per job
C = cut in taxes per job (or the per-job value of credits or other incentives tied to investment or job creation)
I = induced jobs (number of jobs induced by the incentives)

N = noninduced jobs (number of jobs that would have been created in the absence of the incentives)

$(T - C)$ = net tax revenue per new job

Fiscal break-even occurs when the gain equals the loss; that is, when the net revenues obtained from the jobs induced by those incentives equal the cost of the incentives provided for the jobs that would have been created even without incentives:

$$I(T - C) = NC,$$

which, by rearranging terms, could also be written:

$$IT = C(N + I) \quad \text{or}$$

$$I/(N + I) = C/T$$

In other words, fiscal breakeven requires that the percentage increase in employment induced by the incentives is equal to the percentage tax cut. This could also be written as an elasticity:

$$(3) \quad \frac{I/(N + I)}{C/T} = 1 = E.$$

Thus if a locality adopts a property-tax-abatement ordinance that cuts property taxes on new manufacturing plants by 25 percent from their existing level, then at least 25 percent of the gross new manufacturing jobs created in that locality in the future must be attributable to the abatement if the locality is to break even in terms of tax revenue.[1]

The usefulness of this formulation depends on whether or not we can draw inferences about fiscal break-even from the literature on the elasticity of business activity with respect to taxes. The elasticity of Equation 3 is based on break-even conditions that assume cuts in *marginal* tax rates, not cuts in the average tax rate. That is, revenue losses occur only because some *future* jobs that would have been created anyway will benefit from the cuts; the losses do not include reductions in revenue from all existing jobs, as would occur with an across-the-board reduction in the tax rate. Thus, fiscal break-even from incentives is likely if the research on the effects of changes in the marginal tax rate on the gross flow of business activity indicates an elasticity of 1.0 or more.

Much of the research on taxes and business activity has measured changes in the average level of business taxation and changes in the level of employment. Bartik (1991, p. 235) has shown that the two elasticities—the marginal and the average—are equivalent "if all gross new activity responds the same as the dependent variable being considered to taxes, and death rates are roughly constant." The first condition means that we assume that we can draw inferences about the sensitivity of new job creation or establishment birth rates to changes in taxes from studies of the effects of taxes on, for example, gross flows of new investment. The second condition is illustrated with the following equation, where J is total jobs, G is the number of jobs gained, and L is the number of jobs lost:

(4) $J_t = J_{t-1} + G_t - L_t$.

Bartik assumes that the "death rate" or rate of job loss L_t/J_{t-1} is a constant fraction f; this implies that death rates are unaffected by changes in taxes. Then in long-run equilibrium, where J has settled at a new constant level $J^* = J_t = J_{t-1}$, and substituting $(f \times J_{t-1})$ for L_t, Equation 4 becomes:

$J_t = J_t + G_t - fJ_t$,

which can be rearranged:

$J^* = G_t/f$

$G_t/J^* = f$.

In other words, in equilibrium the gross rate of job growth must equal the gross rate of job loss. Bartik concludes: "Hence, a given percentage effect of taxes on gross new activity will imply the same long-run percentage effect of taxes on total business activity" (1991, p. 235).

This conclusion can best be demonstrated with an example. Suppose an economy with 100 jobs is initially in equilibrium with a death rate of 10 percent. Equation 4 would become:

$100 = 100 + 10 - 10$.

Now suppose that the elasticity of gross new activity with respect to taxes is 1.0 so that a 20 percent cut in marginal tax rates produces a 20 percent increase in the gross flow of new jobs G, or an increase from 10 to 12 per period. A new long-run equilibrium will be attained:

$120 = 120 + 12 - 12$.

In other words, total employment will also grow 20 percent, at which point the annual job loss of 10 percent × 120 will just offset the new permanently higher annual job gains. The gross job growth *rate* has also been restored to its original level of 10 percent. The 20 percent tax cut thus produced a 20 percent increase in gross annual job gains *and* in total jobs. Under Bartik's assumptions, the distinction between the marginal and average elasticities becomes moot, and we can legitimately compare and summarize a wide range of elasticity studies. It should also be pointed out that we are talking about long-run elasticities here; a 20 percent increase in the annual gross flow of jobs will *eventually* produce a 20 percent increase in total employment. If this elasticity is equal to 1, fiscal break-even will occur immediately and each year, not just at the point of long-run equilibrium.

One remaining problem appears to stand in the way of drawing inferences about the fiscal effects of incentives: the elasticity research has been based for the most part on studies using a tax variable that represents differences in average tax rates, cross-sectionally or over time, whereas the denominator in Equation 3 is the percentage reduction in tax rates on new investment. This is not as serious a problem as it appears. A 20 percent cut in taxes across the board will also produce a 20 percent cut in taxes on new investment (though the reverse is not true), and it is the cut in taxes on investment that is presumably the cause of the increased economic activity represented by the dependent variable. Thus one could argue that these econometric studies really have been estimating the effects of cuts in taxes on new investment.

This is a valid argument to an extent, but it is likely that the proliferation of investment incentives over the past two decades has meant that the marginal rate has been declining and gradually pulling the average down with it, so that the measured reductions in average rates have understated the reductions in rates on new investment. To the extent that is true, the estimated elasticities are overstated. An observed increase in investment or jobs will have been produced, for example, not by the measured 20 percent reduction in average rates but by the 50 percent reduction in marginal rates that was responsible for pulling the average down. The tax cut in the denominator, if measured properly, would have been 50 percent instead of 20 percent, and therefore the elasticity would have been smaller. The upshot is that incentives are probably even less likely to produce fiscal break-even than we might have concluded by simply comparing Bartik's consensus elasticity of –0.2 to –0.4 with the break-even marginal elasticity of –1.0.

If one is willing to assume that the consensus long-run interstate or intermetropolitan elasticity of about –0.2 to –0.4 can also be interpreted as a reasonable estimate of the marginal elasticity of Equation 3, and that jobs and establishment births and capital investment all respond in approximately the same fashion to changes in taxes, we can then rewrite this elasticity to solve for the average expected percentage increase in establishment births given these elasticities and given a particular percentage tax cut represented by incentives:

$$(5) \quad \frac{I}{N+I} = E \frac{C}{T}.$$

The average tax cut (C/T) among the 75 enterprise zone cities in our sample was 26.4 percent, indicating that we should expect an increase in the birth rate (and, in the long run, in total manufacturing establishments) of 5 percent to 11 percent.

Appendix Note

1. It can be shown that the elasticity of Equation 3 is identical to the standard elasticity formula based on the average over the interval, so that the percentage increase in jobs is equal to induced jobs divided by an average of total new jobs before and after (or with and without) the incentives, and the percentage tax cut is the cut divided by the average of taxes per job with and without the incentives.

Appendix D

The SSEL Data

The purpose of this appendix is to describe in more detail the structure of the SSEL (Standard Statistical Establishment List) data set prepared by the Census Bureau for this research project, and to discuss certain problems with the data. The data set consists of establishment counts for every ZIP code in the United States for three time periods: 1989–1991, 1991–1993, and 1993–1995. The data cover every domestic employer establishment for every 2-digit sector (SIC code) and for industry divisions, with the exception of private households and governments. The data set includes approximately 1.5 million establishments affiliated with about 180,000 multi-establishment firms, and about 5 million single-establishment firms. The data in the SSEL come from a variety of sources, including IRS payroll tax records, annual company organization surveys sent to all multi-unit companies, the Annual Survey of Manufactures, and Current Industrial Reports surveys.

All establishments were further categorized by employment-size class and by seven mutually exclusive status groups: births, deaths, moves in, moves out, expansions, contractions, and constant employment. The latter three groups include only establishments that were in the same ZIP code in the first year and the last year of the period (as, for example, in 1989 and in 1991). Definitions of each of these categories can be found in Chapter 6. We discuss problems with the employment-size categorizations and with the various status classifications below.

EMPLOYMENT-SIZE CLASS

Establishments were categorized by three employment-size classes: 0–19, 20–99, and 100 or more. Establishment employment could change during a two-year period; in most cases, the establishment is categorized by employment in the first year of the period. The only exception is for establishments that were "born" in the second or third year of the period; here the size class must be determined by employment in the last year of the period. Employee counts are always as of the census survey conducted in mid March of each year.

271

The smallest employment-size class includes zero because an establishment could be in the database for 1989, for example, even though it had no employees in mid March of 1989. This could happen if the establishment were created after March, or if it were shut down for seasonal reasons in March. As a result, there will be too many establishments in the smallest size class and too few in the other two classes. This problem does not affect the regression analyses in Chapter 7 since establishments were not broken down by size for this purpose. For the descriptive tables in Chapter 6, however, we made adjustments to the counts of birth and deaths to provide a better picture of establishment turnover by size. Adjustments to the expansion and contraction rates and problems with the moves in and out are discussed in separate sections below.

Birth counts by size class were adjusted by estimating the number of births that occurred in the last 9.5 months of 1991, 1993, or 1995 for the 0–19 size class. We assume that the birth rate is constant over the 24-month period (1990 and 1991, for example) so that 9.5/24 or 40 percent of the births counted for the given time period actually occurred after the mid-March employment reporting date in 1991 or 1993 or 1995 and therefore have an unknown employment size (though they were categorized in 0–19). The estimated number of births that occurred after the point in March at which employment was measured was subtracted from the total number of births in the 0–19 size class. The result is a distribution of births by size class for all establishments for which employment size was known. We assume that the establishments in the unknown category are distributed by size in the same proportions; that is, we assume that births in the last 9.5 months occur in the same proportions by employment size as they did in the first 14.5 months. We then allocate the unknown-size births to the three size classes in accordance with these proportions.

Similar adjustments were made to the death counts. Deaths that occurred in the first 2.5 months of 1989, 1991, and 1993 (after January 1 but prior to the mid March employment count) will show zero March employment. We therefore assume that 2.5/24 or 10.4 percent of the total deaths in a given time period are actually of unknown employment size; these deaths are subtracted from deaths in the 0–19 size class. Once again, the proportions of establishments in each size class, for the remaining cases of known size, are used to allocate the unknown-size establishments among size classes.

Birth rates are calculated by dividing the adjusted birth counts for each size class and SIC code by the estimated number of establishments in that grouping as of the start of the period. For example, births during 1990 and 1991 are divided by the number of establishments as of the beginning of 1990, which is estimated by taking the number of establishments present at some point during 1989 (BEGIN) and subtracting an estimate of the number of deaths during 1989 (assumed to be one-half of the actual deaths during 1989 and 1990 combined). Similarly, death rates are calculated by dividing the adjusted death counts for each size class and SIC code by the estimated number of establishments in that grouping as of the start of the period. For example, deaths during 1989 and 1990 are divided by the number of establishments as of the beginning of 1989, which is estimated by taking the number of establishments present at some point during 1989 (BEGIN) and subtracting an estimate of the number of births during 1989 (assumed to be one-half of the actual births during 1990 and 1991 combined).

Misclassification by employment size should occur less often for moves in and out because these establishments existed elsewhere for part of the period and the employment size should in most cases have been correctly determined by March employment in one ZIP code or the other. For example, an establishment that moved from ZIP A to ZIP B after March 1991 will be recorded as a move into ZIP B for the first time period and will be assigned an employment size based on March 1991 employment in ZIP A. However, if the establishment moved into ZIP B sometime in 1990 and then died after January 1, 1991, but before mid March 1991 it would show up as a move in (because it had payroll some time during 1991 in ZIP B) but with zero employment. This is unlikely to happen very often, but, unfortunately, there is no way to estimate the number of establishments that move and then die within this particular 2.5-month period.

Similarly, an establishment that was born in ZIP A after mid March of 1989 but before December 31, 1989, would show up in the 0–19 size class regardless of actual employment; if this establishment then moved to ZIP B in 1990 or 1991, it would be recorded as a move out of ZIP A for the 1989–1991 period. It is impossible to estimate how many of the establishments moving out of a ZIP code were born within that 9.5-month period. However, moving so soon after being born seems more likely to occur with very small single-establishment firms, which would be correctly classified in the 0–19-size class anyway, rather than larger branch plants. Thus, no adjustments were made to the size-class categorizations for the moves in and out, but it seems doubtful that the overcounting in the smallest size class is very significant.

BIRTHS AND DEATHS

The number of births and deaths recorded in the SSEL data set within a time period will produce reasonably accurate birth or death rates for a 24-

month period and therefore can be divided by two to get annual rates. The two-year death rate is recorded accurately by counting as "present" in 1989 all establishments with payroll for at least one day and counting as "absent" in 1991 only establishments with no payroll for any day that year. All establishments that actually died after January 1, 1989, will get counted as deaths, while no firm that died after January 1, 1991, will be counted as a death, so there will be exactly two years' worth of deaths counted: all those that occurred in 1989 and 1990 (with the minor exceptions noted below). Conversely, the birth rate for 1989–1991 will record as a birth all firms that were actually born after December 31, 1989 (no payroll for any day in 1989) but before January 1, 1992 (at least one day of payroll in 1991). Thus the birth count will record (almost) all births during 1990 and 1991.

The only error for birth and death rates occurs when an establishment that is born in the middle year of a period then dies the same year; such establishments are not counted at all. For example, an establishment that was born in a ZIP code in January 1990 and then died in December 1990 should actually count as a birth and a death for the period 1989–1991. It is not counted as a birth because it had no payroll in the ZIP code at any time during 1991, and it is not counted as a death because it had no payroll in the ZIP code at any time during 1989. On the other hand, firms that are born during 1991 or 1993 and die the same year are counted both ways: as a birth for the earlier period and a death for the later period. The undercounting will occur only for years 1990, 1992 and 1994. For a given year, the sum of uncounted births will exactly equal the sum of uncounted deaths. Unfortunately, we have no way of determining the extent of this undercounting but we assume it is small for the manufacturing sector.

MOVES IN AND OUT

Moves in and out of a ZIP code are determined in a fashion analogous to births and deaths. An establishment that is coded in ZIP A in 1989 and is coded in ZIP B in 1991 is counted as a move out for ZIP A and as a move in for ZIP B for the 1989–1991 period. Thus moves in, like births, should be recorded for establishments that actually moved into the ZIP during 1990 and 1991, and moves out for establishments that left the ZIP during 1989 and 1990. Establishments that move existed in two different ZIP codes during the year of the move, yet the SSEL database records only one location for any one year (with the minor exception of establishments that underwent a reorganization during the year).[1] It is up to the firm to report the address of the establishment.

As a result, moves that occurred in the middle year (such as 1990) will always be recorded correctly, but moves that occurred during 1989 and 1991 may or may not be recorded as moves during the 1989–1991 period. Suppose an establishment moves in mid 1989 from ZIP A to ZIP B; if it is recorded as being in ZIP A for 1989 it will count as a move, but if it is recorded in ZIP B for 1989 (and is still in ZIP B in 1991) then it will not be a move. Instead, it will be included in either the expansion, contraction, or constant employment category. Similarly, if it moved during 1991, then it will count as a move into ZIP B for 1989–1991 if the firm reports the 1991 location as ZIP B. If it is still coded in ZIP A for 1991, it will not be a move for that period, though it will end up as a move for the 1991–1993 period.

The result of these arbitrary classifications during the year of the move is that the "moves in" category for, say, 1989–1991, will include *some* of the moves during 1989, *all* of the moves during 1990, and *some* of the moves during 1991. The same can be said for moves out, of course. For large units of observation, it is likely that the percentage of actual moves during 1989 that are recorded as moves is about equal to one minus the percentage of actual moves during 1990 that are recorded as moves, so that the total approximates two years of moves. Suppose, for example, that firms are more likely to report the new location; this occurs in 60 percent of the cases. Then 40 percent of the 1989 moves into ZIP B will be recorded as moves in (because they had the old ZIP, ZIP A, for 1989), while 60 percent of the moves into ZIP B during 1991 will be recorded as moves in (because they show the new ZIP, ZIP B, for 1991). Then we would end up with approximately two years' worth of moves in, as long as the overall actual moving rates were about the same in 1989 and 1991. The same result would follow if most firms recorded whichever ZIP the establishment was in for the majority of the year, as long as the time pattern of moves over the course of a year was the same in 1989 and 1991. The more disaggregated the data (a single ZIP, a single SIC code, a single size class) the smaller the numbers involved and the less likely it is that the data are an accurate representation of two years' worth of moves.

The data set does not allow us to distinguish establishments that actually moved (in or out of a ZIP code) from those that remained in the same place but had their ZIP codes changed due to ZIP code boundary changes.

EXPANSIONS AND CONTRACTIONS

The data on expansions and contractions overstate the actual number of establishments that increased or reduced employment in a two-year time span.

Expansions counted for the 1989–1991 period, for example, will include some establishments that were born between March 12, 1989, and December 31, 1989. Such establishments will have payroll for some part of 1989 and so will not be counted as births for the 1990–1991 time period, but they will have zero employees in March 1989 and will most likely have more than zero in March 1991. These establishments end up appearing as if they were in the ZIP throughout the period and increased employment. It is even possible that a contraction is reported as an expansion and vice versa. Consider an establishment that went into operation in late 1989 with 50 employees and had cut back to 30 employees by March 1991. It will be counted as an expansion, from zero to 30 employees.

The converse can be said of contractions: establishments that died after January 1 but before mid March 1991 will have zero 1991 employment and will be counted as a contraction for 1989–1991. Expansions and contractions are overcounted since they include some establishments that were born or died rather than only establishments that existed in the same ZIP code for a two-year period (March 1989 to March 1991, for example). This does not mean that the birth or death rates are undercounted, however; they are not. The births that are classified as expansions occurred during 1989, while the birth rate for 1989–1991 measures births occurring during 1990 and 1991. Similarly, the deaths miscounted as contractions occurred during 1991, while death rates for the first period measure deaths during 1989 and 1990.

A correct two-year expansion or contraction rate would consider only firms that existed in the same ZIP code at two different points two years apart—as of mid March 1989 and as of mid March 1991, for example. Employment on those two dates would be compared. This would tell us the percentage of firms that had their employment increased within 24 months.

Expansion rates were adjusted by estimating the number of births that occurred in the last 9.5 months of 1989, 1991, or 1993, based on the adjusted annual birth rates for that sector and firm size. Assuming that all of these later births ended up getting counted as expansions, we subtracted them from the count of expansions for the period (EXPAND). The expansion rate is then found by dividing adjusted expansions by an estimate of the number of establishments in existence as of mid March. To determine the number of establishments that existed in mid March 1989, for example, we subtracted from the number that existed at *some* point during 1989 (BEGIN) the number that we estimated were born from mid March to December (as above) and the number that died between January 1 and mid March (based on adjusted annual death counts).

Similar adjustments were made to the contraction rates, by using annual death rates to estimate the number of deaths that occurred in the first 2.5

months of 1991, 1993, and 1995 (after January 1 but prior to the mid March employment count, thereby producing a zero March employment number and resulting in a mislabeled contraction). To find contraction rates, the adjusted contractions were divided by the same estimate of total establishments in mid March of the first year as was used to calculate expansion rates.

Appendix Note

1. Trey Cole, Census Bureau, phone conversation with Peter Fisher, November 23, 1999.

Appendix E

Translating Enterprise Zone Boundaries and Tax Characteristics of Zones

ENTERPRISE ZONE BOUNDARY FILES

For the various analyses we wished to perform, we needed a variety of data for each zone; unfortunately, these data were available at varying levels of geography. The state and city in which the zone was located determined the appropriate taxes that would apply to a firm in the zone. Some of the economic variables were most appropriately defined at the county, city, or metropolitan area level since they related to the broader labor market or economic region. Data for these sorts of established areas are readily available. However, we also needed establishment counts and demographic data at the enterprise zone level, and here it was necessary to develop boundary files for each enterprise zone. Most of the census data required were from the sample questionnaire section of the *Census of Population* and so were available only at the tract or ZIP-code level (or higher), and the finest geographic scale for the establishment counts was the ZIP-code level (see the description of the SSEL database in Appendix D). Therefore we had to define the actual zone boundaries—in digital format, for use by Geographic Information Systems (GIS) software—and then identify the set of ZIP codes that best approximated the zone. The same process was undertaken for Traffic Analysis Zones (TAZs) in order to analyze commuting patterns using TAZ-based census data. In this section we describe the problems in developing zone boundaries and their approximations.

Enterprise zone computerized boundary files were derived from a number of sources. In a very few cases, the files were provided to us by the city or state (for instance, all enterprise zones in Ohio). Mostly, however, the files had to be hand digitized either from paper maps, pictures, Web pictures or text definitions of zone perimeters. In all cases, the boundaries were not digitized free-hand, but were assembled based on census block (and in a very few instances, block group or tract) files derived from the TIGER/Line system (Bureau of Transportation Statistics 1995). Since blocks are the lowest level of census geography (besides the household), our geographic representation of enterprise zones is generally exact. In a few cases, problems arose. These were usually suburban enterprise zones that included only a part of a large sub-urban-exurban block whose subdivision had not yet been recognized in the 1995 TIGER/Line files. In these few cases, if the majority of the block was in the zone, the block was defined as belonging to the zone, and vice versa. This results in some small degradation of geographical accuracy. Chapters 6, 7, and 8 are the parts of the book that use data derived from these enterprise zone definitions. In almost all cases, the impact of this problem on the results is likely to be small due to the much greater errors in translating the enterprise zone boundaries into ZIP-code region and TAZ region equivalents.

DEFINING ZIP-CODE EQUIVALENTS OF ZONES

Converting enterprise zone boundaries into ZIP-code approximations presents a difficult set of challenges. Enterprise zones tend to be small areas and thus ZIP-code regions are hardly ever coterminous with enterprise zones. Moreover, the shape of many enterprise zone boundaries is highly irregular. As a result ZIP equivalents of enterprise zones will tend to leave out large parts of enterprise zones and include areas not actually designated as enterprise zones. To solve these problems, we developed a two-stage selection process. In the first stage, all ZIPs that had any overlap with enterprise zones in the sample were selected, giving a sample of ZIPs, s_1. We then built a computer algorithm that either assigned or did not assign each ZIP in s_1 to a particular enterprise zone.

After considerable experimentation we finally produced an algorithm implementing the following two decision rules:

1. If 5 percent of the land area of the designated zone was in the ZIP, then ZIP was included in the ZIP definition of the zone, or
2. If at least 10 percent of the ZIP was part of the designated zone, then the ZIP was included in the ZIP definition of the zone.

The rules were written in a commercial GIS using a standard macro language. The result was the final sample of enterprise zone ZIPs, s_f. More stringent rules resulted in too many spatial anomalies—too many ZIP regions not being included that clearly should have been—and less-stringent rules resulted in the opposite. Relying on a single rule also caused problematic definitions, although the addition of any one of the two rules to the other resulted in the inclusion of fewer than 20 new ZIPs to the entire sample.

Many of our results are directly dependent on this translation of enterprise zone blocks into ZIP regions. This is particularly worrisome in Chapter 7, where we build models of the impact of enterprise zone incentives on economic growth in zones. In order to test the sensitivity of our econometric results to the translation algorithm used, we developed models based on progressively more stringent translation rules. In the case of the econometric models we found little evidence of sensitivity to translation criteria.

It is also worth pointing out that previous cross-sectional analyses of enterprise zones and growth have used even broader scales of analysis—usually the county, and sometimes census place. Thus we believe that the problems of geographical definition notwithstanding, our analysis comes significantly closer to accurately representing enterprise zones than previous work.

In the case of the Ohio data, other difficulties arose. Here each enterprise zone was identified by the city that either fully or partly contained it. A sample of ZIPs (s_1) was selected based on any geographic intersection between a ZIP and the enterprise zone city. This sample (s_1) was visually inspected and ZIPs with negligible spatial overlap with enterprise zone cities were removed (creating sample s_2). Given the spatial proximity of many Ohio enterprise zones, this resulted in a situation in which individual ZIPs were assigned to multiple enterprise zone cities. To resolve the problem we wrote a further algorithm that measured, in cases in which multiple enterprise zones had been assigned to a single ZIP, the distance between each ZIP centroid and each of the assigned city centroids. Again a standard GIS programming language was used in algorithm development. The program then assigned the ZIP to the closest enterprise zone city centroid and removed assignments to all other enterprise zones creating our final sample (s_f).

DEFINING TAZ EQUIVALENTS OF ZONES

The ZIP-code data are important to Chapters 6 and 7, which look at the relationship between enterprise zones and growth. The analysis relies on a special tabulation of the SSEL data set undertaken at the ZIP-code level. Chapter 8 focuses on those who live in or commute into enterprise zones. The only national data set of use here is the 1990 *Census Transportation Planning Package* (CTPP) (U.S. Department of Transportation 1990). This is organized around traffic analysis zones (TAZs) in size usually not too dissimilar from tracts (although cities have a lot of discretion in how their TAZs should be defined). The result is that for Chapter 8, the analysis moves from the ZIP-code region to TAZ region level. Thus, enterprise zones must be translated into TAZ equivalents. The problems described in the above two sections arose again, although here in less-extreme form because TAZs are much smaller than ZIPs and are therefore better able to describe enterprise zone geography. It was not necessary to create city TAZ definitions because, in Chapter 8, the broader context in which the enterprise zone operates is not the city, but the commuting region (as defined by the U.S. Department of Transportation). We describe these data in more detail in Chapter 8. Our method for translating enterprise zones into TAZs was similar to that described above, although given the higher level of geographical disaggregation, we relied on visual inspection of the overlap between enterprise zones and TAZ zones.

Table E.1 Tax Rates and Property-Tax Abatements in the Enterprise Zones in 75 Cities, 1994

City	Sales tax rates (%)		Corporate income tax (%)		Local property-tax rates (%)[a]			Local property-tax abatements				
	State	Local	Top state rate	Local rate	Real	Manuf. M&E	Inventory	Buildings	M&E	Inventory	Term[b]	Average percent[b]
Los Angeles, Calif.	6.00	2.25	9.3	NA[c]	1.06	1.06	exempt	NA	NA	NA	NA	NA
Pasadena, Calif.	6.00	2.25	9.3	NA	1.06	1.06	exempt	NA	NA	NA	NA	NA
Porterville, Calif.	6.00	1.25	9.3	NA	1.02	1.02	exempt	NA	NA	NA	NA	NA
Redding, Calif.	6.00	1.25	9.3	NA	1.06	1.06	exempt	NA	NA	NA	NA	NA
Sacramento, Calif.	6.00	1.75	9.3	NA	1.03	1.03	exempt	NA	NA	NA	NA	NA
Stockton, Calif.	6.00	1.75	9.3	NA	1.01	1.01	exempt	NA	NA	NA	NA	NA
Hamden, Conn.	6.00	NA	9.5	NA	2.87	2.87	exempt	Yes	Yes	NA	5	80.0
Hartford, Conn.	6.00	NA	9.5	NA	4.48	4.48	exempt	Yes	Yes	NA	5	80.0
Meriden, Conn.	6.00	NA	9.5	NA	2.88	2.88	exempt	Yes	Yes	NA	5	80.0
New Britain, Conn.	6.00	NA	9.5	NA	3.19	3.19	exempt	Yes	Yes	NA	5	80.0
Norwalk, Conn.	6.00	NA	9.5	NA	1.91	1.91	exempt	Yes	Yes	NA	5	80.0
Norwich, Conn.	6.00	NA	9.5	NA	2.17	2.17	exempt	Yes	Yes	NA	5	80.0
Clearwater, Fla.	6.00	1.00	5.5	NA	2.25	2.25	exempt	NA	NA	NA	NA	NA
Fort Lauderdale, Fla.	6.00	0.00	5.5	NA	2.40	2.40	exempt	NA	NA	NA	NA	NA
Fort Myers, Fla.	6.00	0.00	5.5	NA	2.13	2.13	exempt	NA	NA	NA	NA	NA
Jacksonville, Fla.	6.00	0.50	5.5	NA	2.61	2.61	exempt	NA	NA	NA	NA	NA
Miami Beach, Fla.	6.00	0.50	5.5	NA	2.62	2.62	exempt	NA	NA	NA	NA	NA
Tampa, Fla.	6.00	0.50	5.5	NA	2.58	2.58	exempt	NA	NA	NA	NA	NA
Alton, Ill.	6.25	0.75	4.8	NA	2.58	exempt	exempt	Yes	NA	NA	4	100.0
Champaign, Ill.	6.25	1.00	4.8	NA	2.65	exempt	exempt	Yes	NA	NA	5	100.0
Kankakee, Ill.	6.25	0.00	4.8	NA	2.58	exempt	exempt	Yes	NA	NA	5	60.0
Maywood, Ill.	6.25	0.75	4.8	NA	4.52	exempt	exempt	Yes	NA	NA	10	50.0

Table E.1 (Continued)

City	Sales tax rates (%)		Corporate income tax (%)		Local property-tax rates (%)[a]			Local property-tax abatements				
	State	Local	Top state rate	Local rate	Real	Manuf. M&E	Inventory	Buildings	M&E	Inventory	Term[b]	Average percent[b]
Moline, Ill.	6.25	0.50	4.8	NA	2.85	exempt	exempt	Yes	NA	NA	5	45.0
Pekin, Ill.	6.25	1.00	4.8	NA	3.19	exempt	exempt	Yes	NA	NA	5	100.0
Evansville, Ind.	5.00	NA	7.7	NA	4.23	4.23	1.67	No	No	No	NA	NA
Fort Wayne, Ind.	5.00	NA	7.7	NA	3.59	3.59	1.41	Yes	Yes	No	10	49.5
Hammond, Ind.	5.00	NA	7.7	NA	9.12	9.12	3.59	Yes	Yes	No	10	49.5
Lafayette, Ind.	5.00	NA	7.7	NA	3.62	3.62	1.43	Yes	Yes	No	6	58.7
Muncie, Ind.	5.00	NA	7.7	NA	5.30	5.30	2.09	Yes	Yes	No	3	66.3
South Bend, Ind.	5.00	NA	7.7	NA	5.08	5.08	2.00	Yes	Yes	No	6	58.7
Covington, Ky.	6.00	NA	8.3	2.5	1.45	exempt	0.58	No	No	Yes	20	100.0
Hopkinsville, Ky.	6.00	NA	8.3	1.5	0.75	exempt	0.30	Yes	Yes	Yes	5	100.0
Lexington, Ky.	6.00	NA	8.3	2.0	0.82	exempt	0.33	No	No	No	NA	NA
Louisville, Ky.	6.00	NA	8.3	1.5	1.12	exempt	0.45	No	No	No	NA	NA
Ownesboro, Ky.	6.00	NA	8.3	1.0	1.07	exempt	0.43	No	No	Yes	13	100.0
Joplin, Mo.	4.23	2.13	6.3	NA	1.71	1.42	exempt	Yes	No	NA	20	65.0
Kansas City, Mo.	4.23	2.25	6.3	NA	2.90	2.52	exempt	Yes	No	NA	10	50.0
Springfield, Mo.	4.23	1.75	6.3	NA	2.04	1.76	exempt	Yes	No	NA	10	50.0
St. Joseph, Mo.	4.23	2.60	6.3	NA	1.56	1.61	exempt	Yes	Yes	NA	10	100.0
St. Louis, Mo.	4.23	2.38	6.3	NA	2.50	2.23	exempt	Yes	No	NA	10	100.0
Auburn, N.Y.	4.00	4.00	9.0	NA	3.44	exempt	exempt	Yes	NA	NA	10	27.5
New York City, N.Y.	4.00	4.25	9.0	NA	2.82	exempt	exempt	Yes	NA	NA	10	85.0
Niagara Falls, N.Y.	4.00	3.00	9.0	NA	4.33	exempt	exempt	Yes	NA	NA	10	85.0

Syracuse, N.Y.	4.00	3.00	9.0	NA	2.62	exempt	exempt	Yes	NA	NA	10	85.0
Troy, N.Y.	4.00	3.00	9.0	NA	3.20	exempt	exempt	Yes	NA	NA	10	27.5
Utica, N.Y.	4.00	4.00	9.0	NA	3.64	exempt	exempt	Yes	NA	NA	10	27.5
Canton, Ohio	5.00	0.00	9.1	2.0	1.61	1.63	1.63	Yes	Yes	Yes	10	60.0
Cincinnati, Ohio	5.00	0.50	9.1	2.1	2.07	2.04	2.04	Yes	Yes	Yes	10	100.0
Cleveland, Ohio	5.00	3.00	9.1	2.0	2.27	2.11	2.11	Yes	Yes	Yes	10	67.0
Elyria, Ohio	5.00	0.50	9.1	1.8	1.94	1.89	1.89	Yes	Yes	Yes	10	67.0
Massillon, Ohio	5.00	0.00	9.1	1.5	1.84	1.74	1.74	Yes	Yes	Yes	10	75.0
Warren, Ohio	5.00	0.75	9.1	1.5	1.75	1.54	1.54	Yes	Yes	Yes	10	67.0
Chester, Pa.	6.00	NA	12.3	0.5	0.52	exempt	exempt	Yes	NA	NA	10	43.0
Johnstown, Pa.	6.00	NA	12.3	0.3	0.90	exempt	exempt	Yes	NA	NA	5	84.0
Lancaster, Pa.	6.00	NA	12.3	0.0	0.67	exempt	exempt	Yes	NA	NA	7	59.3
Philadelphia, Pa.	6.00	NA	12.3	0.0	0.73	exempt	exempt	No	NA	NA	NA	NA
Pittsburgh, Pa.	6.00	NA	12.3	0.6	1.01	exempt	exempt	No	NA	NA	NA	NA
Scranton, Pa.	6.00	NA	12.3	0.6	0.76	exempt	exempt	Yes	NA	NA	10	100.0
Amarillo, Tex.	6.25	2.00	4.5	NA	2.35	2.35	2.35	Yes	Yes	NA	10	42.5
El Paso, Tex.	6.25	2.00	4.5	NA	2.49	2.49	2.49	Yes	No	NA	5	50.0
Fort Worth, Tex.	6.25	2.00	4.5	NA	2.71	2.71	2.71	Yes	Yes	NA	10	38.5
Pharr, Tex.	6.25	2.00	4.5	NA	2.41	2.41	2.41	No	No	NA	NA	NA
San Antonio, Tex.[d]	6.25	1.50	4.5	NA	2.53	2.53	2.53	Yes	Yes	NA	10	75.0
Waco, Tex.[d]	6.25	2.00	4.5	NA	2.53	2.53	2.53	Yes	Yes	NA	5	40.0
Danville, Va.	3.50	1.00	6.0	NA	0.76	1.50	exempt	NA	NA	NA	NA	NA
Lynchburg, Va.	3.50	1.00	6.0	NA	1.16	3.00	exempt	NA	NA	NA	NA	NA
Newport News, Va.	3.50	1.00	6.0	NA	1.20	3.00	exempt	NA	NA	NA	NA	NA
Petersburg, Va.	3.50	1.00	6.0	NA	1.49	3.80	exempt	NA	NA	NA	NA	NA
Portsmouth, Va.	3.50	1.00	6.0	NA	1.32	2.50	exempt	NA	NA	NA	NA	NA
Richmond, Va.	3.50	1.00	6.0	NA	1.45	2.30	exempt	NA	NA	NA	NA	NA
Beloit, Wis.	5.00	0.00	7.9	NA	3.81	exempt	exempt	NA	NA	NA	NA	NA
Fond Du Lac, Wis.	5.00	0.00	7.9	NA	3.22	exempt	exempt	NA	NA	NA	NA	NA

Table E.1 (Continued)

City	Sales tax rates (%)		Corporate income tax (%)		Local property-tax rates (%)[a]			Local property-tax abatements				
	State	Local	Top state rate	Local rate	Real	Manuf. M&E	Inventory	Buildings	M&E	Inventory	Term[b]	Average percent[b]
Green Bay, Wis.	5.00	0.00	7.9	NA	3.21	exempt	exempt	NA	NA	NA	NA	NA
Milwaukee, Wis.	5.00	0.50	7.9	NA	3.65	exempt	exempt	NA	NA	NA	NA	NA
Racine, Wis.	5.00	0.00	7.9	NA	3.62	exempt	exempt	NA	NA	NA	NA	NA

[a] Nominal local property-tax rate times assessment ratio. Tax rates on personal property other than manufacturing machinery and equipment and inventory are not shown; such property may be subject to the same rate as real property or the same rate as M&E, or it may be exempt, or it may have its own rate.

[b] Term is the number of years abatement applies; if the locality uses more than one schedule, the typical schedule applied to buildings is shown. Average percent is the simple average percent of taxes abated over the term of the abatement, for the typical schedule applied to buildings.

[c] NA = Not Allowed under state law, or Not Applicable either because it is exempt under state law or locality does not abate that class of property.

[d] Varying schedules apply; the one shown here is for plants creating 60–100 jobs.

Appendix F

Detailed Results

**Table F.1 Effective Tax Rates on New Investment in 1994 for 75
Enterprise Zone Cities (Weighted Average for 16
Manufacturing Sectors)**

City and state	Effective tax rate (%)			Percent reduction in rate	
	After basic taxes	With general incentives	With general & zone incentives	Due to general incentives	Due to zone incentives
California					
Los Angeles	9.1	7.5	6.9	18.1	7.6
Pasadena	9.1	7.5	6.9	18.1	7.6
Porterville	8.7	7.3	6.7	16.6	7.8
Redding	8.8	7.4	6.8	16.4	7.7
Sacramento	8.9	7.4	6.8	17.4	7.7
Stockton	8.9	7.3	6.7	17.4	7.7
Connecticut					
Hamden	8.9	6.6	5.5	25.2	17.1
Hartford	11.4	8.5	7.3	25.6	13.3
Meriden	8.9	6.6	5.5	25.2	17.0
New Britain	9.4	7.0	5.9	25.3	16.2
Norwalk	7.4	5.5	4.4	24.9	20.5
Norwich	7.8	6.7	5.6	13.2	16.8
Florida					
Clearwater	8.0	8.0	6.4	0.0	20.0
Fort Lauderdale	8.2	8.2	6.6	0.0	19.6
Fort Myers	7.5	7.5	6.0	0.0	21.0
Jacksonville	8.7	8.7	7.1	0.0	18.5
Miami Beach	8.8	8.8	7.1	0.0	18.4
Tampa	8.7	8.7	7.0	0.0	18.6
Illinois					
Alton	5.8	5.4	4.3	6.7	20.5
Champaign	5.8	5.5	4.8	6.6	11.5
Kankakee	5.7	5.3	4.4	6.7	17.2
Maywood	7.4	7.0	5.4	5.2	23.4
Moline	6.0	5.6	5.1	6.4	7.9
Pekin	6.3	5.9	4.4	6.1	25.0
Indiana					
Evansville	13.4	10.7	8.3	20.3	22.4
Fort Wayne	12.1	9.4	4.9	22.4	48.0

Table F.1 (Continued)

| City and state | Effective tax rate (%) | | | Percent reduction in rate | |
	After basic taxes	With general incentives	With general & zone incentives	Due to general incentives	Due to zone incentives
Hammond	22.8	20.1	9.5	11.9	52.8
Lafayette	12.2	9.5	5.5	22.2	42.2
Muncie	15.5	12.7	9.2	17.6	27.8
South Bend	15.0	12.3	6.9	18.1	43.8
Kentucky					
Covington	9.1	5.8	5.0	35.4	13.9
Hopkinsville	7.6	4.5	2.7	40.4	39.7
Lexington	7.7	4.9	4.0	36.9	16.5
Louisville	8.2	5.4	4.6	34.3	15.0
Owensboro	7.9	4.6	3.8	41.6	17.4
Missouri					
Joplin	8.9	6.5	4.9	26.8	24.4
Kansas City	12.1	9.8	8.2	19.1	16.2
Springfield	9.5	7.6	6.0	20.0	20.9
St. Joseph	8.8	4.8	3.2	45.8	33.7
St. Louis	12.7	9.7	8.1	23.6	16.4
New York					
Auburn	6.4	3.6	2.9	43.9	20.7
New York City	9.6	5.9	5.2	38.0	12.7
Niagara Falls	7.1	2.7	1.9	62.1	27.9
Syracuse	5.7	2.1	1.4	62.3	35.2
Troy	6.2	3.4	2.6	45.1	22.2
Utica	6.6	3.8	3.0	43.3	20.0
Ohio					
Canton	9.1	8.1	5.8	10.9	28.4
Cincinnati	10.5	9.6	4.7	9.4	50.6
Cleveland	11.0	10.0	6.7	9.0	33.1
Elyria	9.9	8.9	5.9	10.0	33.7
Massillon	9.3	8.4	5.2	10.6	37.4
Warren	8.8	7.9	5.3	11.2	32.1

Table F.1 (Continued)

City and state	Effective tax rate (%)			Percent reduction in rate	
	After basic taxes	With general incentives	With general & zone incentives	Due to general incentives	Due to zone incentives
Pennsylvania					
Chester	11.0	10.4	8.5	6.0	18.2
Johnstown	10.7	10.3	8.4	4.0	18.4
Lancaster	7.4	6.5	4.6	11.5	29.0
Philadelphia	7.5	7.3	5.4	2.4	25.7
Pittsburgh	13.7	13.6	11.7	1.3	13.9
Scranton	13.0	12.3	10.4	6.0	15.4
Texas					
Amarillo	10.6	9.7	8.3	8.7	15.1
El Paso	11.1	10.9	9.5	1.3	13.6
Fort Worth	11.8	10.9	9.4	8.1	13.6
Pharr	10.8	10.8	9.4	0.0	13.7
San Antonio	11.0	9.8	8.4	11.2	14.6
Waco	11.2	10.7	9.3	4.1	13.8
Virginia					
Danville	5.2	5.2	4.4	0.0	16.4
Lynchburg	7.3	7.3	6.4	0.0	11.8
Newport News	7.3	7.3	6.5	0.0	11.7
Petersburg	8.5	8.5	7.6	0.0	10.1
Portsmouth	6.9	6.9	6.0	0.0	12.5
Richmond	6.7	6.7	5.9	0.0	12.7
Wisconsin					
Beloit	7.6	7.6	5.6	0.0	26.7
Fond Du Lac	7.0	7.0	5.0	0.0	28.9
Green Bay	7.0	7.0	5.0	0.0	28.9
Milwaukee	7.5	7.5	5.4	0.0	27.5
Racine	7.4	7.4	5.4	0.0	27.4

Table F.2 The Value of Incentives to Manufacturing Firms in 75 Cities, 1994 (Net Present Value over 20 Years, per Job)

City	Weighted average for 16 sectors		Sector with largest total incentives		Sector with smallest total incentives	
	General plus zone incentives	Additional value of zone incentives	General plus zone incentives	Additional value of zone incentives	General plus zone incentives	Additional value of zone incentives
Hammond, Ind.	22,678	19,193	44,401	41,190	7,540	4,916
South Bend, Ind.	13,295	9,810	25,089	21,878	5,182	2,558
Fort Wayne, Ind.	11,632	8,147	20,957	17,747	4,760	2,136
Lafayette, Ind.	10,758	7,273	19,533	16,322	4,543	1,919
Muncie, Ind.	10,167	6,682	19,883	16,673	4,343	1,719
Cincinnati, Ohio	9,679	8,411	17,037	15,881	3,323	2,350
St. Joseph, Mo.	9,641	2,739	17,337	5,223	3,281	1,022
Niagara Falls, N.Y.	8,378	1,019	19,326	6,043	3,087	604
Hopkinsville, Ky.	8,282	2,780	15,655	4,361	3,094	1,489
Evansville, Ind.	8,085	4,600	15,421	12,211	3,836	1,284
St. Louis, Mo.	7,750	2,699	13,969	5,072	2,618	1,019
Ownesboro, Ky.	7,274	1,407	14,444	2,680	2,178	459
Covington, Ky.	7,120	1,414	14,212	2,689	2,152	461
New York City, N.Y.	7,082	1,021	17,279	6,045	2,720	604
Cleveland, Ohio	7,022	5,754	12,035	10,879	2,572	1,600
Syracuse, N.Y.	6,953	1,024	17,019	6,045	2,676	605

Joplin, Mo.	6,761	2,716	12,350	5,139	2,318	1,020
Hartford, Conn.	6,721	1,817	11,689	3,250	2,404	850
Massillon, Ohio	6,694	5,426	11,401	10,245	2,494	1,521
Kansas City, Mo.	6,628	2,692	12,082	5,053	2,298	1,017
Louisville, Ky.	6,524	1,409	13,373	2,684	2,025	561
Lexington, Ky.	6,515	1,396	13,355	2,658	2,023	559
Elyria, Ohio	6,497	5,229	11,032	9,876	2,435	1,462
Springfield, Mo.	5,947	2,707	10,941	5,105	2,079	1,019
Utica, N.Y.	5,820	1,012	15,229	6,040	2,353	603
New Britain, Conn.	5,819	1,823	10,207	3,269	2,141	850
Auburn, N.Y.	5,762	1,013	15,132	6,041	2,336	603
Troy, N.Y.	5,692	1,016	15,012	6,041	2,315	604
Warren, Ohio	5,648	4,380	9,409	8,253	2,209	1,237
Meriden, Conn.	5,602	1,824	9,851	3,273	2,077	851
Hamden, Conn.	5,595	1,824	9,840	3,273	2,075	851
Canton, Conn.	5,263	3,995	8,705	7,549	2,087	1,114
Norwalk, Conn.	4,924	1,828	8,737	3,288	1,879	851
Scranton, Pa.	4,566	3,239	8,540	5,774	1,286	967
Lancaster, Pa.	4,546	3,240	7,879	5,774	1,494	967
San Antonio, Tex.	4,474	2,340	7,979	3,845	738	738
Chester, Pa.	4,241	3,240	7,346	5,774	1,406	967
Fort Worth, Tex.	4,018	2,382	6,696	3,863	1,196	776
Amarillo, Tex.	3,942	2,367	6,585	3,855	1,172	770
Johnstown, Pa.	3,860	3,236	6,695	5,804	1,296	967
Los Angeles, Calif.	3,810	952	6,791	1,506	858	291
Pasadena, Calif.	3,810	952	6,791	1,506	858	291

Table F.2 (Continued)

City	Weighted average for 16 sectors		Sector with largest total incentives		Sector with smallest total incentives	
	General plus zone incentives	Additional value of zone incentives	General plus zone incentives	Additional value of zone incentives	General plus zone incentives	Additional value of zone incentives
Sacramento, Calif.	3,632	952	6,464	1,506	823	291
Stockton, Calif.	3,628	952	6,457	1,506	822	291
Norwich, Conn.	3,556	1,820	6,435	3,262	1,486	850
Redding, Calif.	3,465	952	6,153	1,506	789	291
Porterville, Calif.	3,458	952	6,141	1,506	788	291
Philadelphia, Pa.	3,452	3,236	6,029	5,804	1,178	967
Pittsburgh, Pa.	3,450	3,234	6,029	5,804	1,178	967
Maywood, Ill.	3,338	2,678	5,605	4,453	1,059	840
Milwaukee, Wis.	3,283	3,283	5,266	5,266	1,315	1,315
Green Bay, Wis.	3,226	3,226	5,159	5,159	1,303	1,303
Fond Du Lac, Wis.	3,226	3,226	5,159	5,159	1,303	1,303
Racine, Wis.	3,225	3,225	5,158	5,158	1,303	1,303
Beloit, Wis.	3,225	3,225	5,157	5,157	1,303	1,303
Waco, Tex.	3,158	2,388	5,276	3,870	957	778
Pekin, Ill.	3,064	2,403	5,143	3,990	978	760
El Paso, Tex.	2,608	2,393	4,199	3,872	857	780
Alton, Ill.	2,462	1,801	4,142	2,988	805	586

City						
Pharr, Tex.	2,390	2,390	3,868	3,868	779	779
Miami Beach, Fla.	2,308	2,308	3,495	3,495	870	870
Jacksonville, Fla.	2,308	2,308	3,495	3,495	870	870
Tampa, Fla.	2,307	2,307	3,495	3,495	870	870
Fort Lauderdale, Fla.	2,300	2,300	3,495	3,495	870	870
Clearwater, Fla.	2,294	2,294	3,495	3,495	870	870
Fort Myers, Fla.	2,289	2,289	3,495	3,495	870	870
Kankakee, Ill.	2,156	1,495	3,633	2,481	717	498
Champaign, Ill.	1,680	1,019	2,839	1,685	558	382
Moline, Ill.	1,381	720	2,345	1,193	441	265
Petersburg, Va.	1,045	1,045	1,117	1,117	573	573
Richmond, Va.	1,045	1,045	1,117	1,117	573	573
Newport News, Va.	1,045	1,045	1,117	1,117	573	573
Portsmouth, Va.	1,045	1,045	1,117	1,117	573	573
Lynchburg, Va.	1,045	1,045	1,117	1,117	573	573
Danville, Va.	1,045	1,045	1,117	1,117	573	573

Table F.3 Variation in City Rankings and Tax Rates by Sector, 75 Cities, 1994 (Cities Ranked by Tax Rate after Enterprise Zone Incentives)

City and state	Highest-ranked sector Sector (SIC)	Rank[a]	Tax rate (%)	Lowest-ranked sector Sector (SIC)	Rank[a]	Tax rate (%)	Highest rate (%)	Lowest rate (%)	Rate spread (%)
California									
Los Angeles	30	42	6.3	27	63	6.1	9.9	4.9	5.0
Pasadena	30	42	6.3	27	63	6.1	9.9	4.9	5.0
Porterville	33	36	7.4	27	58	5.9	9.5	4.8	4.7
Redding	30	40	6.2	27	61	6.0	9.7	4.8	4.9
Sacramento	33	38	7.5	27	60	6.0	9.7	4.8	4.9
Stockton	33	37	7.5	27	59	5.9	9.6	4.8	4.8
Connecticut									
Hamden	23	13	3.8	27	36	4.3	8.4	3.4	5.0
Hartford	31	31	4.1	28	65	7.6	11.5	4.1	7.5
Meriden	23	14	3.8	27	37	4.3	8.4	3.4	5.0
New Britain	23	19	4.0	20	50	8.5	9.0	3.5	5.5
Norwalk	23	10	3.1	26	21	6.4	6.4	3.0	3.5
Norwich	23	18	4.0	25	43	6.5	8.4	3.5	4.9
Florida									
Clearwater	31	10	2.7	33	58	10.9	10.9	2.7	8.2
Fort Lauderdale	31	9	2.7	33	61	11.0	11.1	2.7	8.4
Fort Myers	31	8	2.6	33	55	10.1	10.1	2.6	7.5
Jacksonville	31	13	2.8	33	64	11.9	12.1	2.8	9.3

Miami Beach	31	15	2.8	33	65	11.9	12.2	2.8	9.3
Tampa	31	11	2.8	33	63	11.8	12.0	2.8	9.2
Illinois									
Alton	26	6	3.9	31	37	4.4	5.9	3.0	2.9
Champaign	26	10	4.7	31	44	4.7	7.0	3.5	3.5
Kankakee	26	8	4.1	31	40	4.5	6.2	3.1	3.1
Maywood	26	14	5.4	23	51	5.0	8.2	3.9	4.4
Moline	26	12	5.2	23	49	4.9	7.6	3.7	3.9
Pekin	26	7	4.1	31	38	4.5	6.3	3.1	3.2
Indiana									
Evansville	27	38	4.3	30	73	10.7	14.1	4.3	9.7
Fort Wayne	27	4	1.0	30	46	6.7	7.9	1.0	6.8
Hammond	27	54	5.3	26	75	15.6	15.6	5.3	10.4
Lafayette	27	8	1.6	23	54	5.1	8.9	1.6	7.3
Muncie	27	50	5.2	30	75	11.7	15.6	5.2	10.4
South Bend	27	10	2.9	28	67	7.7	11.4	2.9	8.5
Kentucky									
Covington	36	13	3.9	23	52	5.0	7.4	3.9	3.4
Hopkinsville	37	1	1.8	31	17	3.0	4.7	1.0	3.7
Lexington	34	9	3.8	31	27	3.9	5.9	3.1	2.8
Louisville	34	10	4.2	23	53	5.0	6.8	3.4	3.4
Owensboro	36	6	3.0	33	19	5.7	5.7	3.0	2.8
Missouri									
Joplin	31	7	2.4	33	47	8.3	9.4	2.4	7.0
Kansas City	31	28	3.9	26	73	15.0	15.0	3.9	11.1
Springfield	31	14	2.8	26	54	11.1	11.1	2.8	8.3

Table F.3 (Continued)

City and state	Highest-ranked sector			Lowest-ranked sector			Highest rate (%)	Lowest rate (%)	Rate spread (%)
	Sector (SIC)	Rank[a]	Tax rate (%)	Sector (SIC)	Rank[a]	Tax rate (%)			
St. Joseph	34	2	2.5	26	11	5.2	5.9	1.8	4.1
St. Louis	31	48	4.9	27	73	7.6	13.8	4.9	8.9
New York									
Auburn	24	4	-0.9	20	11	5.8	5.8	-0.9	6.7
New York City	24	6	1.9	31	59	5.3	6.7	1.9	4.7
Niagara Falls	23	2	1.6	20	4	4.2	4.2	-1.8	6.0
Syracuse	20	1	3.0	37	2	2.1	3.0	-2.5	5.5
Troy	24	3	-1.2	20	8	5.4	5.4	-1.2	6.5
Utica	24	5	-0.8	20	14	6.1	6.1	-0.8	6.8
Ohio									
Canton	20	20	6.8	31	61	5.5	8.2	3.8	4.4
Cincinnati	20	6	5.3	31	42	4.6	6.5	2.9	3.6
Cleveland	37	41	5.9	31	65	6.0	9.6	4.5	5.0
Elyria	20	25	7.1	31	62	5.5	8.5	3.9	4.5
Massillon	20	15	6.1	23	56	5.3	7.4	3.4	4.1
Warren	20	17	6.3	23	57	5.3	7.6	3.4	4.1
Pennsylvania									
Chester	26	40	9.5	24	73	10.8	10.8	7.2	3.5
Johnstown	26	46	9.7	24	72	10.1	11.0	7.2	3.8
Lancaster	20	7	5.3	31	47	4.9	5.4	3.9	1.5

Philadelphia	33	18	5.7	31	58	5.3	6.9	4.5	2.3
Pittsburgh	26	68	13.4	20	75	15.7	15.7	9.6	6.1
Scranton	33	60	10.9	23	74	10.5	14.0	8.4	5.7
Texas									
Amarillo	28	42	6.5	37	69	9.2	12.0	5.2	6.8
El Paso	28	66	7.6	33	73	12.8	13.8	6.3	7.5
Fort Worth	28	62	7.5	23	73	9.9	13.7	6.1	7.6
Pharr	28	64	7.6	33	72	12.7	13.7	6.2	7.5
San Antonio	28	48	6.7	24	71	6.8	12.1	5.2	6.8
Waco	28	63	7.5	23	70	9.4	13.5	6.1	7.4
Virginia									
Danville	20	5	5.2	26	28	7.2	7.2	2.8	4.4
Lynchburg	23	24	4.1	32	58	8.5	11.4	3.5	7.8
Newport News	23	25	4.2	32	59	8.6	11.4	3.6	7.9
Petersburg	31	29	4.0	26	70	13.7	13.7	4.0	9.7
Portsmouth	23	20	4.0	26	51	10.3	10.3	3.4	6.9
Richmond	23	17	4.0	26	49	10.0	10.0	3.4	6.6
Wisconsin									
Beloit	33	25	6.0	24	52	5.4	8.5	4.0	4.5
Fond Du Lac	30	15	4.4	24	41	4.8	7.3	3.5	3.8
Green Bay	30	14	4.4	24	40	4.8	7.3	3.5	3.8
Milwaukee	26	22	6.5	24	49	5.2	8.2	3.9	4.3
Racine	26	20	6.4	24	48	5.2	8.1	3.8	4.3
Mean							9.4	3.6	5.8

[a] For rankings, a lower number is better (a lower effective tax rate).

Table F.4 State and Local Direct Revenue Gains and Incentive Costs per New Job for New Manufacturing Plants in 75 Cities, 1994

State	Sector with highest revenue		Sector with lowest revenue	
	Average for all zones in state	Zone with highest revenue	Average for all zones in state	Zone with lowest revenue
Revenue gain per induced job				
Calif.	39,865	40,389	5,316	5,220
Conn.	31,989	39,710	4,072	2,960
Fla.	39,636	41,950	4,244	4,028
Ill.	26,314	29,034	2,990	2,633
Ind.	43,279	53,587	3,343	1,178
Ky.	23,259	29,005	2,903	1,278
Mo.	35,192	46,109	5,056	2,255
N.Y.	20,642	35,521	–481	–2,045
Ohio	40,085	46,202	3,835	3,240
Pa.	58,843	86,675	8,141	3,193
Tex.	50,320	52,738	5,492	4,903
Va.	34,550	41,657	4,112	2,721
Wis.	28,592	30,018	3,412	3,193

State	Sector with largest incentives		Sector with smallest incentives	
	Average for all zones in state	Zone with largest incentive	Average for all zones in state	Zone with smallest incentive
Incentive cost per non-induced job				
Calif.	11,655	12,315	1,432	1,365
Conn.	14,189	17,790	3,010	2,151
Fla.	5,058	5,058	1,259	1,259
Ill.	6,040	8,700	1,167	656
Ind.	37,990	70,423	7,686	5,726
Ky.	22,386	24,496	3,689	3,194
Mo.	21,363	27,833	4,210	3,471
N.Y.	24,450	29,071	3,837	3,402
Ohio	18,391	27,067	3,942	3,233
Pa.	10,449	12,813	1,915	1,705
Tex.	9,043	12,592	1,563	1,207
Va.	1,616	1,616	829	829
Wis.	7,497	7,621	1,889	1,886

**Table F.5 Birth, Death, Expansion, and Contraction Rates
by Establishment Size and Time Period, for
64 Enterprise Zones**

| Rate | Establishment employment | | | |
	0–19	20–99	100+	All sizes
Growth				
1990–91				
Births	15.1	8.0	5.0	11.8
Moves in	6.7	4.1	3.0	5.5
Total growth	21.8	12.1	8.0	17.3
1992–93				
Births	14.1	9.2	5.4	11.7
Moves in	11.0	8.9	5.2	9.7
Total growth	25.2	18.1	10.6	21.4
1994–95				
Births	14.3	7.2	5.4	11.3
Moves in	6.0	4.3	3.8	5.3
Total growth	20.3	11.5	9.2	16.5
Shrinkage				
1989–90				
Deaths	17.5	9.5	7.4	14.0
Moves out	9.8	5.5	3.5	7.8
Total shrinkage	27.4	14.9	10.9	21.7
1991–92				
Deaths	16.4	9.4	5.9	13.2
Moves out	11.2	10.4	7.7	10.5
Total shrinkage	27.6	19.7	13.6	23.7
1993–94				
Deaths	15.8	9.5	5.5	12.9
Moves out	6.1	5.0	4.7	5.6
Total shrinkage	21.9	14.6	10.3	18.5
Expansion				
1989–91	26.0	31.0	33.7	28.4
1991–93	26.5	35.3	34.8	30.0
1993–95	33.7	49.4	45.6	39.5

Table F.5 (Continued)

	Establishment employment			
Rate	0–19	20–99	100+	All sizes
Contraction				
1989–91	28.3	50.3	54.7	37.9
1991–93	26.5	42.1	50.2	33.8
1993–95	23.2	32.2	42.1	28.0

NOTE: All rates represent the number of establishments being born, dying, expanding, and so forth, divided by the total number of establishments at the beginning of the first year of the two-year period (or as of mid March of the first year, for expansion and contraction rates).

Appendix G

Gravity-Based Commuting Models

Gravity or entropy models are widely used as a way of understanding spatial accessibility. In the standard form:

$$(1) \qquad T_{ij} = \alpha \, R_i^{\beta} W_j^{r} / d_{ij}^{\delta} .$$

Commuting flows between origin i (the residence) and destination j (the workplace), T_{ij} are positively related to the number of workers resident in Traffic Analysis Zone (TAZ) i (R) and the number of job opportunities in TAZ j (W), and are inversely related to the distance between them (d_{ij}); the Greek letters indicate parameters. Various justifications for gravity models have been developed over the years. In essence the central argument is that workers and workplaces attract each other, but that the level of attraction is mediated by the friction of distance (Isard et al. 1998). Here it should be noted that distance is usually measured in terms of travel time (though occasionally time is replaced by TAZ centroid-to-centroid distance in miles). Standard transportation demand analysis versions of the model are usually estimated using ordinary least squares regression on a logarithmic version of Equation 1. Data are typically from the Census Transportation Planning Package (CTPP), though sometimes from the PUMS (Public Use Microdata Sample) urban census sample, with R from element 1 data, W from element 2 data, and T_{ij} from element 3.[1] Typically, all TAZ-to-TAZ flows are included with zero observations removed. D_{ij} is derived from TAZ centroid-to-centroid calculations or from road network models. Following Isard (1960), the accessibility of workplaces to workers is:

$$(2) \qquad A_i = \sum_j \hat{T}_{ij} / R_i^{\hat{\beta}} .$$

$\hat{T}$ is calculated from the model. There are more sophisticated ways to model these relationships—in particular the CTPP provides count flows which may better be described by a Poisson distribution (see Smith 1987). However, recent empirical results suggest that the simpler ordinary least squares model may provide estimates of accessibility almost identical to the more complex models.

Clearly this model poses some problems. It might be argued, for instance, that median peak time would be a more appropriate measure. Indeed, most workers travel at peak time. But T_{ij} covers commutes throughout the day and emphasizing median peak time would exaggerate the overall impact of distance on commuting. It is very likely, however, that the δ parameter would change during the course of the day. Insofar as models ignore movements in the δ they may distort the true impact of the friction of distance on commuting flows.

Another problem is that different groups of workers may experience the friction of distance differently. Practically, what this means is that workers in different income-occupational categories may be more or less inclined to travel further. Part of the reason for this appears to be that workers with more skills tend to be rewarded for longer commutes, whereas those with less skills do not. Thus, more-skilled workers may not consider distance as much of an impediment as less-skilled workers do. Ideally, then, different classes of workers should be modeled separately.

Appendix Note

1. See O'Regan and Quigley (1996) for a discussion of accessibility models in a similar context. Our presentation here relies on their work. Note, however, that in the models we develop, R and W are not derived from row and column marginals of the journey-to-work matrix, but from the household and work databases. Also, we are concerned with commutes over the entire day.

Appendix H

Enterprise Zones and Commuting

The analysis presented here has been taken (and modified) from an earlier (and preliminary) research paper undertaken in preparation for this book (Peters and Fisher 1999b). We decided not to repeat this analysis for our final sample of cities because it would take us too far from the central concerns of Chapter 8. Nevertheless, the results are interesting, and they reinforce the conclusions of Chapter 8.

Traditional spatial/transportation models which might be used in other circumstances to measure the accessibility to employment probably do not capture the actual employment functions of zones, since those functions differ so widely. In relation to commuting behavior, at any rate, zones are not homogenous among states or even within states. Thus the building of traditional gravity/entropy models of accessibility using the CTPP data—the only national data set available for this purpose—makes little sense. Instead, we focus on answering a series of broader transportation and accessibility questions. With regard to zone residents:

- Do zones include residential accommodation?
- Are people who live in zones wealthier than those who live outside of zones?
- How do zone residents commute to work, and how long does it take?

With regard to zone workers:

- Are people who work in zones wealthier than those who work outside of zones?
- How do zone workers commute to work and how long does it take?

Then, finally, with regard to flows between zone residents and zone workers:

- Where do zone residents work?
- Where do zone workers reside?

The analysis in this appendix relies on the CTPP, a reorganization of the decennial *Census of Population and Housing* data, allowing households (commuting origins) to be connected, via commuting matrices, to places-of-work (commuting destinations).

Although we are not building models and not testing hypotheses, it would also be useful to state up front what we would hope to find from our descriptive analyses. If enterprise zones do work to mitigate the effects of spatial mismatch, then we would hope that they are located in older inner-city neighborhoods and are partly residential and that they actually contain (or are near) "targetable" people. Moreover, if zones have the desired accessibility effect, then residents should commute shorter distances to work and we would hope that zones attract workers from older inner-city neighborhoods.

ZONE DEMOGRAPHICS AND COMMUTE TIME

Most of the other zones in our original sample of cities are too small (that is, have too few TAZs in their TAZ regions) to conduct a useful commuting analysis. Quite a few of the smaller metropolitan areas had fewer than 10 TAZs, making useful comparisons between enterprise zone and non-enterprise zone TAZs nearly impossible. So this section focuses on enterprise zones in regions with many TAZs (in effect, more than 40) and with a reasonable distribution of zone and non-zone TAZs. In the few instances when we found problems with the CTPP data, the city was removed from the sample. Los Angeles and New York were also excluded. The sample has a few other peculiarities. Most importantly, a few states dominate. This is a function of the original sampling design (oversampling where local variation in incentives was important), and also the way zones are designated in a state.

Table H.1 describes some of the demographic differences between zone and non-zone TAZs. Many of the zones have a much smaller average TAZ population than non-zone TAZs. In only one case, Milwaukee, was the average enterprise zone TAZ population significantly bigger than non-zone TAZs. Zones tend to be in industrial neighborhoods with fewer residential facilities. The housing units variable confirms this picture.

In every case, median household income in zone TAZs was significantly (and substantially) lower than in non-zone TAZs. In one of the more extreme cases, St. Louis, zone TAZs had a median household income of just $7,492, but non-zone TAZs had an income of $30,383. Unsurprisingly, in all but one case (Kankakee) the median earnings of workers resident in zones was significantly less than that of workers resident outside the zones. But the earnings of workers employed *in* the zones was mostly insignificantly different from the earnings of workers employed outside the zone—in six cases the estimate for in-zone earnings was actually greater than out-of-zone earnings, and in two of these six cases, earnings in the zone were significantly higher than earnings out of the zone (Kankakee and Milwaukee). This suggests that zones provide good employment opportunities for workers from an area much broader than the zones themselves and that workers working in the zones earn considerably more than those workers merely resident in the zones.

Travel time to work is either significantly shorter for zone residents than non-zone residents or much the same for zone and non-zone residents. But the travel time to work of those working in the zones was almost always *longer* than those working out of zones (and in five cases the difference was statistically significant). In the case of Champaign, Illinois, workers employed in the zone took an average of 12.6 minutes to get to work, while those employed elsewhere took only 9.7 minutes. In only one case, St. Louis, was the travel time of those working *in* the zone significantly shorter than those working *out* of the zone (this may be a function of the longer, elongated boundaries of the zone, which snake through the city).

The extra commute time of zone workers was not a function of the modal choice of zone residents. Moreover, it was not a function of the relative poverty of zone residents and thus their need to take slower public transit. On the contrary, the commute time of those working in enterprise zones is greater largely because of the long-distance commuters zones attracted from elsewhere in the metropolitan area. Enterprise zones are metropolitan, not neighborhood, employment magnets.

This picture is generally confirmed by the results presented in Table H.2. Here we calculate time-to-work regressions for the 10 cities in our sample.[1] In this table, earnings, mode, and an enterprise zone dummy were the independent variables, time to work was dependent. In every case, the estimate on the enterprise zone dummy was positive, and, except in three cases, statistically significant at $\alpha = 0.05$. In more than half the cases, working in an enterprise zone added more than three minutes to the commute time. While enterprise zones may be providing some special local access (the data are not rich enough to confirm or disconfirm this supposition), the fact remains that they definitely provide work opportunities for broad regional labor markets.

COMMUTING INTO AND OUT OF ENTERPRISE ZONES

Unfortunately, the CTPP does not allow us to look at the labor characteristics of those individuals who commute into and out of the zone for work. So it is difficult to say what sort of workers the enterprise zone is attracting from local residents. The commuting data are restricted to flows with the only attributes being mode—nevertheless the data do extend the analysis presented thus far.

Table H.1 Residential, Income, and Journey-to-Work Differences for Those Working in and Residing in Enterprise Zones, 1990

	Duval, Fla.	Champaign, Ill.	Kankakee, Ill.	Kansas City, Mo.	St. Louis, Mo.	Canton, Ohio	Cincinnati, Ohio	El Paso, Tex.	Forth Worth, Tex.	Milwaukee, Wis.
Persons per TAZ										
In zone	404	441	491	1,427	924	324	1,305	746	647	2,609
Out of zone	1,089*	427	719	1,980*	2,320*	668	1,680	1,014*	571	1,416*
Housing units per TAZ										
In zone	185	194	199	703	460	138	566	231	205	1,005
Out of zone	455*	164	270	821	947*	267*	665	323*	240	563*
Median H/hold income of residents										
In zone	7,690	13,603	20,416	13,972	7,492	13,588	16,119	10,716	16,355	13,769
Out of zone	27,049*	26,386*	28,340*	33,110*	30,383*	26,428*	30,316*	19,332*	24,621*	37,165*
Median earnings of workers resident										
In zone	6,551	8,871	14,124	11,881	6,592	10,716	12,749	6,513	10,359	11,464
Out of zone	15,982*	14,120*	15,510	18,920*	18,134*	16,597*	17,792*	11,190*	14,122*	20,190*
Median earnings of workers employed										
In zone	11,973	11,121	14,291	16,877	11,272	14,589	17,192	10,187	10,753	18,570
Out of zone	14,124*	11,332	7,759*	15,549	17,028*	13,711	15,318	10,113	12,094	15,611*
Median travel time to work of residents										
In zone	13.5	10.3	13.7	17.1	10.1	12.8	18.2	15.4	16.4	18.2
Out of zone	19.2*	12.9*	12.6	19.7*	19.5*	17.0*	19.2	15.2	16.2	18.8

Median travel time to work of those working

In zone	15.1	12.6	14.0	20.5	13.9	15.2	20.3	14.5	13.4	19.2
Out of zone	14.8	9.7*	6.3*	15.8*	18.8*	14.3	16.4*	14.2	13.3	13.7*

NOTE: An asterisk (*) indicates ANOVA F-score significant at 0.05.

**Table H.2 The Effect of Enterprise Zones on Commute Time,
Regression Results for Further Cities**

City	Adjusted R^2	Enterprise zone B	t
Duval, Fla.	0.16	4.6*	5.0
Champaign, Ill.	0.05	3.8*	2.8
Kankakee, Ill.	0.08	4.2*	2.1
Kansas City, Mo.	0.23	3.2*	2.9
St. Louis, Mo.	0.30	1.9*	2.3
Canton, Ohio	0.08	2.7*	3.1
Cincinnati, Ohio	0.22	3.0*	2.5
El Paso, Tex.	0.05	1.6	1.9
Forth Worth, Tex.	0.16	1.1	0.6
Milwaukee, Wis.	0.13	1.6	1.3

NOTE: Log of earnings and mode were the other two independent variables. F test was significant in all cases. An asterisk (*) indicates statistical significance at the 0.05 level (2-tailed test).

For each zone we created maps with two distinct sets of thematic analyses: the first indicated the number of commuters traveling to the TAZ-defined enterprise zone from each TAZ. The data are derived from the CTPP's origin/destination journey-to-work matrices.[2] The second thematic analysis was of median household income (that is, household income of residents) of each TAZ. We do not include the resulting maps here because of their chromatic complexity (they are available from the authors). Unsurprisingly, enterprise zones (particularly those in larger metropolitan areas) attract a large number of commuters (both absolutely and proportionately) from distant and wealthy suburbs. Part of the reason for this is the type of jobs available in the enterprise zones. On the whole, the jobs available in enterprise zones require at least as many skills as jobs elsewhere in the metropolitan area.

Appendix Notes

1. The time-to-work model takes its form from the well-developed journey-to-work literature. Here, commute time is usually seen as a function of income, mode of transportation, and a series of other variables meant to capture various aspects of the commute under investigation, such as the race and gender of commuters and so on. In our restricted model, $t = \int(i, m, e)$; commuting time (t) is a function of the

natural log of earnings (*i*), the mode (*m*) of commute (expressed here as a percentage of workers taking public transit), and, in this case, a dummy (*e*) (whether the journey-to-work destination is an enterprise zone or not). In this form, our model is workplace based; we are concerned with the commuting habits of those working at a particular destination, not residing at a particular origin. Extended tests of OLS regression assumptions were undertaken; the model showed no apparent cause for concern.

In many standard commuting models, occupation rather than income is seen as the important predictor of commuting time. Replacing income with various occupational variables leads to much the same results. For instance, in one equation income was replaced by the proportion of executive, administrative, and managerial occupations and professional specialty occupations in the destination tract— high-end occupations tend to be associated with longer commutes. In most cases the B-value for the enterprise zone variable increased (those working in the zone took longer to get to work than all others). Alterations to the occupational variable—essentially to expand the definition of high-end occupations or to define less-skilled occupations—resulted in fairly consistent Bs.

2.   These are commuters over the entire day, not just peak periods.

References

Ady, Robert. 1997. "Discussion of 'Taxation and Economic Development' and 'The Effects of State and Local Public Services on Economic Development'." *New England Economic Review* (March/April): 77–82.

Anderson, John, and Robert Wassmer. 2000. *Bidding for Business: The Efficacy of Local Economic Development Incentives in a Metropolitan Area.* Kalamazoo, Michigan: W.E. Upjohn Institute for Employment Research.

Armington, Catherine, and Margorie Odle. 1982. "Small Business—How Many Jobs?" *The Brookings Review* 1 (Winter): 14–17.

Bartik, Timothy. 1989. "Small Business Start-Ups in the United States: Estimates of the Effects of the Characteristics of States." *Southern Economic Journal* 55(4): 1004–1018.

———. 1991. *Who Benefits from State and Local Economic Development Policies?* Kalamazoo, Michigan: W.E. Upjohn Institute for Employment Research.

———. 1994. "Jobs, Productivity, and Local Economic Development: What Implications Does Economic Research Have for the Role of Government?" *National Tax Journal* 47 (4): 847–862.

———. 1997. "Discussion of 'Taxation and Economic Development' and 'The Effects of State and Local Public Services on Economic Development'." *New England Economic Review* (March/April): 67–71.

Beaumont, Enid. 1991. "Enterprise Zones and Federalism." In *Enterprise Zones: New Directions in Economic Development*, Roy Green, ed. Newbury Park, California: Sage, pp. 41–58.

Berndt, E.R., and Laurits R. Christensen. 1973. "The Translog Function and the Substitution of Equipment, Structures, and Labor in U.S. Manufacturing 1929–1968." *Journal of Econometrics* 1(1): 81–114.

Birch, David. 1979. *The Job Generation Process.* Cambridge, Massachusetts: MIT Program on Neighborhood and Regional Change.

———. 1981. "Who Creates Jobs." *Public Interest* (Fall): 3–14.

Birdsong, Bret. 1989. *Federal Enterprise Zones: A Poverty Program for the 1990s?* Washington, D.C.: The Urban Institute.

Blackley, P.R. 1990. "Spatial Mismatch in Urban Labor markets: Evidence from Large U.S. Metropolitan Areas." *Social Science Quarterly* 71(1): 39–52.

Blair, John, and Robert Premus. 1987. "Major Factors in Industrial Location: A Review." *Economic Development Quarterly* 1(1): 72–85.

Blumenberg, Evelyn. 2000. "Moving Welfare Participants to Work: Women,

Transportation and Welfare Reform." *Journal of Women and Social Work* 15 (Summer): 259–277.

Boarnet, Marlon, and William Bogart. 1996. "Enterprise Zones and Employment: Evidence from New Jersey." *Journal of Urban Economics* 40(2): 198–215.

Bondonio, Daniele, and John Engberg. 2000. "Enterprise Zones and Local Employment: Evidence from States' Programs." *Regional Science and Urban Economics* 30(5): 519–549.

Briggs, Xavier de Souza. 1997. "Moving Up versus Moving Out: Neighborhood Effects in Housing Mobility Programs." *Housing Policy Debates* 8(1): 195–234.

Brooks, Stephen, Robert Tannenwald, Hilary Sale, and Sandeep Puri. 1986. "The Competitiveness of the Massachusetts Tax System." Interim Report of the Massachusetts Special Commission on Tax Reform, House No. 5148. Boston, Massachusetts.

Brown, C., J. Hamilton, and J. Medoff. 1990. *Employers Large and Small.* Cambridge, Massachusetts: Harvard University Press.

Butler, Stuart. 1981. *Enterprise Zones: Greenlining the Inner Cities.* New York: Universe.

———. 1991. "The Conceptual Evolution of Enterprise Zones." In *Enterprise Zones: New Directions in Economic Development*, Roy Green, ed. Newbury Park, California: Sage, pp. 27–40.

Calzonetti, F., and Robert Walker. 1991. "Factors Affecting Industrial Location Decisions: A Survey Approach." In *Industry Location and Public Policy*, Henry Herzog and Alan Schlottmann, eds. Knoxville, Tennessee: University of Tennessee Press, pp. 221–240.

Chapman, Keith, and David Walker. 1990. *Industrial Location.* Oxford, United Kingdom: Basil Blackwell.

Clark, G.L., and J. Whiteman. 1983. "Why Poor People Do Not Move: Job Search Behavior and Disequilibrium amongst Local Labor Markets." *Environment and Planning A* 15: 85–104.

Clarke, Susan. 1982. "Enterprise Zones: Seeking the Neighborhood Nexus." *Urban Affairs Quarterly* 18(1): 53–71.

Cooke, Thomas J. 1997. "Geographic Access to Job Opportunities and Labor Force Participation Among Women and African Americans in the Greater Boston Metropolitan Area." *Urban Geography* 18(3): 213–227.

Cutler, David, and Edward Glaeser. 1995. "Are Ghettos Good or Bad?" Working Paper 5163, National Bureau of Economic Research, Cambridge, Massachusetts.

Dabney, Dan. 1991. "Do Enterprise Zone Incentives Affect Business Location Decisions?" *Economic Development Quarterly* 5(4): 325–334.

Dowall, David, Marc Beyeler, and Chun-Cheung Wong. 1994. "Evaluation of California's Enterprise Zone and Employment and Economic Incentives Programs." California Policy Seminar, Berkeley, California: University of California.

Duncan, Harley. 1997. "Discussion of 'Taxation and Economic Development' and 'The Effects of State and Local Public Services on Economic Development'." *New England Economic Review* (March/April): 71–75.

Eisinger, Peter K. 1988. *The Rise of the Entrepeneurial State.* Madison, Wisconsin: University of Wisconsin Press.

Elling, Richard, and Ann Sheldon. 1991. "Determinants of Enterprise Zone Success: A Four State Perspective." In *Enterprise Zones: New Directions in Economic Development*, Roy Green, ed. Newbury Park, California: Sage, pp. 136–154.

Ellwood, David. 1986. "The Spatial Mismatch Hypothesis: Are There Teenage Jobs Missing in the Ghetto?" In *The Black Youth Employment Crisis*, Richard B. Freeman and Harry J. Holzer, eds. Chicago, Illinois: University of Chicago Press, pp. 147–185.

Engberg, John, and Robert Greenbaum. 1999. "State Enterprise Zones and Local Housing Markets." *Journal of Housing Research* 10(2): 163–187.

Erickson, Rodney, and Susan Friedman. 1990a. "Enterprise Zones 1: Investment and Job Creation of State Government Programs in the USA." *Environment and Planning C: Government and Policy* 8(3): 251–267.

———. 1990b. "Enterprise Zones 2: A Comparative Analysis of Zone Performance and State Government Policies." *Environment and Planning C: Government and Policy* 8(4): 363–378.

Erickson, Rodney, Susan Friedman, and Richard McCluskey. 1989. *Enterprise Zones: An Evaluation of State Government Policies.* State College, Pennsylvania: The Pennsylvania State University Center for Regional Business Analysis.

Estes, Ralph, and M. Hamond. 1992. "Enterprise Zones: A Critical Analysis—briefing paper." Washington, D.C.: Center for the Advancement of Public Policy and the Institute for Policy Studies.

Fisher, Peter. 1985. "Corporate Tax Incentives: The American Version of Industrial Policy." *Journal of Economic Issues* 19(1): 45–75.

Fisher, Peter and Alan Peters. 1997a. "Tax and Spending Incentives and Enterprise Zones." *New England Economic Review* (March/April): 109–130.

———. 1997b. "Measuring Tax and Incentive Competition: What is the Best Yardstick?" *Regional Studies* 31(8): 751 (14 pp.).

———. 1998. *Industrial Incentives: Competition Among American States and Cities.* Kalamazoo, Michigan: W.E. Upjohn Institute for Employment Research.

Fisher, Ronald. 1997. "The Effects of State and Local Public Services on Economic Development." *New England Economic Review* (March/April): 53–67.

Fix, Michael, and Raymond Struyk. 1994. *Clear and Convincing Evidence: Measurement of Discrimination in America.* Washington, D.C.: Urban Institute.

Foster, Norman, David Forkenbrock, and Thomas Pogue. 1991. "Evaluation of a State Level Road Program to Promote Local Economic Development." *Transportation Quarterly* 45(October): 143–157.

Glaeser, Edward. 1996. "Discussion of 'Spatial Effects upon Employment Outcomes: The Case of New Jersey Teenagers'." *New England Economic Review* (May/June): 58–64.

Glickman, Norman. 1984. "Economic Policy and the Cities: In Search of Reagan's Real Urban Policy." *Journal of the American Planning Association* 59(4): 471–478.

Goldsmith, William. 1982. "Bringing the Third World Home." *New Society Working Papers* 9 (March/April): 24–30.

Gordon, P., A. Kumar, and H.W. Richardson. 1989. "The Spatial Mismatch Hypothesis: Some New Evidence." *Urban Studies* 26: 315–326.

Green, Roy, ed. 1991. *Enterprise Zones: New Directions in Economic Development.* Newbury Park, California: Sage.

Greenbaum, Robert. 1998. "An Evaluation of State Enterprise Zone Policies: Measuring the Impact on Business Decisions and Housing Market Outcomes." Ph.D. dissertation. H. John Heinz III School of Public Policy and Management. Pittsburgh, Pennsylvania: Carnegie Mellon University.

———. 2001. "Selecting the Right Site: Where do States Locate Place-based Economic Development Programs?" In *Proceedings of the Ninety-Third Annual Conference of the National Tax Association, Santa Fe, New Mexico,* November 9–11, 2000, James R. Hines, Jr., ed. Washington, D.C.: National Tax Association, pp. 74–82.

Greenbaum, Robert, and John Engberg. 2000. "An Evaluation of State Enterprise Zone Policies." *Policy Studies Review* 17(2/3): 29–46.

Greene, William H. 1997. *Econometric Analysis.* Upper Saddle River, New Jersey: Prentice Hall.

Hall, Peter. 1977. "Green Fields and Grey Areas." In *Proceeding of the Royal Town Planning Institute Annual Conference.* London: Royal Town Planning Institute.

———. 1982. "Enterprise Zones: A Justification." *International Journal of Urban and Regional Research* 6(3): 417–421.

Hambleton, Robin. 1996. "Empowerment Zones and UK Urban Policy: Competing in the Urban Regeneration Game." Paper presented at the April

1996 Urban Affairs Association Annual Conference held in New York, New York.

Hanson, Susan, and Geraldine Pratt. 1990. "Geographic Perspectives on the Occupational Segregation of Women." *National Geographic Research* 6(4): 376–399.

———. 1991. "Job Search and the Occupational Segregation of Women." *Annals of the Association of American Geographers* 81(12): 229–253.

———. 1995. *Gender, Work and Space*. London: Routledge.

Harris, Richard I.D. 1991. "The Employment Effects of Factor Subsidies: Some Estimates for Northern Ireland Manufacturing Industries, 1955–1983." *Journal of Regional Science* 31(1): 49–64.

Hawkins, Benjamin. 1984. "The Impact of Enterprise Zones on Urban Areas." *Growth and Change* 15(1): 35–40.

Holzer, Harry. 1991. "The Spatial Mismatch Hypothesis: What Has the Evidence Shown?" *Urban Studies* 28(1): 105–122.

Holzer, Harry, and Keith Ihlanfeldt. 1996. "Spatial Factors and the Employment of Blacks at the Firm Level." *New England Economic Review* (May/June): 65–82.

Holzer, Harry, and W. Vroman. 1992. "Mismatches and Urban Labor Markets." In *Urban Labor Markets and Job Opportunity*, G.E. Peterson and W. Vroman, eds. Washington, D.C.: Urban Institute, pp. 81–104.

Hsiao, Cheng. 1986. *Analysis of Panel Data*. Cambridge, United Kingdom: Cambridge University Press.

Huang, Kuo S. 1991. "Factor Demands in U.S. Food Manufacturing Industry." *American Journal of Agricultural Economics* 73(3): 615–620.

Hughes, Mark Alan. 1989. "Misspeaking the Truth to Power: A Geographical Perspective on the 'Underclass' Fallacy." *Economic Geography* 65(3): 187–207.

Hughes, Mark, and Julie Sternberg. 1992. *The New Metropolitan Reality*. Washington, D.C.: Urban Institute.

Humberger, Edward. 1981. "The Enterprise Zone Fallacy." *Journal of Community Action* (September/October): 20–28.

Hunt, Timothy. 1985. *Michigan's Business Tax Costs Relative to the Other Great Lakes States*. Kalamazoo, Michigan: W.E. Upjohn Institute for Employment Research.

Hunt, Timothy, and Christopher O'Leary. 1989. "Experience Rating of Unemployment Insurance in Michigan and Other States: A Microeconomic Comparison for 1988." Kalamazoo, Michigan: W.E. Upjohn Insitute for Employment Research.

Iannone, Donald. 1999. *An Assessment of the Costs, Benefits, and Overall Impacts of the State of Ohio's Economic Development Programs. Final Re-*

port. Cleveland, Ohio: The Urban Center, Maxine Goodman Levin College of Urban Affairs, Cleveland State University.

Ihlanfeldt, K.R. 1994. "The Spatial Mismatch between Jobs and Residential Locations within Urban Areas." *Cityscape* 1(1): 219–244.

Ihlanfeldt, K.R., and L.D. Sjoquist. 1998. "The Spatial Mismatch Hypothesis: A Review of Recent Studies and Their Implications for Welfare Reform." *Housing Policy Debates* 9(4): 849–892.

Immergluck, Daniel. 1998. "Job Proximity and the Urban Employment Problem: Do Suitable Nearby Jobs Improve Neighborhood Employment Rates?" *Uban Studies* 35(1):7–23.

Isard, Walter, Iwan Azis, Matthew Drennan, Ronald Miller, Sidney Saltzman, and Eric Thorbecke. 1998. *Methods of Interregional and Regional Analysis.* Aldershot, United Kingdom: Ashgate.

Isserman, Andrew. 1999. "Making Regional Planning More Effective Through Use of Performance Measures and Control Groups." Paper presented at the *Annual Conference of the Association of Collegiate Schools of Planning* held in Chicago, Illinois, October, 1999.

Jacobs, Susan, and Michael Wasylenko. 1981. "Government Policy to Stimulate Economic Development: Enterprise Zones." In *Financing State and Local Government in the 1980s: Issues and Trends,* N. Walzer and D. Chicoine, eds. Cambridge, Massachusetts: Oelgeschlager, Gunn and Hain.

Jencks, Christopher, and Susan Mayer. 1990. "The Social Consequences of Growing Up in a Poor Neighborhood." In *Inner City Poverty in the United States,* Laurence Lynn, Jr. and Michael McGeary, eds. Washington, D.C.: National Academy Press, pp. 111–186.

Kain, John. 1968. "Housing Segregation, Negro Employment and Metropolitan Decentralization." *Quarterly Journal of Economics* 82(2): 175–192.

———. 1992. "The Spatial Mismatch Hypothesis: Three Decades Later." *Housing Policy Debates* 3(2): 371–462.

Kenyon, Daphne. 1997. "Theories of Interjurisdictional Competition." *New England Economic Review* (March/April): 13–28.

KPMG Peat Marwick. 1994. "The Competitiveness of New York's Business Taxes." *State Tax Notes* 7 (July 18): 161–190.

Lacombe, Annalynn. 1998. "Welfare Reform and Access to Jobs in Boston." Washington, D.C.: Bureau of Transportation Statistics.

Ladd, Helen. 1994. "Spatially Targeted Economic Development Strategies: Do They Work?" *Cityscape* 1(1): 193–211.

Laughlin, James D. 1993. "An Assessment of Indiana's Competitive Position in Business Recruitment." Indianapolis, Indiana: Indiana Economic Development Council.

Levitan, Sarah, and Elizabeth Miller. 1992. "Enterprise Zones: A Promise Based on Rhetoric." Washington, D.C.: Center for Social Policy Studies, The George Washington University.

Luce, Thomas F. 1994. "Local Taxes, Public Services, and the Intrametropolitan Location of Firms and Households." *Public Finance Quarterly* 22(2): 139–176.

MacDonald, Heather. 1999. "Women's Commuting and Employment Patterns." *Journal of Planning Literature* 13(3): 267–283.

Mark, Stephen T., Therese J. McGuire, and Leslie Papke. 2000. "The Influence of Taxes on Employment and Population Growth: Evidence from Washington, D.C. Metropolitan Area." *National Tax Journal* 53(1): 105–123.

Marston, Stephen. 1985. "Two Views of the Geographic Distribution of Unemployment." *Quarterly Journal of Economics* 100 (February): 57–79.

Massey, Doreen. 1982. "Enterprise Zones: A Political Issue." *International Journal of Urban and Regional Research* 6(3): 429–434.

Mayer, Christopher. 1996. "Does Location Matter?" *New England Economic Review* (May/June): 26–40.

McGuire, Therese. 1992. "Review of *Who Benefits from State and Local Economic Development Policies?*" *National Tax Journal* 45(4): 457–459.

———. 1997. "Discussion of 'Taxation and Economic Development' and 'The Effects of State and Local Public Services on Economic Development'." *New England Economic Review* (March/April): 76–77.

McLafferty, Sara, and Valerie Preston. 1996. "Spatial Mismatch and Employment in a Decade of Restructuring." *Professional Geographer* 48(4): 420–431.

Mier, Robert. 1982. "Enterprise Zones: A Long Shot." *Planning* 48 (April): 10–14.

Mieszkowski, P., and E.S. Mills. 1993. "The Causes of Metropolitan Suburbanization." *Journal of Economic Perspectives* 7(3): 135–147.

Minton, Eric. 1999. "On the Road Again." *Planning* (September): 4–8.

Moberg, David. 1995. "No Vacancy!" *Shelter Force* (January/February): 14–16.

Morgan, William, John Mutti, and Mark Partridge. 1989. "A Regional General Equilibrium Model of the United States: Tax Effects on Factor Movements and Regional Production." *Review of Economics and Statistics* 71 (November): 626–635.

Mounts, Richard. 1981. "Urban Enterprise Zones: Will They Work?" *American Review of Public Administration* 15(1): 86–96.

Netzer, Dick. 1991. "An Evaluation of Interjurisdictional Competition Through Economic Development Incentives." In *Competition Among*

States and Local Governments, Daphne Kenyon and John Kincaid, eds. Washington, D.C.: The Urban Institute Press, pp. 221–246.

———. 1997. "Discussion of 'Tax and Spending Incentives and Enterprise Zones'." *New England Economic Review* (March/April): 131–135.

Newman, Robert, and Dennis Sullivan. 1988. "Econometric Analysis of Business Tax Impacts on Industrial Location: What Do We Know, and How Do We Know It?" *Journal of Urban Economics* 23 (March): 215–223.

O'Regan, Katherine, and John Quigley. 1996. "Spatial Effects upon Employment Outcomes: The Case of New Jersey Teenagers." *New England Economic Review* (May/June): 41–58.

Oakland, William, and William Testa. 1996. "State-local Business Taxation and the Benefits Principle." *Economic Perspectives* 19(2): 2–19.

Oates, Wallace, and Robert Schwab. 1991. "The Allocative and Distributive Implications of Local Fiscal Competition." In *Competition Among States and Local Governments*, Daphne Kenyon and John Kincaid, eds. Washington, D.C.: The Urban Institute Press, pp. 127–146.

Papke, James. 1988. "The Indiana Enterprise Zone Experiment: Concepts, Issues, and Impact—A Report to the Indiana Enterprise Zone Board." West Lafayette, Indiana: Department of Economics, Purdue University.

———. 1989. "Interim Report to the Indiana Enterprise Zone Board." West Lafayette, Indiana: Department of Economics, Purdue University.

———. 1995. Interjurisdictional Business Tax-Cost Differentials: Convergence, Divergence and Significance. *State Tax Notes* 9,24: 1701–1711.

Papke, James, and Leslie Papke. 1984. *State Tax Incentives and Investment Location Decisions: Microanalytic Simulations.* Indiana's Revenue Structure: Major Components and Issues, Part II. West Lafayette, Indiana: Center for Tax Policy Studies, Purdue University.

Papke, Leslie. 1987. "Subnational Taxation and Capital Mobility: Estimates of Tax-Price Elasticities." *National Tax Journal* 40(2): 191–203.

———. 1993. "What Do We Know About Enterprise Zones." In *Tax Policy and the Economy*, James Poterba, ed. Cambridge, Massachusetts: National Bureau of Economic Research and MIT Press, pp. 37–72.

———. 1994. "Tax Policy and Urban Development: Evidence from the Indiana Enterprise Zone Program." *Journal of Public Economics* 54(1): 37–49.

———. 1997. "Discussion of 'Tax and Spending Incentives and Enterprise Zones'." *New England Economic Review* (March/April): 135–137.

———. 2000. "The Indiana Enterprise Zone Revisited: Effects on Capital Investment and Land Values," *National Tax Association, Proceedings of the Ninety-Third Annual Conference,* Sante Fe, New Mexico, pp. 83–88. Washington, DC: National Tax Association.

Peirce, Neal, Jerry Hagstrom, and Carol Steinbach. 1979. "Economic Development: The Challenge of the 1980s." Washington, D.C.: Council of State Planning Agencies.

Peters, Alan, and Peter Fisher. 1998. "The Ohio Enterprise Zone Program: Results and Analysis Using the TAIM Model." A Report for the Ohio Economic Development Study. Cleveland, Ohio: The Urban Center, Cleveland State University.

———. 1999a. "Ohio's Business Taxes and Economic Development Incentives: Competitive Effects and Policy Alternatives: An Analysis of Ohio's State and Local Tax System, Corporate Income Tax Credits, Loan and Grant Programs, and Enterprise Zone Incentives Using the TAIM Model." A Report for the Ohio Economic Development Study. Cleveland, Ohio: The Urban Center, Cleveland State University.

———. 1999b. "Enterprise Zones, Incentives and Growth." Paper given to W.E. Upjohn Institute for Employment Research, Kalamazoo, Michigan.

Peterson, G.E., and W. Vroman. 1992. "Urban Labor Markets and Economic Opportunity." In *Urban Labor Markets and Job Opportunity*, G.E. Peterson and W. Vroman, eds. Washington, D.C.: The Urban Institute, pp. 1–29.

Phelps, Edmund. 1972. *Inflation Policy and Unemployment Theory*. New York: Norton.

Pindyck, Robert, and Daniel Rubinfeld. 1998. *Econometric Models and Economic Forecasts*. Boston, Massachusetts: Irwin McGraw-Hill.

Prohofsky, Allen. 2000. "How Quickly Do Corporations Respond to Changes in Tax Law? Evidence from the California Manufacturer's Investment Credit." *Public Budgeting and Finance* 20(3): 119–138.

Rasmussen, David, Marc Bendick, and Larry Ledebur. 1984. "A Methodology for Evaluating Economic Development Incentives." *Growth and Change* 15(2): 18–25.

Rosenbaum, James. 1996. "Discussion of 'Spatial Factors in the Employment of Blacks at the Firm Level'." *New England Economic Review* (May/June): 83–86.

Rosenbaum, James, Susan Popkin, Julie Kaufman, and Jennifer Rusin. 1991. "Social Integration of Low-Income Black Adults in Middle-Class White Suburbs." *Social Problems* 38(4): 448–461.

Rubin, Barry, and C. Kurt Zorn. 1985. "Sensible State and Local Economic Development." *Public Administration Review* 45(2): 333–339.

Rubin, Barry, and Margaret Wilder. 1989. "Urban Enterprise Zones: Employment Impacts and Fiscal Incentives." *Journal of the American Planning Association* 55(4): 418–431.

Rubin, Barry, and Craig Richards. 1992. "A Transatlantic View of Enterprise Zone Impacts: The British and American Experience." *Economic Development Quarterly* 6(4): 431–443.

Rubin, Marilyn Marks. 1991. "Urban Enterprise Zones in New Jersey: Have They Made a Difference?" In *Enterprise Zones: New Directions in Economic Development*, Roy Green, ed. Newbury Park, California: Sage, pp. 105–121.

Rubin, Marilyn, and Regina Armstrong. 1989. "The New Jersey Urban Enterprise Zone Program: An Evaluation." Trenton, New Jersey: New Jersey Department of Commerce, Energy and Economic Development.

Rubin, Marilyn, Steven Brooks, and Richard Buxbaum. 1992. "Indiana Enterprise Zones: A Program Evaluation for 1989 and 1990." Terre Haute, Indiana: Indiana Department of Commerce.

Sayrs, Lois W. 1989. *Pooled Time Series Analysis*. Newbury Park, California: Sage.

Schwartz, Amy Ellen. 1999. "Review of *Industrial Incentives: Competition Among American States and Cities*." *National Tax Journal* 52(1): 145–149.

Sen, Ashish, Paul Metaxatos, Siim Soot, and Vonu Thakuriah. 1999. "Welfare Reform and Spatial Matching Between Client and Jobs." *Papers in Regional Science* 78(2): 195–211.

Shannon, John. 1991. "Federalism's 'Invisible Regulator'-Interjurisdictional Competition." In *Competition Among States and Local Governments*, Daphne Kenyon and John Kincaid, eds. Washington, D.C.: The Urban Institute Press, pp. 117–126.

Sheldon, Ann, and Richard Elling. 1989. "Patterns and Determinants of Enterprise Zone Success in Four States." Paper presented at the 19th Annual Meeting of the Urban Affairs Association held in Baltimore, Maryland.

Smith, Tony E. 1987. "Poisson Gravity Models in Spatial Flows." *Journal of Regional Science* 27(3): 315–340.

Steinnes, Donald. 1984. "Business Climate: Tax Incentives and Regional Economic Development." *Growth and Change* 15(2): 38–47.

Tannenwald, Robert. 1996. "State Business Tax Climate: How Should It be Measured and How Important is It?" *New England Economic Review* (January/February): 23–38.

———. 1997. "State Regulatory Policy and Economic Development." *New England Economic Review* (March/April): 83–99.

Tannenwald, Robert, and Christine Kendrick. 1995. "Taxes and Capital Spending: Some New Evidence." In *Proceedings of the Eighty-Seventh Annual Conference of the National Tax Association, 1994*, Frederick Stocker, ed. Columbus, Ohio: National Tax Association, pp. 113–121.

Tannenwald, Robert, Christopher O'Leary, and Wei-Jang Huang. 1999. "New Ways of Evaluating State Unemployment Insurance." *New England Economic Review* (March/April): 15–40.

Taylor, Brian, and Paul Ong. 1995. "Spatial Mismatch or Automobile Mismatch? An Examination of Race, Residence and Commuting in U.S. Metropolitan Areas." *Urban Studies* 32(9): 1453–1473.

Theodore, N., and V. Carlson. 1996. "Employment Networks and the Creation of Local Labor Markets." Paper presented at the *Annual Meeting of the Association of American Geographers* held in Charlotte, North Carolina.

U.S. Bureau of the Census. 1997. *County Business Patterns 1995.* Washington, D.C.: Census Bureau.

U.S. Department of Housing and Urban Development. 1986. "State-Designated Enterprise Zones: Ten Case Studies." Washington, D.C.: HUD.

———. 1992. *State Enterprise Zone Update.* Washington, D.C.: HUD.

U.S. Department of Transportation, Bureau of Transportation Statistics. *Census Transportation Planning Package.* Urban Element. CD-ROM BTS-15-1 through 33. Washington, D.C.: U.S. Bureau of Transportation Statistics.

Vaughn, Roger. 1979. *State Taxation and Economic Development.* Washington, D.C.: Council of State Planning Agencies.

Walton, John. 1982. "Cities and Jobs and Politics." *Urban Affairs Quarterly* 18 (September): 5–17.

Wasylenko, Michael. 1997. "Taxation and Economic Development: The State of the Economic Literature." *New England Economic Review* (March/April): 37–52.

Wilder, Margaret, and Barry Rubin. 1988. "Targeted Redevelopment Through Urban Enterprise Zones." *Journal of Urban Affairs* 10(1): 1–17.

———. 1996. "Rhetoric Versus Reality: A Review of Studies on State Enterprise Zone Programs." *Journal of the American Planning Association* 62(4): 473–491.

Williams, William. 1967. "A Measure of the Impact of State and Local Taxes on Industry Location." *Journal of Regional Science* 7(1): 49–59.

Wisconsin, Department of Revenue. 1973. *Corporate Tax Climate: A Comparison of Nineteen States.* Madison, Wisconsin.

Wolkoff, Michael. 1992. "Is Economic Development Decision Making Rational?" *Urban Affairs Quarterly* 27(3): 340–355.

Zhang, Zhongcai, and Richard Bingham. 2000. "Metropolitan Employment Growth and Neighborhood Job Access in Spatial and Skills Perspectives: Empirical Evidence from Seven Ohio Metropolitan Regions." *Urban Affairs Review* 35(3): 390–421.

The Authors

Alan H. Peters is an associate professor of urban and regional planning at the University of Iowa. He received his Ph.D. from Rutgers University in 1989. For much of the past decade he has been investigating the effectiveness of state and local economic development policy in the United States. Prior to that he worked on economic development issues in southern Africa and Europe. His major research interest is the application of computer-based micro-simulation models to urban planning problems. Currently he is working on three-dimensional models aimed at showing the visual and spatial consequences of land-use and zoning law.

Peter S. Fisher is a professor of urban and regional planning at the University of Iowa. He holds a bachelor's degree from Haverford College and received a Ph.D. in economics from the University of Wisconsin–Madison in 1978, where he majored in public finance. At the University of Iowa, his research and teaching has focused on state and local government finance and economic development policy. He has served as a consultant on a variety of finance and policy issues for state government agencies and nonprofit organizations. He is co-author, with Alan Peters, of *Industrial Incentives: Competition Among American States and Cities*, published by the Upjohn Institute in 1998.

Subject Index

The italic letters *f*, *n*, and *t* following a page number indicate that the subject information is within a figure, note, or table, respectively, on that page.

Across-the-board tax cuts, 108

Agglomeration economies, 181

Analysis-of-variance approach to zones and growth, 44

Areas. *See* Cities with enterprise zones; Economically depressed areas

Automobile grants to families in poverty, 232–233

Back-loaded incentives, 11, 104, 223

Bartik, Timothy
  hypothetical cost-benefit model, 37–40
  literature review of taxes and location decisions, 162–163
  model of negative fiscal effects of tax cuts, 265–267

BEGIN variable, 276

Beloit, Wisconsin enterprise zone, 208, 209

Benefit-cost ratio of fiscal incentives in zones, 36

Birch, David, *The Job Generation Process*, 25, 26

Births. *See* Firm births

Boston, Massachusetts commuting study, 205

Branch plants. *See* New plants

Break-even elasticity, 115–117
  and front-loading of incentives, 117–118

Business cycles, effect on enterprise zones, 151, 252–254

Business incentives. *See* General incentives; Zone incentives

Business location decisions. *See* Location decisions of firms

Business surveys about zone incentives, 37, 45, 159–160

Business taxes. *See* Taxes on corporations

Butler, Stuart, 24

California, fiscal effect of zone credits in, 121–122

Capital bias in enterprise zones, 8–9, 221
  in seventy-five city sample, 96–99, 100

Capital expense calculations, 97, 98*t*, 242–243

Capital incentives
  authors' recommendations about, 236
  credit ceilings, 94

Capital-matching grants, 89, 92, 93*t*
  in states with seventy-five city sample, 94–96

Case-study methodology, 159, 160

Ceilings on incentives, 68, 94, 201, 204, 254

Census blocks and zone boundaries, 279

Census of Population and Housing, 208

Census Transportation Planning Package (CTPP), 204, 208, 281, 303, 305
  specific features of, 215*n*11, 215*n*12, 310

Cities with enterprise zones
  comparing to non-zone cities, 174–176
  comparing zones to cities where located, 172, 194*n*17
  demographic and time-to-work data for selected, 308–309*t*

About the Institute

The W.E. Upjohn Institute for Employment Research is a nonprofit research organization devoted to finding and promoting solutions to employment-related problems at the national, state, and local levels. It is an activity of the W.E. Upjohn Unemployment Trustee Corporation, which was established in 1932 to administer a fund set aside by the late Dr. W.E. Upjohn, founder of The Upjohn Company, to seek ways to counteract the loss of employment income during economic downturns.

The Institute is funded largely by income from the W.E. Upjohn Unemployment Trust, supplemented by outside grants, contracts, and sales of publications. Activities of the Institute comprise the following elements: 1) a research program conducted by a resident staff of professional social scientists; 2) a competitive grant program, which expands and complements the internal research program by providing financial support to researchers outside the Institute; 3) a publications program, which provides the major vehicle for disseminating the research of staff and grantees, as well as other selected works in the field; and 4) an Employment Management Services division, which manages most of the publicly funded employment and training programs in the local area.

The broad objectives of the Institute's research, grant, and publication programs are to 1) promote scholarship and experimentation on issues of public and private employment and unemployment policy, and 2) make knowledge and scholarship relevant and useful to policymakers in their pursuit of solutions to employment and unemployment problems.

Current areas of concentration for these programs include causes, consequences, and measures to alleviate unemployment; social insurance and income maintenance programs; compensation; workforce quality; work arrangements; family labor issues; labor-management relations; and regional economic development and local labor markets.